Praise for Kelly McGonigal and
The Willpower Instinct

"Tired of the endless debate about whether man possesses free will or is predestined to lounge about gobbling Krispy Kreme donuts while watching TV? If you want action, not theory, *The Willpower Instinct* is the solution for the chronically slothful."

—*USA Today*

"Refreshingly easy to read and peppered with stories of people who have successfully used its methods, *The Willpower Instinct* is a new kind of self-help book. Using science to help explain the "why" and strategies for the "how," McGonigal has created a book that will appeal to those who want to lose a few pounds as well as those who are eager to understand why they just cannot seem to get through their to-do list. A must-read for anyone who wants to change how they live in both small and big ways."

—*Bookpage*

"A fun and readable survey of the field, bringing willpower wisdom out of the labs."

—*Time magazine*

"*The Willpower Instinct* combines the braininess of a Malcolm Gladwell bestseller with the actual helpfulness of an *Idiot's Guide* to not being lazy. If you are trying to lose weight, train for an athletic event, become more successful at work, rid yourself of toxic habits . . . heck, if you're HUMAN, you need to read this book."

—LIBRARYTHING

"This book has tremendous value for anyone interested in learning how to achieve their goals more effectively. McGonigal clearly breaks down a large body of relevant scientific research and its applications, and shows that awareness of the limits of willpower is crucial to our ability to exercise true self-control."

—JEFFREY M. SCHWARTZ, M.D., AUTHOR OF THE BESTSELLING *Brain Lock*

"What a liberating book! Kelly McGonigal explains the scientific reality of willpower, exploding the myths that most of us believe. Stronger willpower—based on inspiring facts, not oppressive nonsense—is finally within everyone's reach."

—GEOFF COLVIN, AUTHOR OF *Talent Is Overrated*

D0089646

THE
WILLPOWER
INSTINCT

THE
WILLPOWER
INSTINCT

How Self-Control Works, Why It Matters,
and What You Can Do to Get More of It

Kelly McGonigal, Ph.D.

AVERY

a member of Penguin Group (USA)

New York

AVERY

Published by the Penguin Group
Penguin Group (USA) LLC
375 Hudson Street
New York, New York 10014

USA · Canada · UK · Ireland · Australia
New Zealand · India · South Africa · China

First trade paperback edition 2013
Copyright © 2012 by Kelly McGonigal, Ph.D.
Penguin supports copyright. Copyright fuels creativity, encourages diverse voices,
promotes free speech, and creates a vibrant culture. Thank you for buying an authorized
edition of this book and for complying with copyright laws by not reproducing, scanning,
or distributing any part of it in any form without permission. You are supporting
writers and allowing Penguin to continue to publish books for every reader.

Brain illustrations by Tina Pavlatos, Visual Anatomy Limited
"Current Self v. Future Self" scale courtesy Hal Ersner-Hershfield and Jon Baron

Most Avery books are available at special quantity discounts for bulk purchase for sales promotions, premiums,
fund-raising, and educational needs. Special books or book excerpts also can be created to fit specific needs.
For details, write: Special.Markets@us.penguingroup.com

The Library of Congress has catalogued the hardcover edition as follows:

McGonigal, Kelly.
The willpower instinct : how self-control works, why it matters, and what
you can do to get more of it / Kelly McGonigal.
p.   cm.
ISBN 978-1-58333-438-6
1. Will.   2. Self-control.   I. Title.
BF632.M363   2012   2011039795
153.8—dc23

ISBN 978-1-58333-508-6 (paperback)

Printed in the United States of America
5   7   9   10   8   6

Book design by Meighan Cavanaugh

All names and identifying characteristics have been changed to protect the privacy of the individuals involved.

Neither the publisher nor the author is engaged in rendering professional advice or services to the individual reader. The ideas, procedures, and suggestions contained in this book are not intended as a substitute for consulting with your physician. All matters regarding your health require medical supervision. Neither the author nor the publisher shall be liable or responsible for any loss or damage allegedly arising from any information or suggestion in this book.

While the author has made every effort to provide accurate telephone numbers, Internet addresses, and other contact information at the time of publication, neither the publisher nor the author assumes any responsibility for errors, or for changes that occur after publication. Further, the publisher does not have any control over and does not assume any responsibility for author or third-party websites or their content.

This book is dedicated to everyone who has ever struggled with temptation,

addiction, procrastination, or motivation—which is to say, all of us.

CONTENTS

The intelligent want self-control; children want candy.

—RUMI

Welcome to Willpower 101

Whenever I mention that I teach a course on willpower, the nearly universal response is, "Oh, that's what I need." Now more than ever, people realize that willpower—the ability to control their attention, emotions, and desires—influences their physical health, financial security, relationships, and professional success. We all know this. We know we're supposed to be in control of every aspect of our lives, from what we eat to what we do, say, and buy.

And yet, most people feel like willpower failures—in control one moment but overwhelmed and out of control the next. According to the American Psychological Association, Americans name lack of willpower as the number-one reason they struggle to meet their goals. Many feel guilty about letting themselves and others down. Others feel at the mercy of their thoughts, emotions, and cravings, their lives dictated by impulses rather than conscious choices. Even the best-controlled feel a kind of exhaustion at keeping it all together and wonder if life is supposed to be such a struggle.

As a health psychologist and educator for the Stanford School of Medicine's Health Improvement Program, my job is to help people manage stress and make healthy choices. After years of watching people struggle to change their thoughts, emotions, bodies, and habits, I realized that much of what people believed about willpower was sabotaging their success and creating unnecessary stress. Although scientific research had much to say that could help them, it was clear that these insights had not yet become part of public understanding. Instead, people continued to rely on worn-out strategies for self-control. I saw again and again that the strategies most people use weren't just ineffective—they actually backfired, leading to self-sabotage and losing control.

This led me to create "The Science of Willpower," a class offered to the public through Stanford University's Continuing Studies program. The course brings together the newest insights about self-control from psychology, economics, neuroscience, and medicine to explain how we can break old habits and create healthy habits, conquer procrastination, find our focus, and manage stress. It illuminates why we give in to temptation and how we can find the strength to resist. It demonstrates the importance of understanding the limits of self-control, and presents the best strategies for training willpower.

To my delight, "The Science of Willpower" quickly became one of the most popular courses ever offered by Stanford Continuing Studies. The first time the course was offered, we had to move the room four times to accommodate the constantly growing enrollment. Corporate executives, teachers, athletes, health-care professionals, and others curious about willpower filled one of the largest lecture halls at Stanford. Students started bringing their spouses, children, and coworkers to class so they could share the experience.

I had hoped the course would be useful to this diverse group, who came to the class with goals ranging from quitting smoking and losing weight to getting out of debt and becoming a better parent. But even I was surprised by the results. A class survey four weeks into the course found that 97 percent of students felt they better understood their own behavior, and 84 percent reported that the class strategies had already given them more will-power. By the end of the course, participants told stories of how they had overcome a thirty-year addiction to sweets, finally filed their back taxes, stopped yelling at their children, stuck to an exercise program, and generally felt better about themselves and more in charge of their choices. Course evaluations called the class life-changing. The consensus of the students was clear: Understanding the science of willpower gave them strategies for developing self-control, and greater strength to pursue what mattered most to them. The scientific insights were as useful for the recovering alcoholic as the e-mail addict, and the self-control strategies helped people resist temptations as varied as chocolate, video games, shopping, and even a married coworker. Students used the class to help meet personal goals such as running a marathon, starting a business, and managing the stresses of job loss, family conflict, and the dreaded Friday morning spelling test (that's what happens when moms start bringing their kids to class).

Of course, as any honest teacher will tell you, I learned a lot from my students as well. They fell asleep when I droned on too long about the wonder of a scientific finding but forgot to mention what it had to do with their willpower challenges. They were quick to let me know which strategies worked in the real world, and which fell flat (something a laboratory study can never tell you). They put creative spins on weekly assignments and showed me new ways for turning abstract theories into useful rules for everyday life. This book combines the best scientific insights and practical exercises from the course, using the latest research and the acquired wisdom of the hundreds of students who have taken the class.

TO SUCCEED AT SELF-CONTROL, YOU NEED TO KNOW HOW YOU FAIL

Most books on changing behavior—whether it's a new diet plan or a guide to financial freedom—will help you set goals and even tell you what to do to reach them. But if identifying what we wanted to change were sufficient, every New Year's resolution would be a success and my classroom would be empty. Few books will help you see why you aren't already doing these things, despite knowing full well that you need to do them.

I believe that the best way to improve your self-control is to see how and why you *lose* control. Knowing how you are likely to give in doesn't, as many people fear, set yourself up for failure. It allows you to support yourself and avoid the traps that lead to willpower failures. Research shows that people who think they have the most willpower are actually the most likely to lose control when tempted.* For example, smokers who are the most optimistic about their ability to resist temptation are the most likely to relapse four months later, and overoptimistic dieters are the least likely to lose weight. Why? They fail to predict when, where, and why they will give in. They expose themselves to more temptation, such as hanging out with smokers or leaving cookies around the house. They're also most likely to be surprised by setbacks and give up on their goals when they run into difficulty.

Self-knowledge—especially of how we find ourselves in willpower trouble—is the foundation of self-control. This is why both "The Science of Willpower" course and this book focus on the most common willpower mistakes we all make. Each chapter dispels a common misconception about self-control and gives you a new way to think about your willpower challenges. For every willpower mistake, we'll conduct a kind of autopsy: When we give in to temptation or put off what we know we should do, what leads to our downfall? What is the fatal error, and why do we make it? Most important, we will look for the opportunity to save our future selves from this fate. How can we turn the knowledge of how we fail into strategies for success?

---

*This bias is not unique to willpower—for example, people who think they are the best at multitasking are actually the most distractible. Known as the Dunning-Kruger effect, this phenomenon was first reported by two Cornell University psychologists who found that people overestimate their abilities in all sorts of areas, including sense of humor, grammar, and reasoning skills. The effect is most pronounced among people who have the least skill; for example, those with a test score in the 12th percentile would, on average, estimate themselves to be in the 62nd percentile. This explains, among other things, a large percentage of *American Idol* auditions.

At the very least, by the time you finish the book, you will have a better understanding of your own imperfect but perfectly human behavior. One thing the science of willpower makes clear is that everyone struggles in some way with temptation, addiction, distraction, and procrastination. These are not individual weaknesses that reveal our personal inadequacies—they are universal experiences and part of the human condition. If this book did nothing else but help you see the common humanity of your willpower struggles, I would be happy. But I hope that it will do far more, and that the strategies in this book will empower you to make real and lasting changes in your life.

HOW TO USE THIS BOOK

BECOME A WILLPOWER SCIENTIST

I'm a scientist by training, and one of the very first things I learned is that while theories are nice, data is better. So I'm going to ask you to treat this book like an experiment. A scientific approach to self-control isn't limited to the laboratory. You can—and should—make yourself the subject of your own real-world study. As you read this book, don't take my word for anything. After I've laid out the evidence for an idea, I'm going to ask you to test that idea in your own life. Collect your own data to find out what is true and what works for you.

Within each chapter, you'll find two kinds of assignments to help you become a willpower scientist. The first I call "Under the Microscope." These prompts ask you to pay attention to how an idea is already operating in your life. Before you can change something, you need to see it as it is. For example, I'll ask you to notice when you are most likely to give in to temptation, or how hunger influences your spending. I'll invite you to pay attention to how you talk to yourself about your willpower challenges, including what you say to yourself when you procrastinate, and how you judge your own willpower failures and successes. I'll even ask you to conduct some field studies, such as sleuthing out how retailers use store design

Observer

to weaken your self-control. With each of these assignments, take the approach of a nonjudgmental, curious observer—just like a scientist peering into a microscope, hoping to discover something fascinating and useful. These aren't opportunities to beat yourself up for every willpower weakness, or to rail against the modern world and all its temptations. (There's no place for the former, and I'll take care of the latter.)

You'll also find "Willpower Experiments" throughout each chapter. These are practical strategies for improving self-control based on a scientific study or theory. You can apply these willpower boosts immediately to real-life challenges. I encourage you to have an open mind about each strategy, even the ones that seem counterintuitive (and there will be plenty). They've been pilot-tested by students in my course, and while not every strategy works for everyone, these are the ones that earned the highest praise. The ones that sounded good in theory but embarrassingly flopped in real life? You won't find them in these pages.

These experiments are a great way to break out of a rut and find new solutions for old problems. I encourage you to try different strategies and collect your own data about which help you the most. Because they are experiments, not exams, you can't fail—even if you decide to try the exact opposite of what the science suggests (after all, science needs skeptics). Share the strategies with your friends, family, and colleagues, and see what works for them. You'll always learn something, and you can use what you've learned to refine your own strategies for self-control.

YOUR WILLPOWER CHALLENGE

To get the most out of this book, I recommend picking a specific willpower challenge to test every idea against. We all have willpower challenges. Some are universal—for example, thanks to our biological instinct to crave sugar and fat, we all need to restrain the urge to single-handedly keep the local bakery in business. But many of our willpower challenges are unique. What you crave, another person might be repulsed by. What you're addicted to, another person might find boring. And what you put off, another person might pay to do. Whatever the specifics, these challenges tend to play out in the same way for each of us. Your craving for chocolate is not so different from a smoker's craving for a cigarette, or a shopaholic's craving to spend. How you talk yourself out of exercising is not so different from how someone else justifies not opening the past-due bills, and another person puts off studying for one more night.

Your willpower challenge could be something you've been avoiding (what we'll call an "I will" power challenge) or a habit you want to break (an "I won't" power challenge). You could also choose an important goal in your life that you'd like to give more energy and focus to (an "I want" power challenge)—whether it's improving your health, managing stress, honing your parenting skills, or furthering your career. Because distraction, temptation, impulse control, and procrastination are such universal human challenges, the strategies in this book will be helpful for any goal you choose. By the time you finish the book, you'll have greater insight into your challenges and a new set of self-control strategies to support you.

I want to further my career in Acting.
5/29/19

TAKE YOUR TIME

This book is designed to be used as if you were taking my ten-week course. It's divided into ten chapters, each of which describes one key idea, the science behind it, and how it can be applied to your goals. The ideas and strategies build on each other, so that what you do in each chapter prepares you for the next.

Although you could read this whole book in one weekend, I encourage you to pace yourself when it comes to implementing the strategies. Students in my class take an entire week to observe how each idea plays out in their own lives. They try one new strategy for self-control each week, and report on what worked best. I recommend that you take a similar approach, especially if you plan to use this book to tackle a specific goal such as losing weight or getting control over your finances. Give yourself time to try out the practical exercises and reflect. Pick one strategy from each chapter—whichever seems most relevant to your challenge—rather than trying out ten new strategies at once.

You can use the ten-week structure of the book anytime you want to make a change or achieve a goal—just as some students have taken the course multiple times, focusing on a different willpower challenge each time. But if you intend to read the whole book first, enjoy—and don't worry about trying to keep up with the reflections and exercises as you go. Make a note of the ones that seem most interesting to you, and return to them when you're ready to put the ideas into action.

LET'S BEGIN

Here's your first assignment: Choose one challenge for our journey through the science of willpower. Then meet me in Chapter 1, where we'll take a trip back in time to investigate where this thing called willpower comes from—and how we can get more of it.

UNDER THE MICROSCOPE:
CHOOSE YOUR WILLPOWER CHALLENGE

If you haven't already, now's the time to pick the willpower challenge to which you'd most like to apply the ideas and strategies in this book. The following questions can help you identify the challenge you're ready to take on:

- "I will" power challenge: What is something that you would like to do more of, or stop putting off, because you know that doing it will improve the quality of your life? *Barres + yoga*
- "I won't" power challenge: What is the "stickiest" habit in your life? What would you like to give up or do less of because it's undermining your health, happiness, or success? *SM intake + negative self talk*
- "I want" power challenge: What is the most important long-term goal you'd like to focus your energy on? What immediate "want" is most likely to distract you or tempt you away from this goal?

I want to further my acting career.

Immediate wants: su scrolling. I do a lot of lounging around.

I Will, I Won't, I Want: What Willpower Is, and Why It Matters

When you think of something that requires willpower, what's the first thing that comes to mind? For most of us, the classic test of willpower is resisting temptation, whether the temptress is a doughnut, a cigarette, a clearance sale, or a one-night stand. When people say, "I have no willpower," what they usually mean is, "I have trouble saying no when my mouth, stomach, heart, or (fill in your anatomical part) wants to say yes." Think of it as "I won't" power. *— I won't power*

But saying no is just one part of what willpower is, and what it requires. After all, "Just say no" are the three favorite words of procrastinators and *— Yes!* coach potatoes worldwide. At times, it's more important to say yes. All those things you put off for tomorrow (or forever)? Willpower helps you put them on today's to-do list, even when anxiety, distractions, or a reality TV show marathon threaten to talk you out of it. Think of it as "I will" power— the ability to do what you need to do, even if part of you doesn't want to.

"I will" and "I won't" power are the two sides of self-control, but they alone don't constitute willpower. To say *no* when you need to say no, and *yes* when you need to say yes, you need a third power: the ability to remember what you really want. I know, you think that what you really want *is* the brownie, the third martini, or the day off. But when you're facing temptation, or flirting with procrastination, you need to remember that what you *really* want is to fit into your skinny jeans, get the promotion, get out of credit card debt, stay in your marriage, or stay out of jail. Otherwise, what's going to stop you from following your immediate desires? To exert self-control, you need to find your motivation when it matters. This is "I want" power. *FIND MY MOTIVATION WHEN IT MATTERS*

Willpower is about harnessing the three powers of I will, I won't, and I want to help you achieve your goals (and stay out of trouble). As we'll see, we human beings are the fortunate recipients of brains that support all of these capacities. In fact, the development of these three powers—I will, I won't, and I want—may define what it means to be human. Before we get down to the dirty business of analyzing why we fail to use these powers, let's begin by appreciating how lucky we are to have them. We'll take a quick peek into the brain to see where the magic happens, and discover how we can train the brain to have more willpower. We'll also take our first look at why willpower can be hard to find, and how to use another uniquely human trait—self-awareness—to avoid willpower failure.

WHY WE HAVE WILLPOWER

Imagine this: It is 100,000 years ago, and you are a top-of-the-line homo sapiens of the most recently evolved variety. Yes, take a moment to get excited about your opposable thumbs, erect spine, and hyoid bone (which allows you to produce some kind of speech, though I'll be damned if I know what it sounds like). Congratulations, too, on your ability to use fire (without setting yourself on fire), and your skill at carving up buffalo and hippos with your cutting-edge stone tools.

Just a few generations ago, your responsibilities in life would have been so simple: 1. Find dinner. 2. Reproduce. 3. Avoid unexpected encounters with a *Crocodylus anthropophagus* (that's Latin for "crocodile that snacks on humans"). But you live in a closely knit tribe and depend on other homo sapiens for your survival. That means you have to add "not piss anyone off in the process" to your list of priorities. Communities require cooperation and sharing resources—you can't just take what you want. Stealing some-one else's buffalo burger or mate could get you exiled from the group, or even killed. (Remember, other homo sapiens have sharp stone tools, too, and your skin is a lot thinner than a hippo's.) Moreover, you might need your tribe to care for you if you get sick or injured—no more hunting and gathering for you. Even in the Stone Age, the rules for how to win friends and influence people were likely the same as today's: Cooperate when your neighbor needs shelter, share your dinner even if you're still hungry, and think twice before saying "That loincloth makes you look fat." In other words, a little self-control, please.

It's not just your life that's on the line. The whole tribe's survival depends on your ability to be more selective about whom you fight with (keep it out of the clan) and whom you mate with (not a first cousin, please—you need to increase genetic diversity so that your whole tribe isn't wiped out by one disease). And if you're lucky enough to find a mate, you're now expected to bond for life, not just frolic once behind a bush. Yes, for you, the (almost) modern human, there are all sorts of new ways to get into trouble with the time-tested instincts of appetite, aggression, and sex.

This was just the beginning of the need for what we now call willpower. As (pre)history marched on, the increasing complexity of our social worlds required a matching increase in self-control. The need to fit in, cooper-ate, and maintain long-term relationships put pressure on our early human brains to develop strategies for self-control. Who we are now is a response to these demands. Our brains caught up, and voilà, we have willpower: the ability to control the impulses that helped us become fully human.

early human species developed self control in order to survive.

WHY IT MATTERS NOW

Back to modern-day life (you can keep your opposable thumbs, of course, though you may want to put on a little more clothing). Willpower has gone from being the thing that distinguishes us humans from other animals to the thing that distinguishes us from each other. We may all have been born with the capacity for willpower, but some of us use it more than others. People who have better control of their attention, emotions, and actions are better off almost any way you look at it. They are happier and healthier. Their relationships are more satisfying and last longer. They make more money and go further in their careers. They are better able to manage stress, deal with conflict, and overcome adversity. They even live longer. When pit against other virtues, willpower comes out on top. Self-control is a better predictor of academic success than intelligence (take that, SATs), a stronger determinant of effective leadership than charisma (sorry, Tony Robbins), and more important for marital bliss than empathy (yes, the secret to lasting marriage may be learning how to keep your mouth *shut*). If we want to improve our lives, willpower is not a bad place to start. To do this, we're going to have to ask a little more of our standard-equipped brains. And so let's start by taking a look at what it is we're working with.

wow.

THE NEUROSCIENCE OF I WILL, I WON'T, AND I WANT

Our modern powers of self-control are the product of long-ago pressures to be better neighbors, parents, and mates. But how exactly did the human brain catch up? The answer appears to be the development of the prefrontal cortex, a nice chunk of neural real estate right behind your forehead and eyes. For most of evolutionary history, the prefrontal cortex mainly controlled physical movement: walking, running, reaching, pushing—a kind of proto-self-control. As humans evolved, the prefrontal cortex got bigger and better connected to other areas of the brain. It now takes up a larger portion of the human brain than in the brains of other species—one reason you'll never see your dog saving kibble for retirement. As the prefrontal cortex grew, it took on new control functions: controlling what you pay attention to, what you think about, even how you feel. This made it even better at controlling what you *do*.

Robert Sapolsky, a neurobiologist at Stanford University, has argued that the main job of the modern prefrontal cortex is to bias the brain—and therefore, you—toward doing "the harder thing." When it's easier to stay on the couch, your prefrontal cortex makes you want to get up and exercise. When it's easier to say yes to dessert, your prefrontal cortex remembers the reasons for ordering tea instead. And when it's easier to put that project off until tomorrow, it's your prefrontal cortex that helps you open the file and make progress anyway.

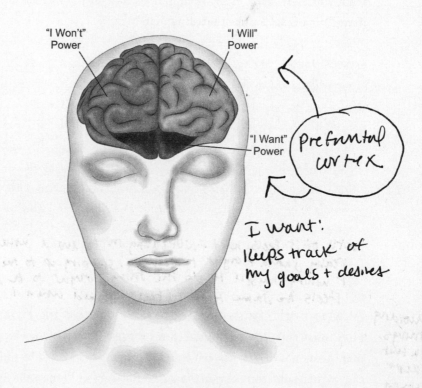

"I Won't" Power

"I Will" Power

"I Want" Power

prefrontal cortex

I want: keeps track of my goals + desires

Willpower in the Brain

The prefrontal cortex is not one unified blob of gray matter; it has three key regions that divvy up the jobs of I will, I won't, and I want. One region, near the upper left side of the prefrontal cortex, specializes in "I will" power. It helps you start and stick to boring, difficult, or stressful tasks, like staying on the treadmill when you'd rather hit the shower. The right side, in contrast, handles "I won't" power, holding you back from following every impulse or craving. You can thank this region for the last time you were tempted to read a text message while driving, but kept your eyes on the road instead. Together, these two areas control what you *do*.

The third region, just a bit lower and in the middle of the prefrontal cortex, keeps track of your goals and your desires. It decides what you *want*. The more rapidly its cells fire, the more motivated you are to take action or resist temptation. This part of the prefrontal cortex remembers what you *really* want, even when the rest of your brain is screaming, "Eat that! Drink that! Smoke that! Buy that!"

UNDER THE MICROSCOPE:
WHAT IS THE HARDER THING?

Every willpower challenge requires doing something difficult, whether it's walking away from temptation or *not* running away from a stressful situation. Imagine yourself facing your specific willpower challenge. What is the harder thing? What makes it so difficult? How do you feel when you think about doing it?

All of it feels hard. Not caving in to avoid what I really should + ought to be doing. Stepping up to the plate + willing myself to do the thing I ought to be doing. Feels the same to me. I feel ashamed when I think about avoiding things. In fact I kept closing this book. when I think about following through, I feel relieved.

A MIND-BLOWING CASE OF WILLPOWER LOST

How important is the prefrontal cortex for self-control? One way to answer that question is to look at what happens when you lose it. The most famous case of prefrontal cortex brain damage is the story of Phineas Gage. And fair warning, this is a gory story. You might want to put down your sandwich.

In 1848, Phineas Gage was a twenty-five-year-old foreman for a gang of rail workers. His employers called him their best foreman, and his team respected and liked him. His friends and family called him quiet and respectful. His physician, John Martyn Harlow, described him as exceptionally strong in both mind and body, "possessing an iron will and an iron frame."

But all that changed on Wednesday, September 13, at four-thirty p.m. Gage and his men were using explosives to clear a path through Vermont for the Rutland and Burlington Railroad. Gage's job was to set up each explosion. This procedure had gone right a thousand times, and yet this time, something went wrong. The explosion happened too soon, and the blast sent a three-foot, seven-inch tamping iron straight into Gage's skull. It pierced his left cheek, blew through his prefrontal cortex, and landed thirty yards behind him, carrying some of Gage's gray matter with it.

You might now be picturing Gage, flat on his back, instantly killed. But he didn't die. By witness reports, he didn't even pass out. Instead, his workers put him in an oxcart and pushed him almost a mile back to the tavern where he was staying. His physician patched him up as well as possible, replacing the largest fragments of skull recovered from the accident site, and stretching the scalp to cover the wounds.

Gage's full physical recovery took over two months (set back perhaps as much by Dr. Harlow's enthusiasm for prescribing enemas as by the persistent fungus growing out of Gage's exposed brain). But by November 17, he was sufficiently healed to return to his regular life. Gage himself reported "feeling better in every respect," with no lingering pain.

Sounds like a happy ending. But unfortunately for Gage, the story doesn't end there. His outer wounds may have healed, but something strange was happening inside Gage's brain. According to his friends and coworkers, his personality had changed. Dr. Harlow described the changes in a follow-up to his original medical report of the accident:

> The balance . . . between his intellectual faculties and his animal propensities seems to have been destroyed. He is fitful, irreverent, indulging at times in the grossest profanity (which was not previously his custom), manifesting

but little deference for his fellows, impatient of restraint or advice when it conflicts with his desires . . . devising many plans of future operation, which are no sooner arranged than they are abandoned. . . . In this regard his mind was radically changed, so decidedly that his friends and acquaintances said he was "no longer Gage."

In other words, when Gage lost his prefrontal cortex, he lost his will power, his won't power, and his want power. His iron will—something that had seemed like an unshakable part of his character—had been destroyed by the tamping iron that blew through his skull.

Most of us don't have to worry about ill-timed railroad explosions robbing us of our self-control, but we all have a little Phineas Gage in us. The prefrontal cortex is not always as reliable as we'd like. Many temporary states—like being drunk, sleep-deprived, or even just distracted—inhibit the prefrontal cortex, mimicking the brain damage that Gage sustained. This leaves us less able to control our impulses, even though our gray matter is still safe in our skulls. Even when our brains are well rested and sober, we aren't fully out of danger. That's because while we all have the capacity to do the harder thing, we also have the desire to do exactly the opposite. This impulse needs to be restrained, and as we'll see, it often has a mind of its own.

Desire has a mind of its own

THE PROBLEM OF TWO MINDS

When we watch our willpower fail—spending too much, eating too much, wasting time, and losing our tempers—well, it can make a person wonder if he has a prefrontal cortex at all. Sure, it might be *possible* to resist temptation, but that doesn't guarantee that we will. It's *conceivable* that we could do today what begs to be done tomorrow, but more often than not, tomorrow wins. For this frustrating fact of life, you can also give evolution a big thanks. As humans evolved, our brains didn't so much change as they grew. Evolution prefers to add on to what it's created, rather than start from scratch. So as humans required new skills, our primitive brain was not replaced with some completely new model—the system of self-control was slapped on top of the old system of urges and instincts.

That means that for any instinct that once served us well, evolution has kept it around—even if it now gets us into trouble. The good news is, evolution has also given us a way to handle the problems we run into. Take, for example, our taste buds' delight in the foods most likely to make us fat. An insatiable sweet tooth once helped humans survive when food was scarce and extra body fat was life insurance. Fast-forward to our modern environment of fast food, junk food, and Whole Foods, and there is more than enough to go around. Extra weight has become a health risk, not an insurance policy, and the ability to *resist* tempting foods is more important for long-term survival. But because it paid off for our ancestors, our modern brains still come equipped with a well-preserved instinct to crave fat and sweets. Fortunately, we can use the brain's more recently evolved self-control system to override those cravings and keep our hands out of the candy bowl. So while we're stuck with the impulse, we're also equipped with the impulse control.

Some neuroscientists go so far as to say that we have one brain but two minds—or even, two people living inside our mind. There's the version of us that acts on impulse and seeks immediate gratification, and the version of us that controls our impulses and delays gratification to protect our long-term goals. They're both us, but we switch back and forth between these two selves. Sometimes we identify with the person who wants to lose weight, and sometimes we identify with the person who just wants the cookie. This is what defines a willpower challenge: Part of you wants one thing, and another part of you wants something else. Or your present self wants one thing, but your future self would be better off if you did something else. When these two selves disagree, one version of us has to override the other. The part of you that wants to give in isn't bad—it simply has a different point of view about what matters most.

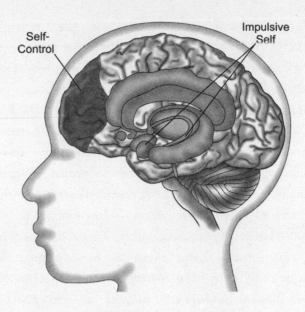

Self-Control

Impulsive Self

The Problem of the Two Minds

UNDER THE MICROSCOPE: MEET YOUR TWO MINDS

Every willpower challenge is a conflict between two parts of oneself. For your own willpower challenge, describe these competing minds. What does the impulsive version of you want? What does the wiser version of you want? Some people find it useful to give a name to the impulsive mind, like "the cookie monster" to the part of you that always wants instant gratification, "the critic" to the part of you that likes to complain about everyone and everything, or "the procrastinator" to the person who never wants to get started. Giving a name to this version of yourself can help you recognize when it is taking over, and also help you call in your wiser self for some willpower support.

THE VALUE OF BOTH SELVES

It's tempting to think about the self-control system as being the infinitely superior "self," and our more primitive instincts as an embarrassing vestige of our evolutionary past. Sure, back when our knuckles dragged in the dirt, those instincts helped us survive long enough to pass on our genes. But now they just get in the way, leading to health problems, empty bank accounts, and sexual encounters we have to apologize for on national television. If only we civilized creatures weren't still burdened with the drives of our long-ago ancestors.

Not so fast. Though our survival system doesn't always work to our advantage, it is a mistake to think we should conquer the primitive self completely. Medical case studies of people who have lost these instincts through brain damage reveal how crucial our primitive fears and desires are for health, happiness, and even self-control. One of the strangest cases involved a young woman who had part of her midbrain destroyed during a brain surgery to stop seizures. She appeared to lose the ability to feel fear and disgust, which robbed her of two of the most instinctive sources of self-restraint. She developed a habit of stuffing herself with food until she got sick, and could frequently be found sexually propositioning family members. Not exactly a model of self-control!

As we'll see throughout this book, without desires we'd become depressed, and without fear we'd fail to protect ourselves from future danger. Part of succeeding at your willpower challenges will be finding a way to take advantage of, and not fight, such primitive instincts. Neuroeconomists—scientists who study what the brain does when we make decisions—have discovered that the self-control system and our survival instincts don't always conflict. In some cases, they cooperate to help us make good decisions. For example, imagine that you're walking through a department store, and something shiny catches your eye. Your primitive brain shrieks, "Buy it!" Then you check out the price tag: $199.99. Before you saw the outrageous price, you would have needed some serious prefrontal cortex intervention to shut down the spending impulse. But what if your brain registers an instinctive pain response to the price? Studies show that this actually happens—the brain can treat a hefty price tag like a physical punch to the gut. That instinctive shock is going to make the job easy for your prefrontal cortex, and you'll barely need to exert any "I won't" power. As we aim to improve our willpower, we'll look for ways to use every bit of what it means to be human—including our most primitive instincts, from the desire for pleasure to the need to fit in—to support our goals.

THE FIRST RULE OF WILLPOWER: KNOW THYSELF

Self-control is one of mankind's most fabulous upgrades, but it's not our only distinction. We also possess self-awareness: the ability to realize what we are doing as we do it, and understand why we are doing it. With any luck, we can also predict what we're likely to do *before* we do it, giving us ample opportunity to reconsider. This level of self-awareness appears to be uniquely human. Sure, dolphins and elephants can recognize themselves in a mirror, but there's little evidence that they search their souls for self-understanding.

Without self-awareness, the self-control system would be useless. You need to recognize when you're making a choice that requires willpower; otherwise, the brain always defaults to what is easiest. Consider a smoker who wants to quit. She needs to recognize the first sign of a craving, and where it's likely to lead her (outside, in the cold, fumbling with a lighter). She also needs to realize that if she gives in to the craving this time, she's more likely to smoke again tomorrow. One more look in the crystal ball, and she'll see that if she continues on this path, she'll end up with all those horrible diseases she learned about in health class. To avoid this fate, she needs to make a conscious choice not to smoke the cigarette. Without self-awareness, she's doomed.

This may sound simple, but psychologists know that most of our choices are made on autopilot, without any real awareness of what's driving them, and certainly without serious reflection on their consequences. Heck, most of the time, we don't even realize we're making a choice. For example, one study asked people how many food-related decisions they made in one day. What would you say? On average, people guessed fourteen. In reality, when these same folks carefully tracked their decisions, the average was 227. That's more than two hundred choices people were initially unaware of—and those are just the decisions related to eating. How can you control yourself if you aren't even aware that there is something to control?

Modern society, with its constant distractions and stimulation, doesn't help. Baba Shiv, a professor of marketing at the Stanford Graduate School of Business, has shown that people who are distracted are more likely to give in to temptations. For example, students trying to remember a telephone number are 50 percent more likely to choose chocolate cake over fruit at a snack cart. Distracted shoppers are more susceptible to in-store promotions, and more likely to go home with items not on their shopping lists.*

When your mind is preoccupied, your impulses—not your long-term goals—will guide your choices. Texting as you stand in line waiting to order at the coffee shop? You might just find yourself asking for a mocha milk shake instead of an iced coffee. (Incoming text msg: Bet u don't want 2 know how many calories r in that drink.) Can't get your mind off work? You might just find yourself agreeing with the salesperson that you need the upgrade and unlimited-service package.

WILLPOWER EXPERIMENT: TRACK YOUR WILLPOWER CHOICES

To have more self-control, you first need to develop more self-awareness. A good first step is to notice when you are making choices related to your willpower challenge. Some will be more obvious, such as, "Do I go to the gym after work?" The impact of other decisions might not be clear until later in

---

*The researchers helpfully point out that anything that "reduces the availability of processing resources in the shopping environment is likely to increase impulse buying by consumers. Marketers . . . could therefore benefit from actions designed to constrain processing resources such as having distracting music or displays in the shopping environment." This, no doubt, explains the chaos that greets me when I walk into the local drugstore.

the day, when you see their full consequences. For example, did you choose to pack your gym bag so you wouldn't have to go home first? (Smart! You'll be less likely to make excuses.) Did you get caught up in a phone call until you were too hungry to go straight to the gym? (Oops! You'll be less likely to exercise if you have to stop for dinner first.) For at least one day, track your choices. At the end of the day, look back and try to analyze when decisions were made that either supported or undermined your goals. Trying to keep track of your choices will also reduce the number of decisions you make while distracted—a guaranteed way to boost your willpower.

AN E-MAIL ADDICT TAKES THE FIRST STEP TO RECOVERY

Michele, a thirty-one-year-old radio show producer, was constantly checking e-mail on her computer or her phone. It was disrupting her productivity at work and annoying her boyfriend, who could never manage to get Michele's full attention. Her willpower challenge for the class was to check e-mail less, and she set an ambitious goal of checking no more than once an hour. After the first week, she reported that she did not come even close to her goal. The problem was that she often didn't even realize that she was checking her e-mail until after she was scrolling through new messages. She could stop once she realized what she was doing, but whatever impulse led her to look at her phone or click over to her e-mail was happening outside of conscious awareness. Michele set the goal to catch herself sooner in the process.

By the next week, she was able to notice when she was reaching for her phone or opening her e-mail. That gave her an opportunity to practice stopping before she got fully sucked in. The impulse to check was more elusive. Michele had trouble recognizing what was prompting her to check *before* she was in the process of checking. With time, though, she came to recognize a feeling almost like an itch—a tension in her brain and body that was relieved when she checked her e-mail. That observation was fascinating to Michele; she had never thought of checking e-mail as a way to relieve tension. She had thought she was just seeking information. As she paid attention to how she felt after she checked, Michele realized that checking her e-mail was as ineffective as scratching an itch—it just made her itch more. With this awareness of both the impulse and her response, she had much more control over her behavior, and even surpassed her original goal to check less often outside of work hours.

> *This week, commit to watching how the process of giving in to your impulses happens. You don't even need to set a goal to improve your self-control yet. See if you can catch yourself earlier and earlier in the process, noticing what thoughts, feelings, and situations are most likely to prompt the impulse. What do you think or say to yourself that makes it more likely that you will give in?*

TRAIN YOUR BRAIN FOR WILLPOWER

It took evolution millions of years to deliver a prefrontal cortex that is capable of everything we humans need. So perhaps it's a little greedy to ask this, but is it possible to make our brains even better at self-control, without having to hang around for another million? If a basic human brain is pretty good at self-control, is there anything we can do right now to improve on the standard model?

Since the dawn of time, or at least since researchers started poking and prodding the human brain, it was assumed that the brain was fixed in structure. Whatever brainpower you had was a done deal, not a work in progress. The only change your brain was going to see was the deterioration of getting old. But over the last decade, neuroscientists have discovered that, like an eager student, the brain is remarkably responsive to experience. Ask your brain to do math every day, and it gets better at math.

Ask your brain to worry, and it gets better at worrying. Ask your brain to concentrate, and it gets better at concentrating.

Not only does your brain find these things easier, but it actually remodels itself based on what you ask it to do. Some parts of the brain grow denser, packing in more and more gray matter like a muscle bulking up from exercise. For example, adults who learn how to juggle develop more gray matter in regions of the brain that track moving objects. Areas of the brain can also grow more connected to each other, so they can share information more quickly. For example, adults who play memory games for twenty-five minutes a day develop greater connectivity between brain regions important for attention and memory.

But brain training isn't just for juggling and remembering where you left your glasses—there is growing scientific evidence that you can train your brain to get better at self-control. What does willpower training for your brain look like? Well, you could challenge your "I won't" power by planting temptation traps around your home—a chocolate bar in your sock drawer, a martini station by your exercise bike, the photo of your very married high school sweetheart taped to the fridge. Or you could build your own "I will" power obstacle course, with stations that require you to drink wheat grass juice, do twenty jumping jacks, and file your taxes early.

Or you could do something a lot simpler and less painful: meditate. Neuroscientists have discovered that when you ask the brain to meditate, it gets better not just at meditating, but at a wide range of self-control skills, including attention, focus, stress management, impulse control, and self-awareness. People who meditate regularly aren't just better at these things. Over time, their brains become finely tuned willpower machines. Regular meditators have more gray matter in the prefrontal cortex, as well as regions of the brain that support self-awareness.

It doesn't take a lifetime of meditation to change the brain. Some researchers have started to look for the smallest dose of meditation needed to see benefits (an approach my students deeply appreciate, since not many are going to head off to the Himalayas to sit in a cave for the next decade).

These studies take people who have never meditated before—even folks who are skeptical of the whole thing—and teach them a simple meditation technique like the one you'll learn just ahead. One study found that just three hours of meditation practice led to improved attention and self-control. After eleven hours, researchers could see those changes in the brain. The new meditators had increased neural connections between regions of the brain important for staying focused, ignoring distractions, and controlling impulses. Another study found that eight weeks of daily meditation practice led to increased self-awareness in everyday life, as well as increased gray matter in corresponding areas of the brain.

It may seem incredible that our brains can reshape themselves so quickly, but meditation increases blood flow to the prefrontal cortex, in much the same way that lifting weights increases blood flow to your muscles. The brain appears to adapt to exercise in the same way that muscles do, getting both bigger and faster in order to get better at what you ask of it. So if you're ready to train your brain, the following meditation technique will get the blood rushing to your prefrontal cortex—the closest we can get to speeding up evolution, and making the most of our brains' potential.

WILLPOWER EXPERIMENT: A FIVE-MINUTE BRAIN-TRAINING MEDITATION

Breath focus is a simple but powerful meditation technique for training your brain and increasing willpower. It reduces stress and teaches the mind how to handle both inner distractions (cravings, worries, desires) and outer temptations (sounds, sights, and smells). New research shows that regular meditation practice helps people quit smoking, lose weight, kick a drug habit, and stay sober. Whatever your "I will" and "I won't" challenges are, this five-minute meditation is a powerful brain-training exercise for boosting your willpower.

Here's how to get started:

1. *Sit still and stay put.*

   Sit in a chair with your feet flat on the ground, or sit cross-legged on a cushion. Sit up straight and rest your hands in your lap. It's important not to fidget when you meditate—that's the physical foundation of self-control. If you notice the instinct to scratch an itch, adjust your arms, or cross and uncross your legs, see if you can feel the urge but not follow it. This simple act of staying still is part of what makes meditation willpower training effective. You're learning not to automatically follow every single impulse that your brain and body produce.

2. *Turn your attention to the breath.*

   Close your eyes or, if you are worried about falling asleep, focus your gaze at a single spot (like a blank wall, not the Home Shopping Network). Begin to notice your breathing. Silently say in your mind "inhale" as you breathe in and "exhale" as you breathe out. When you notice your mind wandering (and it will), just bring it back to the breath. This practice of coming back to the breath, again and again, kicks the prefrontal cortex into high gear and quiets the stress and craving centers of your brain.

3. *Notice how it feels to breathe, and notice how the mind wanders.*

   After a few minutes, drop the labels "inhale/exhale." Try focusing on just the feeling of breathing. You might notice the sensations of the breath flowing in and out of your nose and mouth. You might sense the belly or chest expanding as you breathe in, and deflating as you breathe out. Your mind might wander a bit more without the labeling. Just as before, when you notice yourself thinking about something else, bring your attention back to the breath. If you need help refocusing, bring yourself back to the breath by saying "inhale" and "exhale" for a few rounds. This part of the practice trains self-awareness along with self-control.

   Start with five minutes a day. When this becomes a habit, try ten to fifteen minutes a day. If that starts to feel like a burden, bring it back down to five. A short practice that you do every day is better than a long practice you keep putting off to tomorrow. It may help you to pick a specific time that you will meditate every day, like right before your morning shower. If this is impossible, staying flexible will help you fit it in when you can.

Being Bad at Meditation Is Good for Self-Control

Andrew felt like a terrible meditator. The fifty-one-year-old electrical engineer was convinced that the goal of meditation was to get rid of all thoughts and empty the mind. Even when he was focused on his breath, other thoughts sneaked in. He was ready to give up on the practice because he wasn't getting better at it as quickly as he hoped, and figured he was wasting his time if he wasn't able to focus perfectly on the breath.

Most new meditators make this mistake, but the truth is that being "bad" at meditation is exactly what makes the practice effective. I encouraged Andrew—and all the other frustrated meditators in class—to pay attention not just to how well they were focusing *during* the meditation, but how it was affecting their focus and choices during the rest of the day.

Andrew found that even when his meditation felt distracted, he was more focused after practicing than if he skipped it. He also realized that what he was doing in meditation was exactly what he needed to do in real life: catch himself moving away from a goal and then point himself back at the goal (in this case, focusing on the breath). The meditation was perfect practice for when he was just about to order something salty and deep-fried for lunch, and needed to stop and order something healthier. It was perfect practice for when he had a sarcastic comment on his lips and needed to pause and hold his tongue. And it was perfect practice for noticing when he was wasting time at work and needed to get back on track. All day long, self-control was a process of noticing that he was off-goal and redirecting himself to the goal. With this realization, Andrew no longer cared if his whole ten-minute meditation was spent getting distracted and coming back to the breath. The "worse" the meditation, the better the practice for real life, as long he was able to notice when his mind was wandering.

> *Meditation is not about getting rid of all your thoughts; it's learning not to get so lost in them that you forget what your goal is. Don't worry if your focus isn't perfect when meditating. Just practice coming back to the breath, again and again.*

THE LAST WORD

Thanks to the architecture of the modern human brain, we each have multiple selves that compete for control of our thoughts, feelings, and actions. Every willpower challenge is a battle among these different versions of ourselves. To put the higher self in charge, we need to strengthen the systems of self-awareness and self-control. When we do, we will find the willpower and the *want* power to do the harder thing.

CHAPTER SUMMARY

The Idea: Willpower is actually three powers—I will, I won't, and I want—that help us to be a better version of ourselves.

Under the Microscope

- *What is the harder thing?* Imagine yourself facing your willpower challenge, and doing the harder thing. What makes it hard?
- *Meet your two minds.* For your willpower challenge, describe your two competing selves. What does the impulsive version of you want? What does the wiser version of you want?

Willpower Experiments

- *Track your willpower choices.* For at least one day, try to notice every decision you make related to your willpower challenge.
- *Five-minute brain-training meditation.* Focus on your breath using the words "inhale" and "exhale" in your mind. When your mind wanders, notice, and bring it back to the breath.

What makes it hard is just taking the leap + doing it. It feels uncomfortable - foreign - outside my realm of comfort and security. Part of me wonders if it's this view of unworthiness I have for myself. That I'm undeserving of all good things - so I trap myself / self sabatayne because I've made up in my head that's all that I deserve.

The impulsive side says to relax <u>all</u> the time and it's better to watch TV + look at my phone. To lounge around the house because "I'm too tired + need to rest." The wiser version desires to be proactive and make something of myself. To be proactive in my life, make healthy choices, and build my career. When I begin to think about all the things I need to do to be proactive, I get overwhelmed, and that's when impulsivity creeps in. That's when I watch TV for 6 hrs straight.

I need to remember that it's good to have a big picture ... But I also need to keep my goals <u>actionable</u> and in a do-able time frame.

TWO

The Willpower Instinct: Your Body Was Born to Resist Cheesecake

It starts with a flash of excitement. Your brain buzzes, and your heart pounds in your chest. It's like your whole body is saying *Yes*. Then the anxiety hits. Your lungs tighten and your muscles tense. You start to feel light-headed and a little nauseous. You are almost trembling, you want this so much. But you can't. But you want. *But you can't!* You know what you need to do, but you aren't sure you can handle this feeling without falling apart or giving in.

Welcome to the world of craving. Maybe it's a craving for a cigarette, a drink, or a triple latte. Maybe it's the sight of a last-chance super clearance sale, a lottery ticket, or a doughnut in the bakery window. In such a moment, you face a choice: follow the craving, or find the inner strength to control yourself. This is the moment you need to say "I won't" when every cell in your body is saying "I want."

You know when you've met a real willpower challenge because you feel it in your body. It's not some abstract argument between what is right and what is wrong. It feels like a battle happening inside of you—a battle between two parts of yourself, or what often feels like two very different people. Sometimes the craving wins. Sometimes the part of you that knows better, or wants better for yourself, wins.

Why you succeed or fail at these willpower challenges can seem like a mystery. One day you resist, and the next you succumb. You might ask yourself, "What was I thinking!" But a better question might be, "What was my body doing?" Science is discovering that self-control is a matter of physiology, not just psychology. It's a temporary state of both mind and body that gives you the strength and calm to override your impulses. Researchers are beginning to understand what that state looks like, and why the complexity of our modern world often interferes with it. The good news is that you can learn to shift your physiology into that state when you need your willpower the most. You can also train the body's capacity to stay in this state, so that when temptation strikes, your instinctive response is one of self-control.

A TALE OF TWO THREATS

To understand what happens in the body when we exercise self-control, we need to start with an important distinction: the difference between a saber-toothed tiger and a strawberry cheesecake. In one important respect, the tiger and the cheesecake are alike—both can derail your goal to live a long and healthy life. But in other ways, they are critically different threats. What the brain and body do to deal with them will be very different. Lucky for you, evolution has endowed you with exactly the resources you need to protect yourself from both.

WHEN DANGER STRIKES

Let's start with a little trip back in time, to a place where fierce saber-toothed tigers once stalked their prey.* Imagine you are in the Serengeti in East Africa, minding your own early hominid business. Perhaps you

---

*I am aware that technically, there is no such thing as a saber-tooth tiger. The correct name for this fierce predator is "saber-tooth cat." However, as an early reader pointed out, "saber-tooth cat" brings to mind a long-haired domestic Fluffy wearing a set of Halloween vampire fangs. So I'm sticking with the scientifically questionable but far more threatening saber-tooth tiger.

are scavenging for lunch among the carcasses scattered across the savannah. Things are going well—is that an abandoned, freshly killed antelope you spy?—when all of a sudden, holy shit! A saber-toothed tiger is lurking in the branches of a nearby tree. Perhaps he's savoring his antelope appetizer and contemplating his second course: you. He looks eager to sink those eleven-inch teeth into your flesh, and unlike your twenty-first-century self, this predator has no qualms about satisfying his cravings. Don't expect him to be on a diet, eyeing your curves as a bit too calorie-rich.

Fortunately, you are not the first person to find yourself in this very situation. Many of your long-ago ancestors faced this enemy and others like him. And so you have inherited from your ancestors an instinct that helps you respond to any threat that requires fighting or running for your life. This instinct is appropriately called the fight-or-flight stress response. You know the feeling: heart pounding, jaw clenching, senses on high alert. These changes in the body are no accident. They are coordinated in a sophisticated way by the brain and nervous system to make sure you act quickly and with every ounce of energy you have.

Here's what happened, physiologically, when you spotted that saber-toothed tiger: The information from your eyes first made its way to an area of the brain called the amygdala, which functions as your own personal alarm system. This alarm system sits in the middle of your brain and lives to detect possible emergencies. When it notices a threat, its central location makes it easy to get the message out to other areas of your brain and body. When the alarm system got the signal from your eyeballs that there was a saber-toothed tiger eyeing *you*, it launched a series of signals to your brain and body that prompted the fight-or-flight response. Stress hormones were released from your adrenal glands. Energy—in the form of fats and sugar— was released into your bloodstream from your liver. Your respiratory system got your lungs pumping to fuel the body with extra oxygen. Your cardiovascular system kicked into high gear to make sure the energy in your bloodstream would get to the muscles doing the fighting or the fleeing. Every cell in your body got the memo: time to show what you're made of.

While your body was getting ready to defend your life, the alarm system in your brain was busy trying to make sure that *you* didn't get in the body's way. It focused your attention and senses on the saber-toothed tiger and your surroundings, making sure no stray thoughts distracted you from the threat at hand. The alarm system also prompted a complex change in brain chemicals that inhibited your prefrontal cortex, the area of the brain in charge of impulse control. That's right, the fight-or-flight response wants to make you *more* impulsive. The rational, wise, and deliberative prefrontal cortex is effectively put to sleep—the better to make sure you don't chicken out or overthink your escape. Speaking of escape, I'd say your best bet in this situation is to start running. Now.

The fight-or-flight response is one of nature's greatest gifts to mankind: the built-in ability of your body and brain to devote all of their energy to saving your butt in an emergency. You aren't going to waste energy—physical or mental—on anything that doesn't help you survive the immediate crisis. So when the fight-or-flight response takes over, the physical energy that might a moment ago have been devoted to digesting your morning snack or repairing a hangnail is redirected to the task of immediate self-preservation. Mental energy that was focused on finding your dinner or planning your next great cave painting is rechanneled into present-moment vigilance and rapid action. In other words, the fight-or-flight stress response is an energy-management instinct. It decides how you are going to spend your limited physical and mental energy.

A NEW KIND OF THREAT

Still in the savannah of the Serengeti, fleeing the saber-toothed tiger? Sorry about that. I apologize if our trip back in time was a bit stressful, but it was a necessary detour if we want to understand the biology of self-control. Let's come back to today, away from the prowl of now-extinct predators. Catch your breath, relax a little. Let's find our way somewhere safer and more pleasant.

How about a stroll down your local Main Street? Imagine it now: It's a beautiful day, with bright sun and a gentle breeze. The birds in the trees are singing John Lennon's "Imagine," when all of a sudden—BAM! In a bakery display case, there sits the most delectable strawberry cheesecake you have ever seen. A radiant red glaze glistens over its smooth, creamy surface. A few carefully placed strawberry slices bring to mind the taste of childhood summers. Before you can say, "Oh, wait, I'm on a diet," your feet are moving toward the door, your hand is pulling the handle, and bells chime your tongue-hanging, mouth-drooling arrival.

What's going on in the brain and body *now*? A few things. First, your brain is temporarily taken over by the promise of reward. At the sight of that strawberry cheesecake, your brain launches a neurotransmitter called dopamine from the middle of your brain into areas of the brain that control your attention, motivation, and action. Those little dopamine messengers tell your brain, "Must get cheesecake NOW, or suffer a fate worse than death." This might explain the near-automatic movement of your feet and hands into the bakery. (Whose hand is that? Is that my hand on the door? Yes, it is. Now, how much is that cheesecake?)

While all this is happening, your blood sugar drops. As soon as your brain anticipates your mouth's first creamy bite, it releases a neurochemical that tells the body to take up whatever energy is circulating in the bloodstream. The body's logic is this: A slice of cheesecake, high in sugar and fat, is going to produce a major spike in blood sugar. To prevent an unsightly sugar coma and the rare (but never pretty) death by cheesecake, you need to lower the sugar currently in the bloodstream. How kind of the body to look out for you in this way! But this drop in blood sugar can leave you feeling a little shaky and cranky, making you crave the cheesecake even more. Hmmm, sneaky. I don't want to sound like a cheesecake conspiracy theorist, but if it's a contest between the cheesecake and your good intention to diet, I'd say the cheesecake is winning.

But wait! Just as in the Serengeti, you have a secret weapon: willpower. You remember willpower—the ability to do what really matters, even when it's difficult? Right now, what really matters isn't the momentary pleasure of cheesecake molecules hitting your palate. Part of you knows that you have bigger goals. Goals like health, happiness, and fitting into your pants tomorrow. This part of you recognizes that the cheesecake threatens your long-term goals. And so it will do whatever it can to deal with this threat. This is your willpower instinct.

But unlike the saber-toothed tiger, the cheesecake is not the real threat. Think about it: That cheesecake cannot do anything to you, your health, or your waistline unless you pick up the fork. That's right: This time, the enemy is within. You don't need to flee the bakery (although it might not hurt). And you definitely don't need to kill the cheesecake (or the baker). But you do need to do something about those inner cravings. You can't exactly kill a desire, and because the cravings are inside your mind and body, there's no obvious escape. The fight-or-flight stress response, which pushes you toward your most primitive urges, is exactly what you don't need right now. Self-control requires a different approach to self-preservation—one that helps you handle this new kind of threat.

UNDER THE MICROSCOPE: WHAT IS THE THREAT?

We're used to seeing temptation and trouble outside of ourselves: the dangerous doughnut, the sinful cigarette, the enticing Internet. But self-control points the mirror back at ourselves, and our inner worlds of thoughts, desires, emotions, and impulses. For your willpower challenge, identify the *inner* impulse that needs to be restrained. What is the thought or feeling that makes you want to do whatever it is you *don't* want to do? If you aren't sure, try some field observation. Next time you're tempted, turn your attention inward.

THE WILLPOWER INSTINCT:
PAUSE AND PLAN

Suzanne Segerstrom, a psychologist at the University of Kentucky, studies how states of mind like stress and hope influence the body. She has found that, just like stress, self-control has a biological signature. The need for self-control sets into motion a coordinated set of changes in the brain and body that help you resist temptation and override self-destructive urges. Segerstrom calls those changes the pause-and-plan response, which couldn't look more different from the fight-or-flight response.

You'll recall from our trip to the Serengeti that a fight-or-flight stress response starts when you recognize an external threat. Your brain and body then go into the self-defense mode of attack or escape. The pause-and-plan response differs in one very crucial way: It starts with the perception of an *internal* conflict, not an external threat. You want to do one thing (smoke a cigarette, supersize your lunch, visit inappropriate websites at work), but know you shouldn't. Or you know you *should* do something (file your taxes, finish a project, go to the gym), but you'd rather do nothing. This internal conflict is its own kind of threat: Your instincts are pushing you toward a potentially bad decision. What's needed, therefore, is protection of yourself by yourself. This is what self-control is all about. The most helpful response will be to slow you down, not speed you up (as a fight-or-flight response does). And this is precisely what the pause-and-plan response does. The perception of an internal conflict triggers changes in the brain and body that help you slow down and control your impulses.

THIS IS YOUR BRAIN AND BODY ON WILLPOWER

Like the fight-or-flight response, the pause-and-plan response begins in the brain. Just as the alarm system of your brain is always monitoring what you hear, see, and smell, other areas are keeping track of what's going on inside of you. This self-monitoring system is distributed throughout the brain, connecting the self-control regions of the prefrontal cortex with areas of the brain that keep track of your body sensations, thoughts, and emotions. One important job of this system is to keep you from making stupid mistakes, like breaking a six-month stretch of sobriety, yelling at your boss, or ignoring your overdue credit card bills. The self-monitoring system is just waiting to detect warning signs—in the form of thoughts, emotions, and sensations—that you are about to do something you will later regret. When your brain recognizes such a warning, our good friend the prefrontal cortex jumps into action to help you make the right choice. To help the prefrontal cortex, the pause-and-plan response redirects energy from the body to the brain. For self-control, you don't need legs ready to run or arms ready to punch, but a well-fueled brain ready to flex its power.

As we saw with the fight-or-flight response, the pause-and-plan response doesn't stop in the brain. Remember, your body has already started to respond to that cheesecake. Your brain needs to bring the body on board with your goals and put the brakes on your impulses. To do this, your prefrontal cortex will communicate the need for self-control to lower brain regions that regulate your heart rate, blood pressure, breathing, and other automatic functions. The pause-and-plan response drives you in the opposite direction of the fight-or-flight response. Instead of speeding up, your heart slows down, and your blood pressure stays normal. Instead of hyperventilating like a madman, you take a deep breath. Instead of tensing muscles to prime them for action, your body relaxes a little.

The pause-and-plan response puts your body into a calmer state, but not too sedate. The goal is not to paralyze you in the face of internal conflict, but to give you freedom. By keeping you from immediately following your impulses, the pause-and-plan response gives you the time for more flexible, thoughtful action. From this state of mind and body, you can choose to walk away from the cheesecake, with both your pride and your diet intact.

While the pause-and-plan response is as innate to our human nature as the fight-or-flight response, you've no doubt noticed that it doesn't always *feel* as instinctive as, say, eating the cheesecake. To understand why the willpower instinct doesn't always kick in, we need to dive a little deeper into the biology of both stress and self-control.

THE BODY'S WILLPOWER "RESERVE"

The single best physiological measurement of the pause-and-plan response is something called heart rate variability—a measurement most people have never heard of, but one that provides an amazing window into the body's state of stress or calm. Everybody's heart rate varies to some degree. This is easy to feel when you run up the stairs and your heart rate soars. But if you're healthy, your heart rate has had some normal ups and downs even as you've read this page. We're not talking dangerous arrhythmias here. Just little variations. Your heart speeds up a bit when you inhale: buh-dum buh-dum buh-dum. It slows down again when you exhale: buh-dum buh-dum buh-dum. This is good. This is healthy. It means that your heart is getting signals from both branches of your autonomic nervous system: the sympathetic nervous system, which revs the body into action, and the parasympathetic nervous system, which promotes relaxation and healing in the body.

When people are under stress, the sympathetic nervous system takes over, which is part of the basic biology that helps you fight or flee. Heart rate goes up, and variability goes down. The heart gets "stuck" at a higher rate— contributing to the physical feelings of anxiety or anger that accompany the fight-or-flight response. In contrast, when people successfully exert self-control, the parasympathetic nervous system steps in to calm stress and control impulsive action. Heart rate goes down, but variability goes up. When this happens, it contributes to a sense of focus and calm. Segerstrom first observed this physiological signature of self-control when she asked hungry students not to eat freshly baked chocolate-chip cookies. (It was a cruel setup, actually—the students had been asked to fast in preparation for a taste test. When they arrived, they were taken into a room with a tempting display of warm chocolate-chip cookies, chocolate candy, and carrots. Then they were told: Eat all the carrots you want, but don't touch the cookies or candy. Those are for the next participants. Reluctantly, they had to resist the sweets—and that's when heart rate variability went up. The lucky control participants who were asked to "resist" the carrots but enjoy all the cookies and candy they wanted? No change.)

Heart rate variability is such a good index of willpower that you can use it to predict who will resist temptation, and who will give in. For example, recovering alcoholics whose heart rate variability goes up when they see a drink are more likely to stay sober. Recovering alcoholics who show the opposite response—their heart rate variability *drops* when they see a drink—have a greater risk of relapse. Studies also show that people with higher heart rate variability are better at ignoring distractions, delaying gratification, and dealing with stressful situations. They are also less likely to give up on difficult tasks, even when they initially fail or receive critical feedback. These findings have led psychologists to call heart rate variability the body's "reserve" of willpower—a physiological measure of your capacity for self-control. If you have high heart rate variability, you have more willpower available for whenever temptation strikes.

Why are some people lucky enough to face willpower challenges with high heart rate variability, while others meet temptation at a distinct physiological disadvantage? Many factors influence your willpower reserve, from what you eat (plant-based, unprocessed foods help; junk food doesn't) to where you live (poor air quality decreases heart rate variability—yes, L.A.'s smog may be contributing to the high percentage of movie stars in rehab). *Anything* that puts a stress on your mind or body can interfere with the physiology of self-control, and by extension, sabotage your willpower. Anxiety, anger, depression, and loneliness are all associated with lower heart rate variability and less self-control. Chronic pain and illness can also drain your body and brain's willpower reserve. But there are just as many things you can do that shift the body and mind toward the physiology of self-control. The focus meditation you learned in the last chapter is one of the easiest and most effective ways to improve the biological basis of willpower. It not only trains the brain, but also increases heart rate variability. Anything else that you do to reduce stress and take care of your health— exercise, get a good night's sleep, eat better, spend quality time with friends and family, participate in a religious or spiritual practice—will improve your body's willpower reserve.

WILLPOWER EXPERIMENT: BREATHE
YOUR WAY TO SELF-CONTROL

You won't find many quick fixes in this book, but there is one way to immediately boost willpower: Slow your breathing down to four to six breaths per minute. That's ten to fifteen seconds per breath—slower than you normally breathe, but not difficult with a little bit of practice and patience. Slowing the breath down activates the prefrontal cortex and increases heart rate variability, which helps shift the brain and body from a state of stress to self-control mode. A few minutes of this technique will make you feel calm, in control, and capable of handling cravings or challenges.*

It's a good idea to practice slowing down your breath before you're staring down a cheesecake. Start by timing yourself to see how many breaths you normally take in one minute. Then begin to slow the breath down without holding your breath (that will only increase stress). For most people, it's easier to slow down the exhalation, so focus on exhaling slowly and completely (pursing your lips and imagining that you are exhaling through a straw in your mouth can help). Exhaling fully will help you breathe in more fully and deeply without struggling. If you don't quite get down to four breaths a minute, don't worry. Heart rate variability steadily increases as your breathing rate drops below twelve per minute.

Research shows that regular practice of this technique can make you more resilient to stress and build your willpower reserve. One study found that a daily twenty-minute practice of slowed breathing increased heart rate variability and reduced cravings and depression among adults recovering from substance abuse and post-traumatic stress disorder. Heart rate variability training programs (using similar breathing exercises) have also been used to improve self-control and decrease the stress of cops, stock traders, and

---

*If you want some technological help slowing down your breath, a number of products—from inexpensive smart phone apps (such at the Breath Pacer) to state-of-the-art heart rate variability monitors (such as the EmWave Personal Stress Reliever)—will help you pace your breathing to shift your biology.

customer service operators—three of the most stressful jobs on the planet. And because it takes only one to two minutes of breathing at this pace to boost your willpower reserve, it's something you can do whenever you face a willpower challenge.

WILLPOWER RX

One of my students, Nathan, worked as a physician's assistant at the local hospital. It was a rewarding but stressful job that involved both direct patient care and administrative duties. He found that the slowed-breathing exercise helped him think clearly and make better decisions under pressure. It was so useful, he taught it to his coworkers. They, too, started slowing down their breathing to prepare for stressful situations such as talking to a patient's family, or to help deal with the physical strain of working a long shift without enough sleep. Nathan even started suggesting it to patients, to help them deal with anxiety or get through an uncomfortable medical procedure. Many of the patients felt as though they had no control over what was happening to them. Slowing down the breath gave them a sense of control over their mind and body, and helped them find the courage they needed in difficult situations.

TRAIN YOUR MIND AND YOUR BODY

While there are many things you can do to support the physiology of self-control, this week I'm going to ask you to consider the two strategies that have the biggest bang for their buck. Both are inexpensive and immediately effective, with benefits that only build with time. They also improve a wide set of willpower saboteurs, including depression, anxiety, chronic pain, cardiovascular disease, and diabetes. That makes them good investments for anyone who wants more willpower and doesn't mind the side effects of better health and happiness.

THE WILLPOWER MIRACLE

Megan Oaten, a psychologist, and Ken Cheng, a biologist, had just concluded their first study of a new treatment for enhancing self-control. These two researchers at Macquarie University in Sydney, Australia, were stunned by the findings. While they had hoped for positive results, nobody could have predicted how far-reaching the treatment's effects would be. The trial's guinea pigs were six men and eighteen women, ranging in age from eighteen to fifty years old. After two months of the treatment, they showed improvements in attention and the ability to ignore distractions. In an age of thirty-second attention spans, that would have been reason enough to celebrate. But there was more. They had reduced their smoking, drinking, and caffeine intake—despite the fact that nobody had asked them to. They were eating less junk food and more healthy food. They were spending less time watching television and more time studying. They were saving money and spending less on impulse purchases. They felt more in control of their emotions. They even procrastinated less and were less likely to be late for appointments.

Good God, what is this miracle drug and where can I get a prescription?

The intervention wasn't a drug at all. The willpower miracle was physical exercise. The participants, none of whom exercised regularly before the intervention, were given free membership to a gym and encouraged to make good use of it. They exercised an average of just one time per week for the first month, but were up to three times per week by the end of the two-month study. The researchers did not ask them to make any other changes in their lives, and yet the exercise program seemed to spark newfound strength and self-control in *all* aspects of their lives.

Exercise turns out to be the closest thing to a wonder drug that self-control scientists have discovered. For starters, the willpower benefits of exercise are *immediate*. Fifteen minutes on a treadmill reduces cravings, as seen when researchers try to tempt dieters with chocolate and smokers with cigarettes. The long-term effects of exercise are even more impressive. It not only relieves ordinary, everyday stress, but it's as powerful an antidepressant as Prozac. Working out also enhances the biology of self-control by increasing baseline heart rate variability and training the brain. When neuroscientists have peered inside the brains of new exercisers, they have seen increases in both gray matter—brain cells—and white matter, the insulation on brain cells that helps them communicate quickly and efficiently with each other. Physical exercise—like meditation—makes your brain bigger and faster, and the prefrontal cortex shows the largest training effect.

The first question my students ask when they hear this research is, "How much do I need to do?" My response is always, "How much are you willing to do?" There's no point setting a goal that you're going to abandon in a week, and there's no scientific consensus about how much exercise you need to do. A 2010 analysis of ten different studies found that the biggest mood-boosting, stress-busting effects came from five-minute doses of exercise, not hour-long sessions. There's no shame—and a lot of potential good—in committing to just a five-minute walk around the block.

The next question everyone asks is, "What kind of exercise is best?" To which I respond, "What kind will you actually do?" The body and brain don't seem to discriminate, so whatever you are willing to do is the perfect place to start. Gardening, walking, dancing, yoga, team sports, swimming, playing with your kids or pets—even enthusiastic housecleaning and window-shopping qualify as exercise. If you are absolutely convinced that exercise is not for you, I encourage you to expand your definition to include anything you reasonably enjoy about which you can answer no to the following two questions: 1. Are you sitting, standing still, or lying down? 2. Are you eating junk food while you do it? When you have found an activity that meets this definition, congratulations! You have found your willpower workout.* Anything above and beyond the typical sedentary lifestyle will improve your willpower reserve.

---

*People seem to think I am kidding when I say this. I assure you, I am not. Only 11 percent of Americans currently meet the recommended guidelines for physical exercise, and I am not deluded enough to think everyone is going to start training for a marathon. Ample evidence suggests that a little exercise is better than none, and you can benefit from any physical activity, even if it doesn't involve sneakers or sweat.

WILLPOWER EXPERIMENT: THE FIVE-MINUTE GREEN WILLPOWER FILL-UP

If you want a quick willpower fill-up, your best bet may be to head outdoors. Just five minutes of what scientists call "green exercise" decreases stress, improves mood, enhances focus, and boosts self-control. Green exercise is any physical activity that gets you outdoors and in the presence of Mama Nature. The best news is that when it comes to green exercise, a quick fix really is enough. Shorter bursts have a more powerful effect on your mood than longer workouts. You also don't have to break a sweat or push yourself to exhaustion. Lower-intensity exercise, like walking, has stronger immediate effects than high-intensity exercise. Here are some ideas for your own five-minute green exercise willpower fill-up:

- Get out of the office and head for the closest greenery.
- Cue up a favorite song on your iPod and walk or jog around the block.
- Take your dog outside to play (and chase the toy yourself).
- Do a bit of work in your yard or garden.
- Step outside for some fresh air and do a few simple stretches.
- Challenge your kids to a race or game in the backyard.

A RELUCTANT EXERCISER CHANGES HIS MIND

Antonio, a fifty-four-year-old owner of two successful Italian restaurants, was in my class on doctor's orders. He had high blood pressure and cholesterol, and his waist size crept up an inch every year. If he didn't change his lifestyle, his doctor warned him, he was going to collapse of a heart attack over a plate of veal parmigiana.

Antonio had reluctantly gotten a treadmill for his home office, but it wasn't seeing much use. Exercise seemed like a waste of time; it wasn't fun and it wasn't productive—not to mention the irritation of someone else telling him what he needed to do!

The idea that exercise could increase brain power and willpower intrigued Antonio, though. He was a competitive guy and did not want to slow down. He started to see exercise as a secret weapon, something that could keep him at the top of his game. It didn't hurt that it would improve heart rate variability, which is a major predictor of mortality among people with cardiovascular disease.

He turned his treadmill into a willpower generator by taping a "Willpower" label over the machine's calorie tracker (since he didn't really give a damn how many calories he burned—this was a guy who would throw an entire stick of butter in a pan without thinking twice). As he walked and burned more calories, the "Willpower" number ticked up and he felt stronger. He started to use the treadmill each morning to fuel up with willpower for the day's difficult meetings and long hours.

Antonio's willpower machine did improve his health—what his doctor wanted—but Antonio also got something he wanted. He felt more energized and in control throughout the day. He had assumed that exercise would take away from his energy and time, but found it gave him back far more than he spent.

If you tell yourself that you are too tired or don't have the time to exercise, start thinking of exercise as something that restores, not drains, your energy and willpower.

GAIN WILLPOWER IN YOUR SLEEP!

If you are surviving on less than six hours of sleep a night, there's a good chance you don't even remember what it's like to have your full willpower. Being mildly but chronically sleep deprived makes you more susceptible to stress, cravings, and temptation. It also makes it more difficult to control your emotions, focus your attention, or find the energy to tackle the big "I will" power challenges. (In my classes, there's always one group that immediately recognizes the truth of this statement: new parents.) If you are chronically sleep deprived, you may find yourself feeling regret at the end of the day, wondering why you gave in again to temptation or put off doing what you needed to do. It's easy to let this spiral into shame and guilt. It hardly ever occurs to us that we don't need to become better people, but to become better rested.

Why does poor sleep sap willpower? For starters, sleep deprivation impairs how the body and brain use glucose, their main form of energy. When you're tired, your cells have trouble absorbing glucose from the bloodstream. This leaves them underfueled, and you exhausted. With your body and brain desperate for energy, you'll start to crave sweets or caffeine. But even if you try to refuel with sugar or coffee, your body and brain won't get the energy they need because they won't be able to use it efficiently. This is bad news for self-control, one of the most energy-expensive tasks your brain can spend its limited fuel on.

Your prefrontal cortex, that energy-hungry area of the brain, bears the brunt of this personal energy crisis. Sleep researchers even have a cute nickname for this state: "mild prefrontal dysfunction." Shortchange your sleep, and you wake up with temporary Phineas Gage–like damage to your brain. Studies show that the effects of sleep deprivation on your brain are equivalent to being mildly intoxicated—a state that many of us can attest does little for self-control.

When your prefrontal cortex is impaired, it loses control over other regions of the brain. Ordinarily, it can quiet the alarm system of the brain to help you manage stress and cravings. But a single night of sleep deprivation creates a disconnect between these two regions of your brain. Unchecked, the alarm system overreacts to ordinary, everyday stress. The body gets stuck in a physiological fight-or-flight state, with the accompanying high levels of stress hormones and decreased heart rate variability. The result: more stress and less self-control.

The good news is, all of this is reversible. When the sleep-deprived catch a better night's sleep, their brain scans no longer show signs of prefrontal cortex impairment. In fact, they look just like the brains of the well-rested. Addiction researchers have even started to experiment with sleep interventions as a treatment for substance abuse. In one study, five minutes of breath-focus meditation a day helped recovering addicts fall asleep. This added one hour a night to their quality sleep time, which in turn significantly reduced the risk of drug use relapse. So for better willpower, go to sleep already.

WILLPOWER EXPERIMENT: ZZZZZZZZZZ

If you've been running short on sleep, there are many ways to recharge your self-control. Even if you can't get eight hours of uninterrupted sleep every night, small changes can make a big difference. Some studies show that a single good night's sleep restores brain function to an optimal level. So if you've had a week of late to bed and early to rise, catching up on the weekend can help replenish your willpower. Other research suggests that getting enough sleep early in the week can build a reserve that counteracts sleep deprivation later in the week. And some studies suggest that it's the number of consecutive hours you spend awake that matters most. In a crunch, taking a short nap can restore focus and self-control even if you didn't get much sleep the night before. Try one of these strategies—catching up, stocking up, or napping—to undo or prevent the effects of sleep deprivation.

WHEN SLEEP IS THE WILLPOWER CHALLENGE

One of my students, Lisa, was trying to break the habit of staying up late. At twenty-nine, she was single and lived alone, which meant there was no one setting a sleep schedule for her. She woke up each morning exhausted and dragged herself through her job as an office administrator. She relied on caffeinated diet soda to get through the day, and to her embarrassment, she sometimes nodded off in meetings. By five o'clock, she was wired *and* tired, a combination that left her cranky, distracted, and craving drive-through fast food. The first week of class, she announced that going to sleep earlier would be her willpower challenge for the class.

The next week, she reported no success. Around dinnertime, she would tell herself, "I will definitely go to sleep earlier tonight," but by eleven p.m., that resolve was nowhere to be found. I asked Lisa to describe the process of how she *wasn't* going to bed early. She told me about the million and one things that each seemed more critically urgent the later the night got. Browsing Facebook, cleaning the fridge, tackling the stack of junk mail, even watching infomercials—none of this stuff was actually urgent, but late at night, it felt strangely compelling. Lisa was hooked on doing "one more thing" before she went to sleep. The later it got, and the more tired Lisa got, the less she was able to resist the immediate gratification that each task promised.

When we redefined getting more sleep as a *won't* power challenge, things turned around. Forcing herself to go to sleep wasn't the real problem, it was pulling herself away from the things keeping her up. Lisa set a rule of turning off her computer and TV and not starting any new projects after eleven p.m. This rule was exactly what she needed to feel how tired she really was and give herself permission to go to bed by midnight. With seven hours of sleep each night, Lisa found that infomercials and other late-night temptations lost their appeal. Within a couple of weeks, she had the energy to tackle the next willpower challenge: cutting back on diet soda and drive-through dinners.

If you know you could use more sleep but you find yourself staying up late anyway, consider what you are saying "yes" to instead of sleep. This same willpower rule applies to any task you are avoiding or putting off—when you can't find the will, you might need to find the won't.

THE COSTS OF TOO MUCH SELF-CONTROL

The willpower instinct is a wonderful thing: Thanks to the brain's hard work and the cooperation of your body, your choices can be driven by long-term goals, not panic or the need for instant gratification. But self-control doesn't come cheap. All of these mental tasks—focusing your attention, weighing competing goals, and quieting stress and cravings—require energy, real physical energy from your body, in the same way that your muscles require energy to fight or flee in an emergency.

Everyone knows that too much stress is bad for your health. When you are chronically stressed, your body continues to divert energy from long-term needs such as digestion, reproduction, healing injuries, and fighting off illnesses to respond to the constant stream of apparent emergencies. This is how chronic stress can lead to cardiovascular disease, diabetes, chronic back pain, infertility, or getting every cold and flu that come around. That you never actually have to fight or flee these ordinary stresses (good luck trying to outrun or mortally wound your credit card debt) is beside the point. So long as your brain keeps identifying an external threat, your mind and body will be thrown into a state of high alert and impulsive action.

Because self-control also demands high levels of energy, some scientists speculate that chronic self-control—like chronic stress—can increase your chances of getting sick by diverting resources from the immune system. You heard it here first: Too much willpower can actually be bad for your health. You may be thinking: What about all that stuff in the first chapter about how important willpower is for health? Now you're telling me self-control is going to make me sick? Well, maybe. Just like some stress is necessary for a happy and productive life, some self-control is needed. But just like living under chronic stress is unhealthy, trying to control every aspect of your thoughts, emotions, and behavior is a toxic strategy. It is too big a burden for your biology.

Self-control, like the stress response, evolved as a nifty strategy for responding to specific challenges. But just as with stress, we run into trouble when self-control becomes chronic and unrelenting. We need time to recover from the exertion of self-control, and we sometimes need to spend our mental and physical resources elsewhere. To preserve both your health and happiness, you need to give up the pursuit of willpower perfection. Even as you strengthen your self-control, you cannot control everything you think, feel, say, and do. You will have to choose your willpower battles wisely.

WILLPOWER EXPERIMENT: RELAX TO RESTORE
YOUR WILLPOWER RESERVE

One of the best ways to recover from stress *and* the daily self-control demands of your life is relaxation. Relaxing—even for just a few minutes—increases heart rate variability by activating the parasympathetic nervous system and quieting the sympathetic nervous system. It also shifts the body into a state of repair and healing, enhancing your immune function and lowering stress hormones. Studies show that taking time for relaxation every day can protect your health while also increasing your willpower reserve. For example, people who regularly practiced relaxation had a healthier physiological response to two stressful willpower challenges: a test of mental focus, and a test of pain endurance (keeping one foot immersed in a pan of 39°F water—readers, please do not try this at home). Athletes who relax through deep breathing and physical rest recover more quickly from a grueling training session, reducing stress hormones and oxidative damage to their bodies.

We're not talking about zoning out with television or "relaxing" with a glass of wine and a huge meal. The kind of relaxation that boosts willpower is true physical and mental rest that triggers what Harvard Medical School cardiologist Herbert Benson calls the *physiological relaxation response*. Your heart rate and breathing slow down, your blood pressure drops, and your muscles release held tension. Your brain takes a break from planning the future or analyzing the past.

To trigger this relaxation response, lie down on your back, and slightly elevate your legs with a pillow under the knees (or come into whatever is the most comfortable position for you to rest in). Close your eyes and take a few deep breaths, allowing your belly to rise and fall. If you feel any tension in your body, you can intentionally squeeze or contract that muscle, then let go of the effort. For example, if you notice tension in your hands and fingers, squeeze your hands into fists, then relax them into open hands. If you notice tension in your forehead or jaw, scrunch up your eyes and face, then stretch your mouth wide open before relaxing the face completely.

Stay here for five to ten minutes, enjoying the fact that there is nothing to do but breathe. If you're worried about falling asleep, set an alarm.

Make this a daily practice, especially when you're dealing with high levels of stress or willpower demands. Relaxation will help your body recover from the physiological effects of chronic stress or heroic self-control.

ONE NATION UNDER STRESS

Many of us come to the topic of willpower with ideas about what it is: a personality trait, a virtue, something you either have or you don't, maybe a kind of brute force you muster up in difficult situations. But science is painting a very different picture of willpower. It's an evolved capacity and an instinct that everyone has—a careful calibration of what's happening in your brain and body. But we've also seen that if you are stressed or depressed, your brain and body may not cooperate. Willpower can be disrupted by sleep deprivation, poor diet, a sedentary lifestyle, and a host of other factors that sap your energy, or keep your brain and body stuck in a chronic stress response. To every doctor, diet guru, or nagging spouse convinced that willpower is just a matter of making up your mind, this research should be a reality check. Yes, your mind is important, but your body also needs to get on board.

Science also points us to a critical insight: Stress is the enemy of will-power. So often we believe that stress is the only way to get things done, and we even look for ways to increase stress—such as waiting until the last minute, or criticizing ourselves for being lazy or out of control—to motivate ourselves. Or we use stress to try to motivate others, turning up the heat at work or coming down hard at home. This may seem to work in the short term, but in the long term, nothing drains willpower faster than stress. The biology of stress and the biology of self-control are simply incompatible. Both the fight-or-flight and pause-and-plan responses are about energy management, but they redirect your energy and attention in very different ways. The fight-or-flight response floods the body with energy to act instinctively, and steals it from the areas of the brain needed for wise decision making. The pause-and-plan response sends that energy to the brain—and not just anywhere in the brain, but specifically to the self-control center, the prefrontal cortex. Stress encourages you to focus on immediate, short-term goals and outcomes, but self-control requires keeping the big picture in mind. Learning how to better manage your stress is one of the most important things you can do to improve your willpower.

In recent years, a number of high-profile pundits have claimed that Americans have lost their collective willpower. If this is true, it may have little to do with the loss of core American values, as the pundits have claimed, and more to do with the increased levels of stress and fear in today's society. A 2010 national survey by the American Psychological Association found that 75 percent of people in the United States experience high levels of stress. It's not surprising, given the events of the last decade, from terrorist attacks and flu epidemics to environmental disasters, natural disasters, unemployment, and near economic collapse. These national stresses take a toll on our physiology and self-control. Researchers at Yale University School of Medicine found that during the week after September 11, 2001, patients' heart rate variability decreased significantly. We were a nation overwhelmed, and it's not surprising that rates of drinking, smoking, and drug use increased for months following the attacks of 9/11. The same pattern emerged during the height of the economic crisis of 2008 and 2009. Americans reported indulging in unhealthy foods more often to cope with the stress, and smokers reported smoking more cigarettes and giving up attempts to quit.

We're also an increasingly sleep-deprived nation. According to a 2008 study by the National Sleep Foundation, American adults now get two hours less sleep per night than the average in 1960. Our nation's sleeping habits may be creating an epidemic of poor self-control and focus. Some experts believe that the decrease in average sleep time is also one of the reasons obesity rates have soared over the same time period. Obesity rates are much higher among those who sleep for less than six hours a night, in part because sleep deprivation interferes with how the brain and body use energy. Researchers have also found that too little sleep creates impulse control and attention problems that mimic attention deficit and hyperactivity disorder (ADHD). It may be that children's sleep habits—which typically mirror their parents', despite their even greater need for sleep—are contributing to the dramatic rise in the diagnosis of this disorder.

If we are serious about tackling the biggest challenges that face us, we need to take more seriously the tasks of managing stress and taking better care of ourselves. Tired, stressed-out people start from a tremendous disadvantage, and we are a tired, stressed-out nation. Our bad habits—from overeating to undersleeping—don't just reflect a lack of self-control. By draining our energy and creating more stress, they are stealing our self-control.

UNDER THE MICROSCOPE: STRESS AND SELF-CONTROL

This week, test the theory that stress—whether physical or psychological—is the enemy of self-control. How does being worried or overworked affect your choices? Does being hungry or tired drain your willpower? What about physical pain and illness? Or emotions like anger, loneliness, or sadness? Notice when stress strikes throughout the day or week. Then watch what happens to your self-control. Do you experience cravings? Lose your temper? Put off things you know you should do?

THE LAST WORD

When our willpower challenges overwhelm us, it's tempting to assign the blame to who we are: weak, lazy, willpowerless wimps. But more often than not, our brains and bodies are simply in the wrong state for self-control. When we're in a state of chronic stress, it's our most impulsive selves who face our willpower challenges. To succeed at our willpower challenges, we need to find the state of mind and body that puts our energy toward self-control, not self-defense. That means giving ourselves what we need to recover from stress, and making sure we have the energy to be our best selves.

CHAPTER SUMMARY

The Idea: Willpower is a biological instinct, like stress, that evolved to help us protect ourselves from ourselves.

Under the Microscope

- *What is the threat?* For your willpower challenge, identify the *inner* impulse that needs to be restrained.
- *Stress and self-control.* Notice when stress strikes throughout the day or week, and watch what happens to your self-control. Do you experience cravings? Lose your temper? Put off things you know you should do?

Willpower Experiments

- *Breathe your way to self-control.* Slow down your breathing to four to six breaths per minute to shift into the physiological state of self-control.
- *The five-minute green willpower fill-up.* Get active outdoors—even just a walk around the block—to reduce stress, improve your mood, and boost motivation.
- *Zzzzzzzzzz.* Undo the effects of sleep deprivation with a nap or one good night's sleep.
- *Relax to restore your willpower reserve.* Lie down, breathe deeply, and let the physiological relaxation response help you recover from the demands of self-control and daily stress.

THREE

Too Tired to Resist: Why Self-Control Is Like a Muscle

It's a familiar sight on college campuses across the country: Haggard-looking students slump over library desks and laptops. Zombie-like, they lurch across campus in search of caffeine and sugar. The gyms are empty, beds unslept in. At Stanford, it's called "Dead Week"—the seven-day final examination period at the end of every quarter. Students cram their heads with facts and formulas, pull all-nighters, and push themselves to study hard enough to make up for ten weeks of dorm parties and Frisbee golf. However, studies show that these heroic efforts come at a cost (beyond the nightly pizza deliveries and pricey espresso drinks). During final exam periods, many students seem to lose the capacity to control anything other than their study habits. They smoke more cigarettes and ditch the salad bar for the french fry line. They're prone to emotional outbursts and bike accidents. They skip showering and shaving, and rarely make the effort to change clothes. Dear God, they even stop flossing.

Welcome to one of the most robust, if troubling, findings from the science of self-control: People who use their willpower seem to run out of it. Smokers who go without a cigarette for twenty-four hours are more likely to binge on ice cream. Drinkers who resist their favorite cocktail become physically weaker on a test of endurance. Perhaps most disturbingly, people who are on a diet are more likely to cheat on their spouse. It's as if there's only so much willpower to go around. Once exhausted, you are left defenseless against temptation—or at least disadvantaged.

This finding has important implications for your willpower challenges. Modern life is full of self-control demands that can drain your willpower. Researchers have found that self-control is highest in the morning and steadily deteriorates over the course of the day. By the time you get to the stuff that really matters to you, like going to the gym after work, tackling the big project, keeping your cool when your kids turn the couch into a finger paint masterpiece, or staying away from the emergency pack of cigarettes stashed in your drawer, you may find yourself out of willpower. And if you try to control or change too many things at once, you may exhaust yourself completely. This failure says nothing about your virtue—just about the nature of willpower itself.

THE MUSCLE MODEL
OF SELF-CONTROL

The first scientist to systematically observe and test the limits of willpower was Roy Baumeister, a psychologist at Florida State University with a long-standing reputation for studying puzzling phenomena. He had tackled questions like why sports teams show a home court disadvantage during championships, and why good-looking criminals are more likely to be found not guilty by a jury.* His work has even touched on satanic ritual

---

*Curious about the answers? Athletes become more self-conscious during high-stakes competitions in front of a hometown audience, and this interferes with their ability to respond instinctively and automatically to the game. Juries are more likely to assume that an attractive person is basically a "good" person, and that external factors influenced his or her "bad" behavior—providing the benefit of that all-important reasonable doubt.

abuse, sexual masochism, and UFO abductions—topics that would scare away most researchers. You could argue, however, that his most frightening findings have little to do with the occult, and everything to do with ordinary human weakness. For the last fifteen years, he has been asking people to exert their willpower in the laboratory—turning down cookies, tuning out distractions, holding back their anger, and holding their arms in ice water. In study after study, no matter what task he used, people's self-control deteriorated over time. A concentration task didn't just lead to worse attention over time; it depleted physical strength. Controlling emotions didn't just lead to emotional outbursts; it made people more willing to spend money on something they didn't need. Resisting tempting sweets didn't just trigger cravings for chocolate; it prompted procrastination. It was as if every act of willpower was drawing from the same source of strength, leaving people weaker with each successful act of self-control.

These observations led Baumeister to an intriguing hypothesis: that self-control is like a muscle. When used, it gets tired. If you don't rest the muscle, you can run out of strength entirely, like an athlete who pushes himself to exhaustion. Since that early hypothesis, dozens of studies by Baumeister's laboratory and other research teams have supported the idea that willpower is a limited resource. Trying to control your temper, stick to a budget, or refuse seconds all tap the same source of strength. And because every act of willpower depletes willpower, using self-control can lead to *losing* control. Refraining from gossiping at work may make it more difficult to resist the cafeteria dessert table. And if you do turn down that tempting tiramisu, you may find it more difficult to focus when you're back at your desk. By the time you're driving home, and the idiot in the next lane almost runs into you because he's looking at his cell phone—yeah, that'll be you screaming out your window that he should be sure to program 911 into his phone, the jackass.

Many things you wouldn't typically think of as requiring willpower also rely on—and exhaust—this limited well of strength. Trying to impress a date or fit into a corporate culture that doesn't share your values. Navigating a stressful commute, or sitting through another boring meeting. Anytime you have to fight an impulse, filter out distractions, weigh competing goals, or make yourself do something difficult, you use a little more of your willpower strength. This even includes trivial decisions, like choosing between the twenty brands of laundry detergent at the market. If your brain and body need to pause and plan, you're flexing the metaphorical muscle of self-control.

The muscle model is at once reassuring and discouraging. It's nice to know that not every willpower failure reveals our innate inadequacies; sometimes they point to how hard we've been working. But while it's comforting to know that we can't expect ourselves to be perfect, this research also points to some serious problems. If willpower is limited, are we doomed to fail at our biggest goals? And thanks to the near-constant self-control demands of our society, are we destined to be a nation of willpower-drained zombies, wandering the world seeking instant gratification?

Luckily there are things you can do to both overcome willpower exhaustion and increase your self-control strength. That's because the muscle model doesn't just help us see why we fail when we're tired; it also shows us how to train self-control. We'll start by considering why willpower gets exhausted. Then we'll take a lesson from endurance athletes—who regularly push past exhaustion—and explore training strategies for greater self-control stamina.

UNDER THE MICROSCOPE: THE HIGHS AND LOWS OF WILLPOWER

The muscle model of willpower predicts that self-control drains throughout the day. This week, pay attention to when you have the most willpower, and when you are most likely to give in. Do you wake up with willpower and steadily drain it? Or is there another time of the day when you find yourself recharged and refreshed? You can use this self-knowledge to plan your schedule wisely, and limit temptations when you know you'll be the most depleted.

A Would-Be Entrepreneur
Puts First Things First

When Susan woke up at five-thirty a.m., the first thing she did was check her work e-mail at her kitchen table. She would spend a good forty-five minutes over coffee responding to questions and identifying her priorities for the day. Then she headed off on an hour-long commute to put in a ten-hour day as a key account manager for a large commercial shipping company. Her job was demanding—conflicts to be negotiated, egos to be soothed, fires to be put out. By six p.m., she was already drained, but more often than not, she felt obligated to stay late or go out for dinner or drinks with coworkers. Susan wanted to start her own consulting business, and was taking steps to prepare herself financially and professionally. But most evenings she was too tired to make much progress on her business plan, and she feared that she'd be stuck in her job forever.

When Susan analyzed how she was spending her willpower, it was obvious that her job was getting a hundred percent, starting with the early-morning e-mail and ending with her long commute home. The kitchen-table e-mail session was an old habit from when she was new to the job and eager to exceed expectations. But now, there was no good reason those e-mails couldn't wait until she got to the office at eight a.m. Susan decided that the only time of day she was likely to have the mental energy to pursue her own goals was before her workday. She made it her new routine to spend the first hour of the day building her business, not taking care of everyone else's needs.

This was a smart move for Susan, who needed to put her willpower where her goals were. It also demonstrates an important willpower rule: *If you never seem to have the time and energy for your "I will" challenge, schedule it for when you have the most strength.*

WHY IS SELF-CONTROL LIMITED?

Obviously we don't have an actual self-control muscle hidden underneath our biceps, keeping our hands from reaching for dessert or our wallet. We do, however, have something like a self-control muscle in our brain. Even though the brain is an organ, not a muscle, it does get tired from repeated acts of self-control. Neuroscientists have found that with each use of willpower, the self-control system of the brain becomes less active. Just like a tired runner's legs can give out, the brain seems to run out of the strength to keep going.

Matthew Gailliot, a young psychologist working with Roy Baumeister, wondered whether a tired brain was essentially a problem of energy. Self-control is an energy-expensive task for the brain, and our internal energy supply is limited—after all, it's not like we have an intravenous sugar drip into our prefrontal cortex. Gailliot asked himself: Could willpower exhaustion simply be the result of the brain running out of energy?

To find out, he decided to test whether giving people energy—in the form of sugar—could restore exhausted willpower. He brought people into the laboratory to perform a wide range of self-control tasks, from ignoring distractions to controlling their emotions. Before and after each task, he measured their blood sugar levels. The more a person's blood sugar dropped after a self-control task, the worse his performance on the next task. It appeared as if self-control was draining the body of energy, and this energy loss was weakening self-control.

Gailliot then gave the willpower-drained participants a glass of lemonade. Half of them received sugar-sweetened lemonade to restore blood sugar; the other half received a placebo drink that was artificially sweetened and would not supply any usable energy. Amazingly, boosting blood sugar restored willpower. The participants who drank sugar-sweetened lemonade showed improved self-control, while the self-control of those who drank the placebo lemonade continued to deteriorate.

Low blood sugar levels turn out to predict a wide range of willpower failures, from giving up on a difficult test to lashing out at others when you're angry. Gailliot, now a professor at Zirve University in Turkey, has found that people with low blood sugar are also more likely to rely on stereotypes and less likely to donate money to charity or help a stranger. It is as if running low on energy biases us to be the worst versions of ourselves. In contrast, giving participants a sugar boost turns them back into the best versions of themselves: more persistent and less impulsive; more thoughtful and less selfish.

Well, as you can imagine, this is just about the most best-received finding I've ever described in class. The implications are at once counterintuitive and delightful. Sugar is your new best friend. Eating a candy bar or drinking soda can be an act of self-control! (Or at least restoring self-control.) My students love these studies and are only too happy to test the hypothesis themselves. One student used a steady supply of Skittles to get through a difficult project. Another kept a tin of Altoids (one of the last breath mints to contain real sugar) in his pocket, popping them during long meetings to outlast his colleagues. I applaud their enthusiasm for translating science into action and empathize with their sweet tooth. And I even confess that for years, I brought candy to every Introduction to Psychology class, hoping to get the undergraduate students focused and off Facebook.*

If sugar were truly the secret to more willpower, I'm sure I'd have a runaway bestseller on my hands and a lot of eager corporate sponsors. But as my students and I were trying our own willpower-replenishing experiments, some scientists—including Gailliot—started to raise some smart questions. How much energy, exactly, was getting used up during acts of mental self-control? And did restoring that energy really require consuming a substantial amount of sugar? University of Pennsylvania psychologist Robert Kurzban has argued that the actual amount of energy your brain needs to exert self-control is less than half a Tic Tac per minute. This may

---

*Did plying students with candy work? I'm not entirely sure, although it did pay off on the end-of-quarter course evaluations.

be more than the brain uses for other mental tasks, but it is far less than your body uses when it exercises. So assuming you have the resources to walk around the block without collapsing, the absolute demands of self-control couldn't possibly deplete your entire body's store of energy. And surely it wouldn't require refueling with a sugar-laden 100-calorie drink. Why, then, does the brain's increased energy consumption during self-control seem to deplete willpower so quickly?

ENERGY CRISIS

To answer this question, it may be helpful to recall the American banking crisis of 2009. After the 2008 financial meltdown, banks received an influx of money from the government. These funds were supposed to help the banks cover their own financial obligations so they could start lending again. But the banks refused to lend money to small businesses and individual borrowers. They weren't confident in the money supply, so they hoarded the resources they had. Stingy bastards!

It turns out that your brain can be a bit of a stingy bastard, too. The human brain has, at any given time, a very small supply of energy. It can store some energy in its cells, but it is mostly dependent on a steady stream of glucose circulating in the body's bloodstream. Special glucose-detecting brain cells are constantly monitoring the availability of energy. When the brain detects a drop in available energy, it gets a little nervous. What if it runs out of energy? Like the banks, it may decide to stop spending and save what resources it has. It will keep itself on a tight energy budget, unwilling to spend its full supply of energy. The first expense to be cut? Self-control, one of the most energy-expensive tasks the brain performs. To conserve energy, the brain may become reluctant to give you the full mental resources you need to resist temptation, focus your attention, or control your emotions.

University of South Dakota researchers X. T. Wang, a behavioral economist, and Robert Dvorak, a psychologist, have proposed an "energy budget" model of self-control. They argue that the brain treats energy like money. It will spend energy when resources are high, but save energy when resources are dropping. To test this idea, they invited sixty-five adults—ranging in age from nineteen to fifty-one—into the laboratory for a test of their willpower. Participants were given a series of choices between two rewards, such as $120 tomorrow or $450 in a month. One reward was always smaller, but participants would get it faster than the larger reward. Psychologists consider this a classic test of self-control, as it pits immediate gratification against more-favorable long-term consequences. At the end of the study, the participants had the opportunity to win one of their chosen rewards. This ensured that they were motivated to make real decisions based on what they wanted to win.

Before the choosing began, the researchers measured participants' blood sugar levels to determine the baseline status of available "funds" for self-control. After the first round of decisions, participants were given either a regular, sugary soda (to boost blood sugar levels) or a zero-calorie diet soda. The researchers then measured blood sugar levels again, and asked the participants to make another series of choices. The participants who drank the regular soda showed a sharp increase in blood sugar. They also became more likely to delay gratification for the bigger reward. In contrast, blood sugar dropped among the participants who drank the diet soda.* These participants were now more likely to choose the immediate gratification of the quicker, smaller reward. Importantly, it wasn't the absolute level of blood sugar that predicted a participant's choices—it was the direction of change. The brain asked, "Is available energy increasing or decreasing?" It then made a strategic choice about whether to spend or save that energy.

---

*This is a little-known effect of diet soda that contributes to hunger, overeating, and weight gain. The sweet taste tricks the body into taking up glucose from the bloodstream in anticipation of a blood sugar spike. You're left with less energy and less self-control, while your body and brain wonder what happened to the sugar rush they were promised. This may be why recent studies show that diet soda consumption is associated with weight gain, not weight loss.

PEOPLE WHO ARE STARVING SHOULDN'T SAY NO TO A SNACK

The brain may have a second motivation behind its reluctance to exert self-control when the body's energy levels are dropping. Our brains evolved in an environment very different from our own—one in which food supplies were unpredictable. (Remember our trip to the Serengeti, when you were scavenging for antelope carcasses?) Dvorak and Wang argue that the modern human brain may still be using blood sugar levels as a sign of scarcity or abundance in the environment. Are the bushes full of berries, or barren? Is dinner dropping dead at our feet, or do we have to chase it across the plains? Is there enough food for everyone, or do we have to compete with bigger and faster hunters and gatherers?

Way back when the human brain was taking shape, dropping blood sugar levels had less to do with whether you'd been using your energy-guzzling prefrontal cortex to resist a cookie, and more to do with whether food was available at all. If you hadn't eaten in a while, your blood sugar was low. To an energy-monitoring brain, your blood sugar level was an indicator of how likely you were to starve in the near future if you didn't find something to eat, quick.

A brain that could bias your decisions toward immediate gratification when resources are scarce, but toward long-term investment when resources are plenty, would be a real asset in a world with an unpredictable food supply. Those who were slower to listen to their hunger, or too polite to fight for their share, may have found the last bone already scraped clean. In times of food scarcity, early humans who followed their appetites and impulses had a better chance of survival. He who takes the biggest risks—from exploring new land to trying new foods and new mates—is often the most likely to survive (or at least have his genes survive). What appears in our modern world as a *loss* of control may actually be a vestige of the brain's instinct for strategic risk-taking. To prevent starvation, the brain shifts to a more risk-taking, impulsive state. Indeed, studies show that modern humans are more likely to take *any* kind of risk when they're hungry. For example, people make riskier investments when they're hungry, and are more willing to "diversify their mating strategies" (evolutionary psychologist–speak for cheating on their partner) after a fast.

Unfortunately, in modern Western society, this instinct no longer pays off. Internal changes in blood sugar levels rarely signal famine or the need to quickly pass on your genes in case you don't survive winter. But when your blood sugar drops, your brain will still favor short-term thinking and impulsive behavior. Your brain's priority is going to be getting more energy, not making sure you make good decisions that are in line with your long-term goals. That means stockbrokers may make some stupid buys before lunch, dieters may be more likely to "invest" in lottery tickets, and the politician who skips breakfast may find his intern irresistible.

WILLPOWER EXPERIMENT: THE WILLPOWER DIET

Yes, it's true that a shot of sugar can give you a short-term willpower boost in an emergency. In the long run, though, mainlining sugar is not a good strategy for self-control. During stressful times, it's especially tempting to turn to highly processed, high-fat, and high-sugar "comfort" food. Doing so, however, will lead to a self-control crash and burn. In the long term, blood sugar spikes and crashes can interfere with the body's and brain's ability to use sugar—meaning that you could end up with high blood sugar, but low energy (as is the case for the millions of Americans with type 2 diabetes*). A better plan is to make sure that your body is well-fueled with food that gives you lasting energy. Most psychologists and nutritionists recommend a low-glycemic diet—that is, one that helps you keep your blood sugar steady. Low-glycemic foods include lean proteins, nuts and beans, high-fiber grains and cereals, and most fruits and vegetables—basically, food that looks like its

---

*In fact, type 2 diabetes is for all practical purposes the same as chronic low blood sugar, because the brain and body cannot efficiently use the energy that is available. This is likely one reason people with uncontrolled diabetes show impaired self-control and deficits in prefrontal cortex function.

natural state and doesn't have a ton of added sugar, fat, and chemicals. It may take some self-control to shift in this direction, but whatever steps you take (say, eating a hearty and healthy breakfast during the workweek instead of skipping breakfast, or snacking on nuts instead of sugar) will more than pay you back for any willpower you spend making the change.

TRAINING THE WILLPOWER MUSCLE

Any muscle in your body can be made stronger through exercise—whether you're building your biceps by lifting barbells, or training your thumbs by text messaging. If self-control is a muscle (even a metaphorical muscle), it should be possible to train it, too. As with physical exercise, using your self-control muscle may be tiring, but over time, the workout should make it stronger.

Researchers have put this idea to the test with willpower-training regimes. We're not talking military boot camp or Master Cleanses here. These interventions take a simpler approach: Challenge the self-control muscle by asking people to control one small thing that they aren't used to controlling. For example, one willpower-training program asked participants to create and meet self-imposed deadlines. You could do this for any task you've been putting off, such as cleaning your closet. The deadlines might be: Week 1, open the door and stare at the mess. Week 2, tackle anything that's on a hanger. Week 3, throw out anything that predates the Reagan administration. Week 4, find out if Goodwill accepts skeletons. Week 5—well, you get the picture. When the willpower trainees set this kind of schedule for themselves for two months, not only did closets get cleaned and projects completed, but they also improved their diets, exercised more, and cut back on cigarettes, alcohol, and caffeine. It was as if they had strengthened their self-control muscle.

Other studies have found that committing to any small, consistent act of self-control—improving your posture, squeezing a handgrip every day to exhaustion, cutting back on sweets, and keeping track of your spending—can increase overall willpower. And while these small self-control exercises may seem inconsequential, they appear to improve the willpower challenges we care about most, including focusing at work, taking good care of our health, resisting temptation, and feeling more in control of our emotions. One study, led by a team of psychologists at Northwestern University, even tested whether two weeks of willpower training could reduce violence against a romantic partner.* They randomly assigned forty adults (ages eighteen to forty-five, all in romantic relationships) to one of three training groups. One group was asked to use their nondominant hand for eating, brushing their teeth, and opening doors. The second group was told to avoid swearing and to say "yes" instead of "yeah." The third group received no special instructions. After two weeks, participants in both self-control groups were less likely to respond to typical triggering events, like jealousy or feeling disrespected by their partner, with physical violence. The third group, in contrast, showed no change. Even if you don't personally struggle with physical violence, we all know what it's like to lose our cool and do something out of anger that we later regret.

The important "muscle" action being trained in all these studies isn't the specific willpower challenge of meeting deadlines, using your left hand to open doors, or keeping the F-word to yourself. It's the habit of noticing what you are about to do, and choosing to do the more difficult thing instead of the easiest. Through each of these willpower exercises, the brain gets used to pausing before acting. The triviality of the assignments may even help this process. The tasks are challenging, but they're not overwhelming. And while the self-restraints require careful attention, they're unlikely to trigger strong feelings of deprivation. ("What do you mean I'm

---

*The same research team is responsible for one of the most creative studies of interpersonal aggression I've seen. Scientists can't invite participants to beat up their romantic partners in the laboratory (thank goodness), but they still need to be able to observe acts of physical aggression. So in one study, these researchers asked participants to choose what uncomfortable yoga pose their partners would have to do, and how long they would have to hold it.

not allowed to say 'yeah'?!?!? That's the only thing that gets me through the day!") The relative unimportance of the willpower challenges allowed participants to exercise the muscle of self-control without the internal angst that derails so many of our attempts to change.

WILLPOWER EXPERIMENT: A WILLPOWER WORKOUT

If you want to put yourself through your own willpower-training regime, test the muscle model of self-control with one of the following willpower workouts:

- *Strengthen "I Won't" Power:* Commit to not swearing (or refraining from any habit of speech), not crossing your legs when you sit, or using your nondominant hand for a daily task like eating or opening doors.
- *Strengthen "I Will" Power:* Commit to doing something every day (not something you already do) just for the practice of building a habit and not making excuses. It could be calling your mother, meditating for five minutes, or finding one thing in your house that needs to be thrown out or recycled.
- *Strengthen Self-Monitoring:* Formally keep track of something you don't usually pay close attention to. This could be your spending, what you eat, or how much time you spend online or watching TV. You don't need fancy technology—pencil and paper will do. But if you need some inspiration, the Quantified Self movement (www.quantifiedself.com) has turned self-tracking into an art and science.

For any of these willpower-training exercises, you could choose something related to your main willpower challenge. For example, if your goal is to save money, you might keep track of what you spend. If your goal is to exercise more often, you might decide to do ten sit-ups or push-ups before your morning shower. But even if you don't match this experiment to your biggest goals, the muscle model of self-control suggests that exercising your willpower each day, even in silly or simple ways, will build strength for all your willpower challenges.

A CANDY ADDICT CONQUERS HIS SWEET TOOTH

Jim, a thirty-eight-year-old freelance graphic designer, had what he called a lifelong addiction to sweets—he never met a jelly bean he didn't like. He was intrigued by a study I mentioned in class that found that leaving candy out in a visible place can increase people's general self-control (if they routinely resist the temptation). Jim worked from home, and often moved between his office and other rooms in his house. He decided to put a glass jar of jelly beans in the hallway that he would have to pass every time he left or returned to his office. He didn't ban all sweets, but did institute a "no candy from the candy jar" rule to challenge his self-control muscle.

The first day, the instinct to pop a few jelly beans in his mouth was automatic and difficult to stop. But over the week, saying no got easier. Seeing the candy reminded Jim of his goal to exercise his won't power. Surprised by his success, he started stepping away from his desk more often just to get some extra "exercise" in. Though Jim had initially worried that the visible temptation would exhaust his willpower, he found the process energizing. When he returned to his office after resisting the candy jar, he felt motivated. Jim was astonished that something he thought was completely out of his control could change so quickly when he set a small challenge for himself and committed to it.

When you're trying to make a big change or transform an old habit, look for a small way to practice self-control that strengthens your willpower, but doesn't overwhelm it completely.

HOW REAL ARE THE "LIMITS" OF SELF-CONTROL?

Whether you look to science or your own life for evidence, it is clear that we humans have a tendency to run out of willpower. But one thing that isn't clear is whether we run out of *power*, or whether we just run out of *will*. Is it really impossible for a smoker to stick to a budget when she's trying to give up cigarettes? Is the dieter depriving himself of his favorite foods really too weak to resist an illicit affair? There is always a difference between what is difficult and what is impossible, and the limits of self-control could reflect either. To answer this question, we need to step back for a moment from the metaphorical muscle of self-control and take a closer look at why actual muscles—such as the ones in your arms and legs—get tired and give up.

MAKING THE FINISH LINE

Halfway through the 26.2-mile run of her first Ironman triathlon, thirty-year-old Kara felt great. She had already survived the 2.4-mile swim and the 112-mile bike ride, and running was her best event. She was going faster than she had expected she'd be able to at this point in the race. Then she hit the turnaround point of the run, and the physical reality of what she had done hit her body hard. Everything hurt, from her aching shoulders to the blisters on her feet. Her legs felt heavy and hollow, as if they didn't have the strength to go on. It was as if a switch in her body had been flipped, telling her, "You're done." Her optimism deflated, and she began to think to herself, *This is not going to end as well as it began.* But despite the feeling of exhaustion that made it seem as though her feet and legs would not cooperate, they did. Whenever she thought, *I can't do this,* she said to herself, "You *are* doing this," and just kept putting one foot in front of the other, all the way to the finish line.

Kara's ability to finish the triathlon is a perfect example of how deceptive fatigue can be. Exercise physiologists used to believe that when our bodies give up, it is because they literally cannot keep working. Fatigue was muscle failure, pure and simple: The muscles run out of energy stores. They can't take in enough oxygen to metabolize the energy they have. The pH level of the blood becomes too acidic or too alkaline. All these explanations made sense in theory, but no one could ever prove that this was what was causing exercisers to slow down and give up.

Timothy Noakes, a professor of exercise and sports science at the University of Cape Town, had a different idea. Noakes is known in the athletic world for challenging deeply held beliefs. (For example, he helped show that drinking too many fluids during endurance competitions could kill an athlete by diluting the essential salts in the body.) Noakes is an ultramarathon competitor himself, and he became interested in a little-known theory put forth in 1924 by Nobel Prize–winning physiologist Archibald Hill. Hill had proposed that exercise fatigue might be caused not by muscle failure, but by an overprotective monitor in the brain that wanted to prevent exhaustion. When the body was working hard, and putting heavy demands on the heart, this monitor (Hill called it "the governor") would step in to slow things down. Hill didn't guess at how the brain produced the feeling of fatigue that led athletes to give up, but Noakes was intrigued with the implication: Physical exhaustion was a trick played on the body by the mind. If this was true, it meant that the physical limits of an athlete were far beyond what the first message from the body to give up suggested.

Noakes, with several colleagues, began to review evidence of what happens to endurance athletes under extreme conditions. They found no evidence for physiological failure happening within the muscles; instead, it appeared that the brain was telling the muscles to stop. The brain, sensing an increased heart rate and rapidly depleting energy supply, literally puts the brakes on the body. At the same time, the brain creates an overwhelming feeling of fatigue that has little to do with the muscles' capacity to keep working. As Noakes puts it, "Fatigue should no longer be considered a physical event but rather a sensation or emotion." Most of us interpret exhaustion as an objective indicator that we cannot continue. This theory says it is just a feeling generated by the brain to motivate us to stop, in much the same way that the feeling of anxiety can stop us from doing something dangerous, and the feeling of disgust can stop us from eating something that will make us sick. But because fatigue is only an early warning system, extreme athletes can routinely push past what seems to the rest of us like the natural physical limits of the body. These athletes recognize that the first wave of fatigue is never a real limit, and with sufficient motivation, they can transcend it.

What does this have to do with our original problem of college students cramming their heads with knowledge and their mouths with junk food? Or with dieters cheating on their spouses, and office workers losing their focus? Some scientists now believe that the limits of self-control are just like the physical limits of the body—we often feel depleted of willpower before we actually are. In part, we can thank a brain motivated to conserve energy. Just as the brain may tell the body's muscles to slow down when it fears physical exhaustion, the brain may put the brakes on its own energy-expensive exercise of the prefrontal cortex. This doesn't mean we're out of willpower; we just need to muster up the motivation to use it.

Our beliefs about what we are capable of may determine whether we give up or soldier on. Stanford psychologists have found that some people do not believe the feeling of mental fatigue that follows a challenging act of self-control. These willpower athletes also do not show the typical deterioration in self-control that the muscle model predicts—at least, not during the types of moderate willpower challenges that researchers can ethically test in the laboratory. Based on these findings, the Stanford psychologists have proposed an idea as jarring to the field of self-control research as Noakes's claims were to the field of exercise physiology: The widely observed scientific finding that self-control is limited may reflect people's beliefs about willpower, not their true physical and mental limits. The research on this idea is just beginning, and no one is claiming that humans have an unlimited capacity for self-control. But it is appealing to think that we often have more willpower than we believe we do. It also raises the possibility that we can, like athletes, push past the feeling of willpower exhaustion to make it to the finish line of our own willpower challenges.

UNDER THE MICROSCOPE: IS YOUR EXHAUSTION REAL?

All too often, we use the first feeling of fatigue as a reason to skip exercise, snap at our spouses, procrastinate a little longer, or order a pizza instead of cooking a healthy meal. To be sure, the demands of life really do drain our willpower, and perfect self-control is a fool's quest. But you may have more willpower than the first impulse to give in would suggest. The next time you find yourself "too tired" to exert self-control, challenge yourself to go beyond that first feeling of fatigue. (Keep in mind that it's also possible to overtrain—and if you find yourself constantly feeling drained, you may need to consider whether you have been running yourself to real exhaustion.)

WHEN THERE'S A WANT, THERE'S A WILL

When Kara, the first-time triathlete, felt too exhausted to continue, she remembered how much she wanted to finish and imagined the crowd cheering her across the finish line. It turns out that the metaphorical "muscle" of willpower can also be coaxed into persevering longer with the right inspiration. University at Albany psychologists Mark Muraven and Elisaveta Slessareva have tested a number of motivations on willpower-drained students. Not surprisingly, money helps undergraduates find a reserve of willpower, and they will do for cash what moments earlier they had been too exhausted to do. (Imagine someone offering you $100 to say no to a package of Girl Scout cookies. Not so irresistible now, huh?) Self-control also surged when students were told that doing their best would help researchers discover a cure for Alzheimer's disease, not unlike endurance athletes who race for a cure. Finally, the mere promise that practice would improve performance on a difficult task helped the students push past will-power exhaustion. While this is a less obvious motivator, it's one that plays a big role in determining whether or not people stick with difficult changes in real life. If you think that not smoking is going to be as hard one year from now as it is that first day of nicotine withdrawal, when you would claw your own eyes out for a cigarette, you're much more likely to give up. But if you can imagine a time when saying no will be second nature, you'll be more willing to stick out the temporary misery.

WILLPOWER EXPERIMENT: WHAT'S YOUR "WANT" POWER?

When your willpower is running low, find renewed strength by tapping into your want power. For your biggest willpower challenge, consider the following motivations:

1. *How will you benefit from succeeding at this challenge?* What is the payoff for you personally? Greater health, happiness, freedom, financial security, or success?
2. *Who else will benefit if you succeed at this challenge?* Surely there are others who depend on you and are affected by your choices. How does your behavior influence your family, friends, coworkers, employees or employer, and community? How would your success help them?
3. *Imagine that this challenge will get easier for you over time if you are willing to do what is difficult now.* Can you imagine what your life will be like, and how you will feel about yourself, as you make progress on this challenge? Is some discomfort now worth it if you know it is only a temporary part of your progress?

As you face your challenges this week, ask yourself which motivation holds the most power for you in that moment. Are you willing to do something difficult for others, when you might not for yourself? Is the dream of a better future—or the fear of a terrible fate—the only thing that keeps you going? When you find your biggest want power—the thing that gives you strength when you feel weak—bring it to mind whenever you find yourself most tempted to give in or give up.

A Frustrated Mom Finds Her Want Power

Erin was a stay-at-home mom of twin boys going through the terrible twos. She was exhausted by the demands of parenting, and frazzled by the boys' discovery of the word "No!" She frequently found herself pushed to her breaking point, losing her cool with the twins over minor but endless battles. Her willpower challenge for the class was learning how to stay calm when she was ready to erupt.

When Erin thought about her biggest motivation for controlling her temper, the obvious answer seemed to be, "To be a better parent." In the moment of frustration, however, this motivation wasn't working. She would remember that she wanted to be a better parent, but this made her even more frustrated! Erin realized that an even bigger motivation was the desire to enjoy being a parent—which is not exactly the same thing as being a better parent. Erin was yelling out of frustration not just for what the boys were doing, but also for the many ways she felt she wasn't living up to her ideal of the perfect mom. Half the time, she was angry at herself, but she was taking it out on her sons. She also resented giving up her job—where she felt very effective—for something that made her feel so out of control. Reminding herself that she wasn't a perfect mom did nothing to give her more self-control—it just made her feel worse.

To find the willpower not to explode, Erin had to realize that staying calm was as much for herself as it was for her sons. It wasn't fun to yell, and she didn't like who she was when she lost control. She was getting so frustrated by the gap between her ideals and the reality of daily life that she had started to question whether she even wanted to be a parent. And

Erin *wanted* to want to be a parent. Taking the effort to stop, breathe, and find a less stressful response was not just about giving her sons a better mom. It was about enjoying being with her sons, and feeling good about what she had given up to be a stay-at-home mom. With this insight, Erin found that it was easier to keep her cool. Not yelling at her boys became a way of not yelling at herself, and of finding the joy in the messy reality of mommyhood.

Sometimes our strongest motivation is not what we think it is, or think it should be. If you're trying to change a behavior to please someone else or be the right kind of person, see if there is another "want" that holds more power for you.

EVERYDAY DISTRACTIONS AND THE COLLAPSE OF A CIVILIZATION

We've seen ample evidence that the self-control demands of everyday life can drain the willpower we need to resist ordinary, everyday temptations like cookies and cigarettes. This, of course, is not good news. But as much as these temptations threaten our personal goals, they are small potatoes compared with the collective consequences of a society in which most people are chronically drained of willpower. One of the most troubling studies of willpower fatigue raised the stakes by using a "public goods" measure of self-control called the "Forest Game." In this economic simulation, players became owners of a timber company for a game period of twenty-five years. They were given 500 acres the first year, and were told that the forest would grow at a rate of 10 percent each year. In any given year, each owner could cut down up to 100 acres. For every acre a player cut down, they would be paid six cents. Don't worry about the exact math, but under these terms, it makes the most economic (not to mention environmental) sense to allow the forest to grow rather than to cut it down and sell it off quickly. However, this strategy requires patience and the willingness to cooperate with other players, so no one tries to chop down the whole forest to make a quick buck.

Before the game, some groups of players completed a self-control task that required blocking out mental distractions—a classic willpower-depletion setup. They came to the game a bit willpower-exhausted. In the game, these players went on to decimate their forests for short-term financial gain. By the tenth year in the simulation, they were down from 500 to 62 acres. By year fifteen, the forest was completely destroyed, and the simulation had to be ended early. The players had not cooperated with each other; they had defaulted to a take-what-you-can-get-before-the-others-sell-it strategy. In contrast, players who had not performed the distraction task still had a forest when the simulation ended at twenty-five years, and they had made more money while saving a few trees. Cooperation, economic success, environmental stewardship—I don't know about you, but I know which players I'd put in charge of my forest, business, or country.

The Forest Game is just a simulation, but one cannot help being reminded of the eerily similar demise of the Easter Island forest. For centuries, the lush, densely forested island in the Pacific Ocean supported a thriving civilization. But as the population grew, the island's inhabitants started cutting down trees for more land and wood. By the year 800 C.E., they were cutting down trees faster than the forest could regenerate. By the 1500s, the forest was wiped out, along with many species the inhabitants depended on for food. Starvation and cannibalism became widespread. By the late 1800s, 97 percent of the population had died or left the barren island.

Since then, many people have wondered, what were the residents of Easter Island thinking as they destroyed their forests and society? Couldn't they see the long-term consequences of what they were doing? We can't imagine ourselves making such obviously shortsighted decisions, but we shouldn't be so sure. Humans have a natural tendency to focus on immediate gains, and changing course to prevent future disaster takes enormous self-discipline from all members of a society. It's not just a matter of caring; change requires *doing*. In the Forest Game study, all the players expressed the same values of cooperation and the desire to protect the long-term good. The willpower-depleted players just didn't act on those values.

The psychologists who ran this study suggest that people who are willpower-depleted cannot be counted on to make good decisions for society. This is a troubling claim, given what we know about how easy it is to exhaust willpower, and how many minor decisions in our daily lives demand self-control. We are not going to solve national or global crises like economic growth, health care, human rights, and climate change if we are exhausted by grocery shopping and dealing with difficult coworkers.

As individuals, we can take steps to strengthen our personal self-control, and this will make no small difference in our personal lives. Knowing how to strengthen the limited self-control of a nation is a trickier thing. Rather than hope that we as a nation develop more willpower in order to meet our biggest challenges, our best bet might be to take self-control out of the equation whenever possible—or at least reduce the self-control demands of doing the right thing. Behavioral economist Richard Thaler and legal scholar Cass Sunstein have argued persuasively for "choice architecture," systems that make it easier for people to make good decisions consistent with their values and goals. For example, asking people to become organ donors when they renew a driver's license or register to vote. Or having health insurance companies automatically schedule annual check-ups for their members. These are things most people mean to do, but put off because they are distracted by so many other more pressing demands.

Retailers already use choice architecture to influence what you buy, although usually not for any noble purpose but to make a profit. If there were sufficient incentive, stores might more prominently feature healthy or environmentally friendly products. Instead of lining the checkout area with indulgent impulse purchases like candy and gossip magazines, stores could use that real estate to make it easier for people to pick up dental floss, condoms, or fresh fruit. This kind of simple product placement has been shown to dramatically increase healthy purchases.

Choice architecture designed to manipulate people's decisions is a controversial proposition. Some see it as restricting individual freedom or ignoring personal responsibility. And yet, people who are free to choose anything most often choose against their long-term interests. Research on the limits of self-control suggests that this is not because we are innately irrational, or because we are making deliberate decisions to enjoy today and screw tomorrow. Instead, we may simply be too tired to act against our worst impulses. If we want to strengthen self-control, we may need to think about how we can best support the most exhausted version of ourselves—and not count on an ideal version of ourselves to show up and save the day.

The Last Word

The limits of self-control present a paradox: We cannot control everything, and yet the only way to increase our self-control is to stretch our limits. Like a muscle, our willpower follows the rule of "Use it or lose it." If we try to save our energy by becoming willpower coach potatoes, we will lose the strength we have. But if we try to run a willpower marathon every day, we set ourselves up for total collapse. Our challenge is to train like an intelligent athlete, pushing our limits but also pacing ourselves. And while we can find strength in our motivation when we feel weak, we can also look for ways to help our tired selves make good choices.

CHAPTER SUMMARY

The Idea: Self-control is like a muscle. It gets tired from use, but regular exercise makes it stronger.

Under the Microscope

- *The highs and lows of willpower.* Keep track of your self-control strength this week, with special interest in when you have the most willpower, and when you are most likely to give in or give up.
- *Is your exhaustion real?* The next time you find yourself "too tired" to exert self-control, examine whether you can go beyond that first feeling of fatigue to take one more step.

Willpower Experiments

- *The willpower diet.* Make sure that your body is well fueled with food that gives you lasting energy.
- *A willpower workout.* Exercise your self-control muscle by picking one thing to do (I will power) or not do (I won't power) this week, or keeping track of something you aren't used to paying close attention to.
- *Find your "want" power.* When you find your biggest want power—the motivation that gives you strength when you feel weak—bring it to mind whenever you find yourself most tempted to give in or give up.

FOUR

License to Sin:
Why Being Good Gives
Us Permission to Be Bad

Whenever I teach the Science of Willpower course, the universe provides a perfect willpower scandal to illustrate the theories of why we lose control. Gifts from the past include Ted Haggard, Eliot Spitzer, John Edwards, and Tiger Woods. These stories may be old news now,* but hardly a week goes by without breaking news about some upstanding citizen—a politician, religious leader, cop, teacher, or athlete—who shocks the world with an epic willpower failure.

It's tempting to interpret these stories in light of the limits of self-control. Each of these men was under tremendous pressure, from the demands of a punishing professional schedule to the need to control his public image

---

*For those who have forgotten (or never knew) the scandals these men were caught in, here's the short version: Haggard was a popular minister fighting against gay rights who got caught having sex and doing drugs with a male prostitute; Spitzer was the governor and former attorney general of New York State who relentlessly prosecuted corruption, and then turned out to be the regular client of a prostitution ring under federal investigation; Edwards was a failed Democratic presidential candidate who campaigned on the strength of his family values, all the while cheating on a wife dying of cancer; and Woods was the celebrated golfer known for his self-discipline, but revealed to be a sex addict.

twenty-four hours a day. Surely their self-control muscles were exhausted, their willpower drained, their blood sugar low, their prefrontal cortices shriveling up in protest. Who knows, maybe they were all on diets.

This would be too easy an answer (though I'm sure a defense attorney will eventually try it out on a grand jury). Not every lapse of self-control reflects an actual loss of control. Sometimes we make a conscious choice to give in to temptation. To fully understand why we run out of will-power, we need another explanation, one that is more psychological than physiological.

Though you may not be in danger of a sex scandal worthy of national hysteria, we are all at risk for a little willpower hypocrisy—even if it's just cheating on our New Year's resolutions. To avoid following in the footsteps of our headline-making heroes, we need to rethink the assumption that every willpower failure is caused by weakness. In some cases, we are the victims of our own self-control success. We'll consider how progress can paradoxically undermine our motivation, how optimism can give us a license to indulge, and why feeling good about our virtue is the fastest path to vice. In each case, we'll see that giving in is a choice, and not an inevitable one. By seeing how we give ourselves permission, we can also discover how to keep ourselves on track.

FROM SAINTS TO SINNERS

I'd like you to rate the following statements on a scale of strongly disagree, somewhat disagree, somewhat agree, and strongly agree. First up: *Most women are not really smart.* And what about: *Most women are better suited to stay at home taking care of the children than to work.*

Now imagine you've asked these questions to Princeton University undergraduates. If you're lucky, the female students won't tell you to shove your survey up your asinine assumptions. Even the male students will reject these sexist statements. But what if you had asked them instead to rate slightly different statements: *Some women are not really smart,* and

Some women are better suited to stay at home taking care of the children. It's not so easy to reject these statements. They might seem a little sexist, but it's hard to argue with "some."

These surveys were part of a study by psychologists Benoît Monin and Dale Miller, who were investigating stereotypes and decision making. As you might predict, Princeton students who were asked to rate the first two statements were quick to denounce them. But students who were asked to rate the qualified "*some* women" statements were more neutral on the matter.

After rating the statements, the students were asked to make a decision in a hypothetical hiring situation. Their assignment was to assess the suitability of several candidates—male and female—for a high-level job in a stereotypically male-dominated industry like construction or finance. This seems like a straightforward task, especially for the students who had just rejected sexist statements. Surely they would not discriminate against a qualified woman. But the Princeton researchers found exactly the opposite. The students who had strongly disagreed with the obviously sexist statements were more likely to favor a man for the job than the students who had somewhat reluctantly agreed with the less sexist "some women" statements. The same pattern emerged when the researchers asked students about racist attitudes and then gave them an opportunity to discriminate against racial minorities.

These studies shocked a lot of people. Psychologists had long assumed that once you expressed an attitude, you would be likely to act in line with it. After all, who wants to feel like a hypocrite? But the Princeton psychologists had uncovered the exception to our usual desire to be consistent. When it comes to right and wrong, most of us are not striving for moral perfection. We just want to feel good enough—which then gives us permission to do whatever we want.

The students who had rejected obviously sexist or racist statements felt they had established their moral credentials. They had proven to themselves that they were not sexist or racist, but this left them vulnerable to what psychologists call *moral licensing*. When you do something good, you feel good about yourself. This means you're more likely to trust your impulses—which often means giving yourself permission to do something bad. In this case, the students felt so good about themselves for rejecting the sexist and racist statements, they became less vigilant about making a sexist or racist decision. They were more likely to listen to an instinctive bias and less likely to consider whether a decision was consistent with their broader goal to be fair. It wasn't that they wanted to discriminate—they simply let the glow of their earlier good behavior blind them to the harm of their decisions.

Moral licensing doesn't just give us permission to do something bad; it also lets us off the hook when we're asked to do something good. For example, people who first remember a time when they acted generously give 60 percent less money to a charitable request than people who have not just recalled a past good deed. In a business simulation, managers of a manufacturing plant are less likely to take costly measures to reduce the plant's pollution if they have recently recalled a time when they acted ethically.

The moral licensing effect might explain why some people who have obvious moral credentials—a minister, a family values politician, an attorney general prosecuting corruption—can justify to themselves some serious moral lapses, whether it's the married televangelist having sex with his secretary, the fiscal conservative using public funds to remodel his home, or the police officer using extreme force against a nonresisting criminal. Most people don't question their impulses when they're feeling virtuous, and some people's positions permanently remind them of their virtue.

Why are we suddenly talking about discrimination and sex scandals instead of dieting and procrastination? Because what is a willpower challenge if not a battle between virtue and vice? Anything you moralize becomes fair game for the effect of moral licensing. If you tell yourself that you're "good" when you exercise and "bad" when you don't, then you're more likely to skip the gym tomorrow if you work out today. Tell yourself you're "good" for working on an important project and "bad" for procrastinating, and you're more likely to slack off in the afternoon if you made progress in the morning. Simply put: Whenever we have conflicting desires, being good gives us permission to be a little bit bad.

Importantly, this is not just a matter of running out of blood sugar or willpower. When psychologists ask people about their licensed indulgences, the indulgers report feeling in control of their choices, not out of control. They also don't feel guilty. Instead, they report feeling proud of themselves for earning a reward. They offer the justification, "I was so good, I deserve a little treat." This sense of entitlement too often becomes our downfall. Because we're quick to view self-indulgence as the best reward for virtue, we forget our real goals and give in to temptation.

THE WARM AND FUZZY LOGIC OF LICENSING

The logic of licensing is not, strictly speaking, logical. For one thing, we rarely require a connection between our "good" behavior and the "bad" behavior we're justifying. Shoppers who restrain themselves from buying something tempting are more likely to go home and *eat* something tempting. Employees who put in extra time on a project may feel justified putting a personal expense on the company credit card.

Anything that makes us feel warm and fuzzy about our virtue—even just thinking about doing something good—can license us to follow our impulses. In one study, people were asked to choose which type of volunteer work they would prefer: teaching children in a homeless shelter or improving the environment. Even though they weren't signing up for any actual service, just imagining the choice increased their desire to splurge on a pair of designer jeans. Another study found that merely considering donating money to a charity—without actually handing over any cash—increased people's desire to treat themselves at the mall. Most generously, we even give ourselves credit for what we could have done, but didn't. We *could* have eaten the whole pizza, but we only ate three slices. We *could* have bought a new wardrobe, but we made do with just a new jacket. Following this ridiculous line of logic, we can turn any act of indulgence into something to be proud of. (Feeling guilty about your credit card debt? Hey, at least you haven't robbed a bank to pay it off!)

Studies like this demonstrate that there is no careful accountant in our brains, calculating exactly how good we've been and what kind of self-indulgence we've earned. Instead, we trust the *feeling* that we have been good, and that we are a good person. Psychologists who study moral reasoning know this is how we make most judgments of right or wrong. We have a gut response, and we only look to logic if we are forced to explain our feelings. Many times, we can't even come up with a logical reason to defend our judgment—but we stick with our feelings anyway. Take, for example, one of the morally dubious scenarios psychologists use to study how we decide what is right and what is wrong. Do you think it is morally acceptable for an adult brother and sister to have sex, if they both want to and they use birth control? For most of us, this question triggers an instant inner ick. That's just *wrong*. Then we strain our brains to explain why it must be immoral.

If we don't get an inner ick, a sharp pang of guilt, or a twinge of anxiety when we think about something, it doesn't feel wrong. Returning to more mundane willpower challenges, if a behavior—like having another slice of birthday cake or putting one more little thing on our credit cards—doesn't trigger that instinctive feeling of "wrongness," we don't tend to question our impulses. This is how feeling good about ourselves for past good behavior helps us justify future indulgences. When you feel like a saint, the idea of self-indulgence doesn't feel wrong. It feels right. Like you earned it. And *if the only thing motivating your self-control is the desire to be a good enough person*, you're going to give in whenever you're already feeling good about yourself.

The worst part of moral licensing is not just its questionable logic; the problem is how it tricks us into acting against our best interests. It convinces us that self-sabotaging behavior—whether breaking your diet, blowing your budget, or sneaking a smoke—is a "treat." This is lunacy, but it's an incredibly powerful trick of a mind that turns your wants into shoulds.

Moral judgments are also not nearly as motivating as our culture likes to believe. We idealize our own desire to be virtuous, and many people believe that they are most motivated by guilt and shame. But who are we kidding? We are most motivated by getting what we want and avoiding what we don't want. Moralizing a behavior makes us more, not less, likely to feel ambivalent about it. When you define a willpower challenge as something you should do to be a better person, you will automatically start to come up with arguments for why you shouldn't have to do it. It's just human nature—we resist rules imposed by others for our own good. If you try to impose those rules on yourself, from a moralizing, self-improvement point of view, you're going to hear very quickly from the part of you that doesn't want to be controlled. And so when you tell yourself that exercising, saving money, or giving up smoking is the *right* thing to do—not something that will help you meet your goals—you're less likely to do it consistently.

To avoid the moral licensing trap, it's important to separate the true moral dilemmas from the merely difficult. Cheating on your taxes or your spouse may be morally flawed, but cheating on your diet is not a mortal sin. And yet, most people think of all forms of self-control as a moral test. Giving in to dessert, sleeping late, carrying a credit card balance—we use them to determine whether we are being good or bad. None of these things carry the true weight of sin or virtue. When we think about our willpower challenges in moral terms, we get lost in self-judgments and lose sight of how those challenges will help us get what we want.

UNDER THE MICROSCOPE: VIRTUE AND VICE

This week, watch how you talk to yourself and others about your willpower failures and successes:

- Do you tell yourself you've been "good" when you succeed at a willpower challenge, and "bad" when you give in to procrastination or temptation?
- Do you use your "good" behavior to give yourself permission to do something "bad"? Is this a harmless reward, or is it sabotaging your larger willpower goals?

WHEN EXERCISE LICENSES EATING, A BRIDE-TO-BE GAINS WEIGHT

Cheryl, a thirty-five-year-old financial adviser, was getting married in eight months. She wanted to lose fifteen pounds before the wedding, and had started working out at the gym three days a week. The problem was, she knew exactly how many calories every minute on the stair climber was worth. As she burned more calories, she couldn't help imagining the food she was earning the right to eat. Although she had planned to cut back on calories, too, she felt free to eat a little more on workout days. If she exercised an extra five minutes, she could get chocolate chips on her frozen yogurt, or have a second glass of wine with dinner. Exercise began to equal a license to indulge. As a result, the scale had budged three pounds—in the wrong direction.

By thinking about exercise as earning food, Cheryl was undermining her goal to lose weight. To get out of this licensing trap, she needed to see exercise as a necessary step to achieving her goal, and healthier eating as a *second, independent* step she also had to take. They weren't interchangeable "good" behaviors, and succeeding at one didn't license her to take it easier on the other.

> *Don't mistake a goal-supportive action for the goal itself. You aren't off the hook just because you did one thing consistent with your goal. Notice if giving yourself credit for positive action makes you forget what your actual goal is.*

THE PROBLEM WITH PROGRESS

Even if you aren't turning your willpower challenges into measures of your moral worth, it's still possible to fall into the trap of moral licensing. That's because there's one thing *all* Americans instinctively moralize. No, not sex. Progress! Progress is good, and making progress on our goals feels good. So good that we like to congratulate ourselves: Well done, you!

Maybe we should think twice before we hand ourselves the gold star. While most of us believe that making progress on our goals spurs us on to greater success, psychologists know we are all too quick to use progress as an excuse for taking it easy. Ayelet Fishbach, professor at the University of Chicago Graduate School of Business, and Ravi Dhar, professor at the Yale School of Management, have shown that making progress on a goal motivates people to engage in goal-sabotaging behavior. In one study, they reminded successful dieters of how much progress they had made toward their ideal weight. They then offered the dieters a thank-you gift of either an apple or a chocolate bar. Eighty-five percent of the self-congratulating dieters chose the chocolate bar over the apple, compared with only 58 percent of dieters who were not reminded of their progress. A second study found the same effect for academic goals: Students made to feel good about the amount of time they had spent studying for an exam were more likely to spend the evening playing beer pong with friends.

Progress can cause us to abandon the goal we've worked so hard on because it shifts the power of balance between our two competing selves. Remember that by definition, a willpower challenge involves two conflicting goals. Part of you is thinking about your long-term interests (e.g., weight loss); the other part wants immediate gratification (chocolate!). In the moment of temptation, you need your higher self to argue more loudly than the voice of self-indulgence. However, self-control success has an unintended consequence: It temporarily satisfies—and therefore silences—the higher self. When you make progress toward your long-term goal, your brain—with its mental checklist of many goals—turns off the mental processes that were driving you to pursue your long-term goal. It will then turn its attention to the goal that has not yet been satisfied—the voice of self-indulgence. Psychologists call this *goal liberation*. The goal you've been suppressing with your self-control is going to become stronger, and any temptation will become more tempting.

In practical terms, this means that one step forward gives you permission to take two steps back. Setting up your automatic retirement investment may satisfy the part of you that wants to save, liberating the part of you that wants to shop. Getting your files organized may satisfy the part of you that wants to work, liberating the part of you that wants to watch the game on TV. You were listening to the angel on your shoulder, but now the devil seems much more compelling.

Even the most trusty tool of goal pursuit, the To Do list, can backfire. Have you ever made a list of everything you need to do on a project, and then felt so good about yourself that you considered your work on that project done for the day? If so, you're not alone. Because it's such a relief to make that list, we mistake the satisfaction of identifying what needs to be done with actual effort toward our goals. (Or, as one of my students said, he loves productivity seminars because they make him *feel* so productive— never mind that nothing has been produced yet.)

Although it runs counter to everything we believe about achieving our goals, focusing on progress can hold us back from success. That's not to say that progress itself is a problem. The problem with progress is how it makes us feel—and even then, it's only a problem if we listen to the feeling instead of sticking to our goals. Progress can be motivating, and even inspire future self-control, but only if you view your actions as evidence that *you are committed* to your goal. In other words, you need to look at what you have done and conclude that you must really care about your goal, so much so that you want to do even more to reach it. This perspective is easy to adopt; it's just not our usual mind-set. More typically, we look for the reason to stop.

These two mind-sets have very different consequences. When people who have taken a positive step toward meeting a goal—for example, exercising, studying, or saving money—are asked, "How much *progress* do you feel you have made on your goal?" they are more likely to then do something that conflicts with that goal, like skip the gym the next day, hang out with friends instead of studying, or buy something expensive. In contrast, people who are asked, "How *committed* do you feel to your goal?" are not tempted by the conflicting behavior. A simple shift in focus leads to a very different interpretation of their own actions—"I did that because *I wanted to*," not "I did that, great, now I can do what I really want!"

WILLPOWER EXPERIMENT: TO REVOKE YOUR LICENSE, REMEMBER THE WHY

How do you focus on commitment instead of progress? A study by researchers at Hong Kong University of Science and the University of Chicago provides one strategy. When they asked students to remember a time they turned down a temptation, moral licensing ensued, and 70 percent took the next opportunity to indulge. But when they also asked the participants to remember *why* they had resisted, the licensing effect disappeared—69 percent resisted temptation. Like magic, the researchers had discovered a simple way to boost self-control and help the students make a choice consistent with their overall goals. Remembering the "why" works because it changes how you feel about the reward of self-indulgence. That so-called treat will start to look more like the threat to your goals that it is, and giving in won't look so good. Remembering the why will also help you recognize and act on other opportunities to accomplish your goal.

The next time you find yourself using past good behavior to justify indulging, pause and remember the why.

WHEN TOMORROW LICENSES TODAY

Whether it's patting ourselves on the back for making progress, or remembering how we resisted temptation yesterday, we are quick to give ourselves credit for past good behavior. But the fuzzy math of moral licensing doesn't limit us to taking only past actions into account. We just as easily look into the future, and credit ourselves with our planned virtuous behavior. For example, people who merely *intend* to exercise later are more likely to overeat at dinner. This habit allows us to sin today, and make up for it later—or so we tell ourselves.

DON'T COUNT YOUR GRILLED CHICKEN SALAD BEFORE IT'S HATCHED

Imagine this: It's lunchtime, you're in a rush, and the most convenient place to pick something up is a fast-food restaurant. You're trying to watch your weight and improve your health, so your plan is to avoid the most fattening foods on the menu. When you get in line, you're delighted to see that along with the usual indulgent fare, the restaurant is offering a new line of salads. This restaurant is close to your office, so you come here more often than has probably been good for your waistline. You're thrilled that you'll now have options you won't have to feel guilty about. You stand in line, considering your choices, weighing a garden salad against a grilled chicken salad. Then, when you're finally in front of the register, you hear the words "double cheeseburger and fries" coming out of your mouth.

What just happened?

It might seem like old habits kicked in, or maybe the aroma of french fries overpowered your good intentions. But would you believe that the healthy items on the menu actually made you more likely to order the cheeseburger and fries?

This is the conclusion of several studies by marketing researchers at Baruch College, City University of New York. The researchers were intrigued by reports that when McDonald's added healthier items to its menu, sales of Big Macs skyrocketed. To find out why, the researchers designed their own fast-food menus and set up a mock restaurant. Diners were given a menu and asked to select one item. All the menus had a range of standard fast-food fare, such as french fries, chicken nuggets, and a baked potato with fixings. Half the participants were given a special menu that also included a healthy salad. When the salad was an option, the percentage of participants choosing the *least healthy* and most fattening item on the menu increased. The researchers found the same effect for vending machine choices. When a reduced-calorie package of cookies was added to a set of standard junk-food options, participants were *more* likely to choose the least healthy snack (which, in this case, happened to be chocolate-covered Oreos).

How can this be? Sometimes the mind gets so excited about the *opportunity* to act on a goal, it mistakes that opportunity with the satisfaction of having actually accomplished the goal. And with the goal to make a healthy choice out of the way, the unmet goal—immediate pleasure— takes priority. You feel less pressure to actually order the healthy item, and you feel a stronger desire for the indulgent item. Add this up, and although it makes no rational sense, you give yourself permission to order the most artery-clogging, waist-expanding, and life-span-shortening thing on the menu. These studies call into question the public health push to offer at least one healthy choice in school cafeterias, vending machines, and chain restaurants. Unless the change is widespread, and all of the offerings are made healthier, there is a risk that people will end up making even worse choices than if nothing had been done.

Maybe you think you wouldn't be susceptible to this effect—surely you have more self-control than the suckers in these studies! If so, then you're really in trouble. The participants who rated themselves as having the best self-control, especially around food, were the most likely to end up ordering the least healthy item when a healthy choice was available. While only 10 percent of these self-identified willpower wonders chose the least healthy item when the menu did not include a salad, 50 percent chose the least healthy item when the salad was an option. Perhaps they were so confident that they would order the healthy item in the future, they felt comfortable ordering the french fries today.

This illustrates a fundamental mistake we make when thinking about our future choices. We wrongly but persistently expect to make different decisions tomorrow than we do today. I'll smoke this one cigarette, but starting tomorrow, I'm done. I'll skip the gym today, but I'm sure I'll go tomorrow. I'll splurge on holiday gifts, but then no more shopping for at least three months.

Such optimism licenses us to indulge today—especially if we know we will have the opportunity to choose differently in the near future. For example, researchers at Yale University gave students the choice between a fat-free yogurt and a large Mrs. Fields cookie. When the students were told they would have the same options the following week, 83 percent chose the cookie, compared with only 57 percent of students who thought the snacks were a one-time opportunity. Students showed the same pattern when the choice was between lowbrow and highbrow entertainment ("I can be educated and enlightened next week"), and between an immediate, smaller financial reward and a larger, delayed financial reward ("I need the cash now, but next week I'll wait for the bigger payoff").

In fact, 67 percent of students who were told they'd have the same choice the following week predicted that they would choose the more virtuous option. But when the experimenters actually brought them back to the lab for a second choice, only 36 percent made a different choice. Nevertheless, they felt much less guilt over that initial indulgent choice when they thought they could make up for it later.

UNDER THE MICROSCOPE: ARE YOU BORROWING CREDIT FROM TOMORROW?

As you go about making decisions related to your willpower challenge, notice if the promise of future good behavior comes up in your thinking. Do you tell yourself you will make up for today's behavior tomorrow? What effect does this have on your self-control today? For extra credit, keep paying attention—all the way to tomorrow. Do you actually do what you said you would, or does the cycle of "indulge today, change tomorrow" begin again?

WHY THERE'S ALWAYS TIME TO DO IT TOMORROW

Our optimism about the future extends not just to our own choices, but to how easy it will be to do what we say we will do. Psychologists have shown that we wrongly predict we will have much more free time in the future than we do today. This trick of the mind has been best demonstrated by two marketing professors—Robin Tanner at the University of Wisconsin, Madison, and Kurt Carlson at Duke University—who were intrigued by the mistakes consumers make in predicting how much they will use exercise equipment, 90 percent of which is destined to collect dust in the basement. They were curious what people thought about when they imagined their future use of those barbells or ab machines. Did they imagine a future much like the present, full of competing time commitments, distractions, and daily fatigue? Or did they imagine some alternate reality?

To find out, they asked a whole bunch of people to predict, "How many times per week (on average) will you exercise in the next month?" Then they asked another group of people the same question, with one important preface: "*In an ideal world*, how many times per week will you exercise in the next month?" The two groups showed no differences in their estimates—people were, by default, answering the question "in an ideal world" even when they had been asked to predict their actual, not ideal, behavior. We look into the future and fail to see the challenges of today. This convinces us that we will have more time and energy to do in the future what we don't want to do today. We feel justified in putting it off, confident that our future behavior will more than make up for it.

This psychological tendency is difficult to shake. The experimenters tried to prompt more realistic self-predictions by giving some people the explicit instructions, "Please do *not* provide an idealistic prediction, but rather the most realistic prediction of your behavior that you can." People who received these instructions showed even *more* optimism about their behavior, reporting the highest estimates yet. The experimenters decided they had to give these optimists a reality check, so they invited them back two weeks later to report how many times they had actually exercised. Not surprisingly, this number was lower than predicted. People had made their predictions for an ideal world, but lived through two weeks in the real world.

The experimenters then asked these same people to predict how many times they would exercise in the *next* two weeks. Ever the optimists, they made estimates *even higher than their initial predictions*, and much higher than their actual reports from the past two weeks. It's as if they took their original predicted average seriously, and were assigning their future selves extra exercise to make up for their "unusually poor" performance. Rather than view the past two weeks as reality, and their original estimates as an unrealistic ideal, they viewed the past two weeks as an anomaly.

Such optimism is understandable—if we expected to fail at every goal we set, we'd give up before we got started. But if we use our positive expectations to justify present inaction, we might as well not have even set the goal in the first place.

WILLPOWER EXPERIMENT:
A TOMORROW JUST LIKE TODAY

Behavioral economist Howard Rachlin proposes an interesting trick for overcoming the problem of always starting a change tomorrow. When you want to change a behavior, aim to reduce the *variability* in your behavior, not the behavior itself. He has shown that smokers asked to try to smoke the same number of cigarettes every day gradually decrease their overall smoking—even when they are explicitly told not to try to smoke less. Rachlin argues that this works because the smokers are deprived of the usual cognitive crutch of pretending that tomorrow will be different. Every cigarette becomes not just one more smoked today, but one more smoked tomorrow, and the day after that, and the day after that. This adds new weight to every cigarette, and makes it much harder to deny the health consequences of a single smoke.

Apply Rachlin's advice to your own willpower challenge this week: Aim to reduce the variability of your behavior day to day. View every choice you make as a commitment to all future choices. So instead of asking, "Do I want to eat this candy bar now?" ask yourself, "Do I want the consequences of eating a candy bar every afternoon for the next year?" Or if you've been putting something off that you know you should do, instead of asking "Would I rather do this today or tomorrow?" ask yourself, "Do I really want the consequences of always putting this off?"

VEGETARIAN BEFORE DINNER

Jeff, a thirty-year-old network systems analyst, was a conflicted carnivore. He kept reading about the health benefits of eating less meat, not to mention the horrors of the food-processing industry. But then there was the joy of a steak burrito, sausage-and-pepperoni pizza, a fast-food burger, and bacon at breakfast. Jeff knew becoming a vegetarian would ease his ethical concerns, but when a slice of pizza was within arm's reach, the desire to be a better person dissolved in the steam rising off the melted cheese.

His early attempts to eat less meat resulted in some creative moral licensing. He found himself using one vegetarian item to cancel out the "badness" of a nonvegetarian item—such as ordering a side of vegetable chili to ease his guilt about ordering a steak burrito. Or he would use whatever he ate at breakfast to determine whether this would be a "good day" or a "bad day"—if he ate a bacon-and-egg sandwich for breakfast, it was going to be a bad day, which meant he was free to eat meat at lunch and dinner, too. Tomorrow (he told himself) would be a good day from start to finish.

Rather than giving himself permission to be good on some days and bad on others (which, predictably, led to more bad days than good), he decided to take the challenge of reducing the variability in his behavior. He settled on the strategy of "vegetarian before dinner." He would stick to vegetarian foods until six p.m., then eat whatever he wanted to for dinner. With this rule, he couldn't eat a burger at noon and tell himself dinner would be nothing but broccoli—and he couldn't use the morning's cereal as an excuse to have chicken wings for lunch.

This approach is a great way to end the endless internal debate about whether you've earned a reward. When Jeff was deciding between the ham-and-cheese sandwich and the hummus wrap at lunch, the new rule made it easy to decide. Lunch is vegetarian, no conversation. Using a daily rule also helps you see through the illusion that what you do tomorrow will be totally different from what you do today. Jeff knew that if he broke his rule one day, he would—according to the experiment's instructions—have to break it every day for the rest of the week. Even though the ham-and-cheese sandwich looked tempting, he really didn't want to abandon his goal for the whole week. Seeing the sandwich as the beginning of a new rule, not the exception, made it less appetizing.

> *Is there a rule you can live with that will help you end the kind of inner debate that talks you right out of your goals?*

WHEN SIN LOOKS LIKE VIRTUE

There's one last licensing trap we must learn to avoid, and unlike all of the traps we've seen so far, it has nothing to do with our own virtuous behavior. It has to do with our deep desire to convince ourselves that what we want isn't so bad. As you'll see, we are far too eager to give the object of our temptation its own moral credentials, licensing us to indulge guilt-free.

THE HALO EFFECT

Imagine you are in the grocery store, picking up a few things for the weekend. You round the corner from the cereal aisle into the frozen foods section, where you encounter a most unusual in-store promotion. A veritable angel—of the holy variety, not some blonde teen-dream fantasy—holds a tray of food samples. The golden glow of her halo illuminates a plate of mini hot dogs. Harp music seems to be coming out of her pores. "Try one," the angel entreats you. You look at the plump appetizers, and thoughts of saturated fat, nitrites, and cholesterol run through your head. You know these hot dogs are not good for your diet, but surely, an angel wouldn't steer you wrong? Maybe just one bite . . .

Congratulations: You have just met, and fallen for, the halo effect. This form of moral licensing looks for any reason to say "yes" to temptation. When we want permission to indulge, we'll take any hint of virtue as a justification to give in.

To see this in action, you don't have to look any further than dinner. Studies show that people who order a main dish advertised as a healthy choice also order more indulgent drinks, side dishes, and desserts. Although their goal is to be healthy, they end up consuming more calories than people who order a regular entrée. Dieting researchers call this a *health halo*. We feel so good about ordering something healthy, our next indulgence doesn't feel sinful at all.* We also see virtuous choices as negating indulgences— literally, in some cases. Researchers have found that if you pair a cheese- burger with a green salad, diners estimate that the meal has fewer calories than the same cheeseburger served by itself. This makes no sense, unless you believe that putting lettuce on a plate can magically make calories disappear. (Though judging by what people order at the movies and restaurants, I'd say many of us believe diet sodas have a similar calorie-negating effect.)

What's really happening is that the salad is clouding the diners' judg- ment. It's giving them a *feeling* that the meal they're eating is virtuous. Those lettuce leaves come with a health halo that casts a glow on the burger, making it more likely that they will underestimate the health "cost" of the meal. Dieters—who in theory should be the most likely to know the calorie counts of foods—were the most susceptible to the halo effect, taking 100 calories off their estimates when a salad was added.

Halo effects pop up all over the place, whenever something indulgent is paired with something more virtuous. For example, studies also show that shoppers who buy chocolate for a charity will reward their good deed by eating more chocolate. The altruistic donation shines its halo glow on the candy bars, and the do-gooders enjoy them, guilt-free. Bargain-hunters

---

*The researchers also point out that diners were way too quick to accept the designation "healthy" on an entrée. On average, the dishes labeled healthy choices were actually higher in calories than the other entrées, but no one questioned the label.

who get a good deal may feel so virtuous for saving money that they buy more than they intended, and gift-givers may feel so generous that they decide they, too, deserve a gift. (This may explain why women's shoes and clothing make up the largest percentage of early holiday shopping.)

MAGIC WORDS

The problem here is that when we think of food or products in terms of "good" and "bad," we let a good feeling take the place of common sense. This allows restaurants and marketers to add 1 percent virtue to 99 percent vice and make us feel good about ourselves even as we sabotage our long-term goals. Because we're already conflicted about our goals (Health! No, pleasure!), we're happy to be complicit in this charade.

The SnackWells cookie craze of 1992 is a perfect example of this kind of moral licensing. When dieters saw the words "Fat Free!" on the outside of the package, it more than canceled out the sin of the chocolate devil's food cookies on the inside. People watching their weight irrationally consumed whole boxfuls of the high-sugar treats, blinded by the light of the fat-free halo (OK, I admit, I was one of them). Medical researchers dubbed this confusion, and the unintentional weight gain that followed, the "SnackWell Syndrome." Nowadays, "fat free" may not have the same effect on jaded dieters, but we aren't necessarily any wiser. Recent research suggests that we've merely traded old magic words for new ones. Oreo cookies labeled "organic" are judged to have fewer calories than regular Oreos, and are perceived as more appropriate to eat every day. Call it a green glow—eating organic is not just healthy, but the right thing to do for the planet. The environmental friendliness of the cookies canceled out any nutritional sins. The more pro-environment a person was, the more they underestimated the calories in the organic cookies and approved of eating them daily—just like the dieters were most susceptible to the health halo of adding a salad to a burger. The more we care about a particular virtue, the more vulnerable we are to ignoring how a "virtuous" indulgence might threaten our long-term goals.

> ## UNDER THE MICROSCOPE:
> ## ARE YOU HANDING OUT HALOS?
>
> Do you give yourself permission to indulge in something by focusing on its most virtuous quality? Do you have any magic words that give you permission to indulge, like "Buy 1 Get 1 Free," "All Natural," "Light," "Fair Trade," "Organic," or "For a Good Cause"? This week, see if you can catch yourself in the act of handing out a halo to something that undermines your goals.

A Shopper Seduced by Savings Spends More

Margaret, a recently retired pharmacist, was a discount shopping club junkie. The steeper the discount, the bigger the high. Rolling her cart through the warehouse aisles, grabbing items in bulk off the shelves, she felt good about scoring a deal. Toilet paper, cereal, wrapping paper—it didn't matter, as long as it was a bargain. Everything about the store, from the visibly slashed prices to the no-frills decor, screamed, "You are saving money, you shopping genius!" And yet when Margaret took a cold, hard look at the receipts from her weekly trip to the discount store, it was clear she was spending way more than she ever had at the regular grocery store. She had gotten so used to focusing on the "You saved _____!" tally at the end of each receipt, she was ignoring the total amount she was spending. Margaret realized that just by stepping foot in the discount store, she was falling under the store's halo effect. This was liberating her to spend without guilt, and she had been all too happy to indulge. To find her way out of this trap, she redefined what it meant to save. No longer would getting a good deal qualify—she had to stay under a set spending limit *and* get a good deal. She still felt good about saving, but no longer let the glow of savings turn her weekly trips into shopping sprees.

When a halo effect is getting in the way of your willpower challenge, look for the most concrete measure (e.g., calories, cost, time spent or wasted) of whether a choice is consistent with your goals.

THE RISKS OF GOING GREEN

How many times have you been asked to save the planet by taking one small action, from changing your lightbulbs to carrying reusable shopping bags? You may even have been asked to purchase something called a "carbon offset"—basically, a financial penance for your energy use and overconsumption. For example, travelers who feel guilty about the environmental impact of flying first class can kick in a little extra money for the airline to plant a tree in South America.

All of these actions, on their own, are good for the environment. But what happens if these actions change the way we think about ourselves? Will they convince us that we care about the planet, and motivate us to go green whenever possible? Or could these virtuous choices be contributing to environmental harm by serving as constant reminders of our green credentials?

I first started worrying about this when a study came out showing a moral licensing effect for going green. Just browsing a website that sells green products, like rechargeable batteries and organic yogurt, makes people feel good about themselves. But going green doesn't always lead to virtuous action. The study found that people who actually chose to purchase an eco-friendly product were more likely to then cheat on a test that paid them for each correct answer. They were also more likely to steal extra money out of the envelope they were told to collect their payout from. Somehow the virtue of green shopping justified the sins of lying and stealing.

Even if you don't think driving a Prius is going to turn you into a liar,* the findings of this study are troubling. Yale economist Matthew J. Kotchen has raised concerns that small "green" actions will reduce both consumers' and businesses' guilt, licensing larger harmful behaviors. We may be concerned about the environment, but making significant life-style changes is not easy. It can be overwhelming to think about the magnitude of climate change and energy shortages, and what needs to happen to prevent disaster. Anything that lets us feel like we have done our part—so we can stop thinking about the problem—we will jump at. And once our guilt and anxiety are gone, we will feel free to resume our usual wasteful ways. So a reusable shopping bag can become license to buy more, planting a tree can become license to travel more, and changing your lightbulbs can become license to live in a bigger, energy-hungry house.

The good news is, not all green acts are likely to inspire conspicuous consumption and guilt-free carbon binges. University of Melbourne economists have found that a licensing effect is most likely when people pay a "penance" for *bad* behavior—for example, paying an extra $2.50 to plant a tree to make up for the carbon costs of your home electricity use. The consumer's general eco-guilt is relieved, increasing the chance that they will feel licensed to consume more energy. A similar effect has been found with other well-intentioned penalty policies. For example, daycare centers that charge parents a fine for picking up their children late find that the policy actually *increases* late pickups. Parents are able to buy the right to be late, erasing their guilt. And because most of us would rather pay a little to do what's easiest, these programs license us to pass the buck to someone else.

However, when people are given a chance to pay for something that *replaces a harmful act* with something good for the environment—for example, paying 10 percent more on your electricity bill to use green sources of energy—no

---

*But be advised, it may make you a worse driver. A 2010 report by an auto insurance analytics company found that drivers of hybrid cars are involved in more collisions, receive 65 percent more traffic tickets, and drive 25 percent more miles than other drivers. Is this a case of a green halo licensing road recklessness? Hard to say, but while you're patting yourself on the back for your eco-friendly wheels, be sure to keep an eye on the speedometer.

such licensing effect is seen. Why not? Economists speculate that this kind of green act doesn't so much reduce guilt as it strengthens the consumer's sense of commitment to the environment. When we pay that extra money to use wind or solar energy, we think, *I'm the kind of person who does good things for the planet!* And then we carry that identity with us, looking for more ways to live our values and achieve our goals. If we want to motivate green behavior in others, we would be wise to focus more on strengthening a person's identity as someone who cares about the environment, and less on giving people the opportunity to buy the right to melt the polar ice caps.

This goes for any type of positive change, including how we try to motivate ourselves. We need to feel like the kind of person who *wants* to do the right thing. Moral licensing turns out to be, at its core, an identity crisis. We only reward ourselves for good behavior if we believe that *who we really are* is the self that wants to be bad. From this point of view, every act of self-control is a punishment, and only self-indulgence is a reward. But why must we see ourselves this way? Moving beyond the traps of moral licensing requires knowing that who we are is the self that wants the best for us—and the self that wants to live in line with our core values. When this happens, we will no longer view the impulsive, lazy, or easily tempted self as the "real" us. We will no longer act like someone who must be bribed, tricked, or forced to pursue our goals, and then rewarded for making any effort at all.

UNDER THE MICROSCOPE: WHO DO YOU THINK YOU ARE?

When you think about your willpower challenge, which part of you feels more like the "real" you—the part of you who wants to pursue the goal, or the part of you who needs to be controlled? Do you identify more with your impulses and desires, or with your long-term goals and values? When you think about your willpower challenge, do you feel like the kind of person who can succeed—or do you feel like you need to fundamentally suppress, improve, or change who you are?

THE LAST WORD

In the quest for self-control, it is a mistake to frame every willpower challenge in moral terms. We are too quick to give ourselves moral credit for good deeds done or merely contemplated, and too good at justifying giving in. Thinking in terms of "right" and "wrong" instead of remembering what we really want will trigger competing impulses and license self-sabotaging behavior. For change to stick, we need to identify with the goal itself, not the halo glow we get from being good.

CHAPTER SUMMARY

The Idea: When we turn willpower challenges into measures of moral worth, being good gives us permission to be bad. For better self-control, forget virtue, and focus on goals and values.

Under the Microscope

- *Virtue and vice.* Do you tell yourself you've been "good" when you succeed at a willpower challenge, then give yourself permission to do something "bad"?
- *Are you borrowing credit from tomorrow?* Do you tell yourself you will make up for today's behavior tomorrow—and if so, do you follow through?
- *Halo effects.* Do you justify a vice because of one virtuous aspect (e.g., discount savings, fat-free, protects the environment)?
- *Who do you think you are?* When you think about your willpower challenge, which part of you feels like the "real" you—the part of you who wants to pursue the goal, or the part of you who needs to be controlled?

Willpower Experiments

- *To revoke your license, remember the why.* The next time you find yourself using past good behavior to justify indulging, pause and think about why you were "good," not whether you deserve a reward.
- *A tomorrow just like today.* For your willpower challenge, aim to reduce the variability of your behavior day to day.

FIVE

The Brain's Big Lie:
Why We Mistake
Wanting for Happiness

In 1953, James Olds and Peter Milner, two young scientists at McGill University in Montreal, were trying to make sense of a very puzzling rat. The scientists had implanted an electrode deep into the rat's brain, through which they could send shocks. They were trying to activate an area of the brain that other scientists had discovered would create a fear response in rats. According to previous reports, lab rats hated the shocks so much, they would avoid anything associated with the moment of brain stimulation. Olds and Milner's rat, on the other hand, kept returning to the corner of the cage where it had been shocked. It was as if their rat was hoping for another shock.

Stymied by the rat's curious behavior, they decided to test the hypothesis that the rat wanted to be shocked. They rewarded the rat with a mild jolt every time it moved a little bit to the right and away from the corner. The rat quickly caught on, and in just a few minutes, it was all the way in the other corner of the cage. Olds and Milner found that the rat would move in any direction if they rewarded it with a shock. Pretty soon, they could operate the rat like a joystick.

Were the other researchers wrong about the effects of stimulating this area of a rat's midbrain? Or had they somehow ended up with a masochistic rat?

Actually, they had stumbled on an unexplored area of the brain, thanks to a bit of clumsiness during the implanting procedure. Olds was trained as a social psychologist, not a neuroscientist, and had yet to develop real laboratory skill. He had implanted the electrode in the wrong area. By mistake, they had found an area of the brain that seemed to produce incredible pleasure when stimulated. What else could explain why the rat would go anywhere to get another shock? Olds and Milner called their discovery the pleasure center of the brain.

But Olds and Milner did not yet understand what they had tapped into. That rat wasn't experiencing bliss—it was experiencing desire. What neuroscientists eventually learned about that rat's experience provides a fascinating window into our own experience of cravings, temptation, and addiction. As we look through that window, we'll see that when it comes to happiness, we cannot trust our brains to point us in the right direction. We'll also explore how the new field of neuromarketing is using this science to manipulate our brains and manufacture desire, and what we can do to resist.

THE PROMISE OF REWARD

Once Olds and Milner had discovered the "pleasure" center of their rat's brain, they set to work demonstrating just how euphoric stimulating this area of the brain was. First they starved the rat for twenty-four hours, then placed him in the middle of a short tunnel with food at both ends. Normally, the rat would run to one end and gobble down the rat chow. But if they shocked the rat before he made it to the food, he would stop at that spot and never budge. He preferred to wait for the possibility of another shock rather than the guaranteed reward of food.

The scientists also tested whether the rat would shock himself if given the opportunity. They set up a lever that, when pressed, would electrically stimulate the rat's pleasure center. Once the rat figured out what the lever did, he began giving himself shocks every five seconds. Other rats given free access to self-stimulation showed no signs of satiation, and would continue to press the lever until they collapsed from exhaustion. Rats even found self-torture acceptable if it led to brain stimulation. Olds put self-stimulating levers at the opposite ends of an electrified grid, and set it up so that a rat could only receive one shock at a time from each lever. Rats willingly ran back and forth across the electrified grid until their charred feet were so injured they could not continue. Olds became even more convinced that the only thing that could produce this behavior was bliss.

It didn't take long for a psychiatrist to think this experiment would be a pretty neat thing to try with humans.* At Tulane University, Robert Heath implanted electrodes into his patients' brains, and gave them a control box to self-stimulate the newly discovered pleasure center. Heath's patients behaved remarkably like Olds and Milner's rats. When given permission to self-stimulate at any rate they liked, they averaged forty shocks per minute. When a food tray was brought in for a break, the patients—who admitted they were hungry—didn't want to stop the self-stimulation to eat. One patient put up vigorous protests whenever the experimenter tried to end the session and disconnect the electrodes. Another participant continued to press the button over two hundred times *after* the current was turned off, until the experimenter finally demanded that he stop.† Somehow these

---

*Although Heath's research was strange, it wasn't the strangest thing going on in psychology laboratories in the 1960s. Over at Harvard, Timothy Leary was studying the spiritual benefits of LSD and hallucinogenic mushrooms. At the Maimonides Medical Center in Brooklyn, Stanley Krippner was furthering ESP research by training subjects to send telepathic messages to a person dreaming in another room. And Ewen Cameron at Allen Memorial Institute in Montreal was trying to erase the memories of housewives held against their will as part of CIA-sponsored research on mind control.

†One of the most interesting things about Heath's report is how he interpreted the patient's continued pressing of the button after the current was turned off. Heath thought it demonstrated that the patient was too mentally disturbed to be an adequate test subject. He did not yet have sufficient understanding of the brain region he was stimulating to recognize that this behavior was the first sign of addiction and compulsion.

results convinced Heath that self-stimulation of the brain was a viable therapeutic technique for a wide range of mental disorders (heck, they seemed to like it), and he decided it would be a good idea to leave the electrodes in his patients' brains and give them small portable self-stimulators they could wear on their belts and use whenever they wanted.

At this point, we should consider the context of this research. The dominant scientific paradigm at the time was behaviorism. Behaviorists believed the only thing worth measuring—in animals or humans—was *behavior*. Thoughts? Feelings? Waste of time. If an objective observer couldn't see it, it wasn't science, and it wasn't important. This may be why early reports of Heath's work lack any detailed firsthand reports from his patients about what the self-stimulation felt like. Heath, like Olds and Milner, assumed that because his subjects continuously self-stimulated, and ignored food for the opportunity to keep shocking themselves, they were being "rewarded" for it with euphoric pleasure. And it's true that the patients said the shocks felt good. But their near-constant rates of self-stimulation, combined with anxiety about having the current turned off, suggested something other than true satisfaction. What few details we have about his patients' thoughts and feelings reveal another side to this seemingly blissful experience. One patient, who suffered from narcolepsy and was given the portable implant to help him stay awake, described the feeling of self-stimulation as intensely frustrating. Despite his "frequent, sometimes frantic pushing of the button," he was never able to achieve the sense of satisfaction he felt he was close to experiencing. The self-stimulation left him anxious, not happy. His behavior looked more like compulsion than a man experiencing pleasure.

What if Olds and Milner's rats weren't self-stimulating to exhaustion because it felt so good that they didn't want to stop? What if the area of the brain they were stimulating wasn't rewarding them with the experience of profound pleasure, but simply *promising* them the experience of pleasure? Is it possible the rats were self-stimulating because their brains were telling them that if they just pressed that lever one more time, something wonderful was going to happen?

Olds and Milner hadn't discovered the pleasure center—they had discovered what neuroscientists now call the *reward* system. The area they were stimulating was part of the brain's most primitive motivational system, one that evolved to propel us toward action and consumption. That's why Olds and Milner's first rat kept hanging around the corner where he was first stimulated, and why the rats were willing to forgo food and electrocute their feet for the chance at another brain jolt. Each time the area was activated, the rat's brain said, "Do this again! This will make you feel good!" Every stimulation encouraged the rat to seek more stimulation, but the stimulation itself never brought satisfaction.

As you will see, it's not just electrodes in the brain that can trigger this system. Our whole world is full of stimuli—from restaurant menus and catalogs to lottery tickets and television ads—that can turn us into the human version of Olds and Milner's rat chasing the promise of happiness. When that happens, our brains become obsessed with "I want," and it gets harder to say, "I won't."

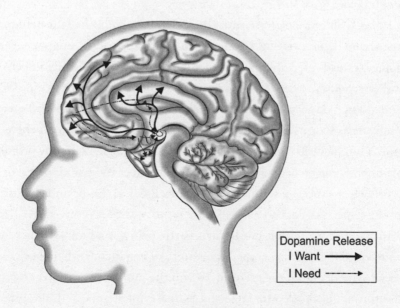

Dopamine Release
I Want ⟶
I Need ---⟶

"Promise of Reward" System of Midbrain

THE NEUROBIOLOGY OF "I WANT"

How does the reward system compel us to act? When the brain recognizes an opportunity for reward, it releases a neurotransmitter called dopamine. Dopamine tells the rest of the brain what to pay attention to and what to get our greedy little hands on. A dopamine rush doesn't create happiness itself—the feeling is more like arousal. We feel alert, awake, and captivated. We recognize the possibility of feeling good and are willing to work for that feeling.

In the last few years, neuroscientists have given the effect of dopamine release many names, including *seeking*, *wanting*, *craving*, and *desire*. But one thing is clear: It is not the experience of liking, satisfaction, pleasure, or actual reward. Studies show that you can annihilate the entire dopamine system in a rat's brain, and it will still get a goofy grin on its face if you feed it sugar. What it won't do is work for the treat. It likes the sugar; it just doesn't *want* it before it has it.

In 2001, Stanford neuroscientist Brian Knutson published the definitive experiment demonstrating dopamine's role in anticipating, but not experiencing, reward. He borrowed his method from a famous study in behavioral psychology, Ivan Pavlov's classical conditioning of dogs. In 1927, Pavlov observed that if he rang a bell before feeding his dogs, they started to salivate as soon as they heard the bell ring, even if food was nowhere in sight. They had learned to associate the sound of the bell with the promise of dinner. Knutson had a hunch that the brain does its own kind of salivation when it expects a reward—and, critically, that this brain response is not the same as the brain's response when the reward is received.

In his study, Knutson put human participants in a brain scanner and conditioned them to expect the opportunity to win money when they saw a special symbol appear on a screen. To win the money, they'd have to press a button to get the reward. As soon as the symbol appeared, the brain's dopamine-releasing reward center lit up, and the participants pressed the button to get their reward. When the participants actually won money, however, this area of the brain quieted down. The joy of winning was registered in different areas of the brain. Knutson had proven that dopamine is for action, not happiness. The promise of reward guaranteed that participants wouldn't miss out on the reward by failing to act. What they were feeling when the reward system lit up was *anticipation*, not pleasure.

Anything we think is going to make us feel good will trigger the reward system—the sight of tempting food, the smell of coffee brewing, the 50-percent-off sign in a store window, a smile from a sexy stranger, the infomercial that promises to make you rich. The flood of dopamine marks this new object of desire as critical to your survival. When dopamine hijacks your attention, the mind becomes fixated on obtaining or repeating whatever triggered it. This is nature's trick to make sure you don't starve because you can't be bothered to pick a berry, and that you don't hasten human extinction because seducing a potential mate seems like too much of a hassle. Evolution doesn't give a damn about happiness itself, but will use the promise of happiness to keep us struggling to stay alive. And so the promise of happiness—not the direct experience of happiness—is the brain's strategy to keep you hunting, gathering, working, and wooing.

Of course, as with many of our primitive instincts, we find ourselves in a very different environment now than the one the human brain evolved in. Take, for example, the flood of dopamine we experience whenever we see, smell, or taste high-fat or high-sugar food. That dopamine release guarantees we will want to stuff ourselves silly. This is a great instinct if you live in an environment where food is scarce. But when you live in a world where food is not only widely available but also specifically engineered to maximize your dopamine response, following every burst of dopamine is a recipe for obesity, not longevity.

Or consider the effects of sexually graphic images on our reward system. For much of human history, you weren't going to see a naked person posing seductively for you unless the opportunity for mating was real. Certainly a little motivation to act in this scenario would be smart if you wanted to keep your DNA in the gene pool. Fast-forward a few hundred thousand years, and we find ourselves in a world where Internet porn is always available, not to mention constant exposure to sexual images in advertisements and entertainment. The instinct to pursue every one of these sexual "opportunities" is how people end up addicted to X-rated websites—and victims of advertising campaigns that use sex to sell everything from deodorant to designer jeans.

DOPAMINE ON DEMAND

When we add the instant gratification of modern technology to this primitive motivation system, we end up with dopamine-delivery devices that are damn near impossible to put down. Some of us are old enough to remember the thrill of pressing a button on an answering machine to find out if we had any new messages. Then there was the anticipation of connecting by modem to AOL, hoping the computer would tell us, "You've got mail!" Well, now we have Facebook, Twitter, e-mail, and text messaging—the modern equivalent of psychiatrist Robert Heath's self-stimulating devices.

Because we know there's a chance we'll have a new message, or because the very next YouTube video may be the one that makes us laugh, we keep hitting refresh, clicking the next link, and checking our devices compulsively. It's as if our cell phones, BlackBerrys, and laptops have a direct line into our brains, giving us constant jolts of dopamine. There are few things ever dreamed of, smoked, or injected that have as addictive an effect on our brains as technology. This is how our devices keep us captive and always coming back for more. The definitive Internet act of our times is a perfect metaphor for the promise of reward: We search. And we search. And we search some more, clicking that mouse like—well, like a rat in a cage seeking another "hit," looking for the elusive reward that will finally feel like enough.

Cell phones, the Internet, and other social media may have accidentally exploited our reward system, but computer and video game designers intentionally manipulate the reward system to keep players hooked. The promise that the next level or big win could happen at any time is what makes a game compelling. It's also what makes a game hard to quit. One study found that playing a video game led to dopamine increases equivalent to amphetamine use—and it's this dopamine rush that makes both so addictive. The unpredictability of scoring or advancing keeps your dopamine neurons firing, and you glued to your seat. Depending on your point of view, this makes for either incredible entertainment or unethical exploitation of gamers. While not everyone who picks up an Xbox controller gets hooked, for those who are vulnerable, games can be as addictive as any drug. In 2005, a twenty-eight-year-old Korean boiler repairman, Lee Seung Seop, died from cardiovascular failure after playing the game Star-Craft for fifty hours straight. He had refused to eat or sleep, wanting only to continue. It's impossible to hear this story and not think about Olds and Milner's rats pressing the lever to exhaustion.

UNDER THE MICROSCOPE: WHAT GETS YOUR DOPAMINE NEURONS FIRING?

Do you know what your own dopamine triggers are? Food? Alcohol? Shopping? Facebook? Something else? This week, pay attention to what captures *your* attention. What unleashes that promise of reward that compels you to seek satisfaction? What gets you salivating like Pavlov's dogs or obsessed like Olds and Milner's rats?

A Prescription for Addiction

Perhaps the most striking evidence of dopamine's role in addiction comes from patients being treated for Parkinson's disease, a common neurodegenerative disorder caused by the loss of dopamine-producing brain cells. The main symptoms reflect dopamine's role in motivating action: slow or impaired movement, depression, and occasionally complete catatonia. The standard treatment for Parkinson's disease is a two-drug combo: L-dopa, which helps the brain make dopamine, and a dopamine agonist, which stimulates dopamine receptors in the brain to mimic the action of dopamine. When patients begin drug therapy, their brains are flooded with way more dopamine than they've seen in a long time. This relieves the main symptoms of the disease, but also creates new problems that no one expected.

Medical journals are full of case studies documenting the unintended side effects of these drugs. There is the fifty-four-year-old woman who developed insatiable cravings for cookies, crackers, and pasta, and would stay up late into the night binge-eating. Or the fifty-two-year-old man who developed a daily gambling habit, staying at the casino for thirty-six hours straight and running through his life's savings.* Or the forty-nine-year-old man who all of a sudden found himself afflicted with an increased appetite, a taste for alcohol, and what his wife called "an excessive sex urge" that required calling the cops to get him to leave her alone. All of these cases were completely resolved by taking the patients off the dopamine-enhancing drug. But in many cases, confused loved ones and doctors first sent patients to psychotherapy and Alcoholics or Gamblers Anonymous. They were unable to see that the new addictions were a brain glitch, not a deep-seated emotional problem that required psychological and spiritual counseling.

While these cases are extreme, they aren't so different from what happens in your brain whenever you get hooked by the promise of reward. The drugs that the Parkinson's patients were on simply exaggerated the natural effect that all these things—food, sex, alcohol, gambling, work—have on the reward system. We are driven to chase pleasure, but often at the cost of our well-being. When dopamine puts our brains on a reward-seeking mission, we become the most risk-taking, impulsive, and out-of-control version of ourselves.

Importantly, even if the reward never arrives, the promise of reward—combined with a growing sense of anxiety when we think about stopping—is

---

*He also become completely obsessed with his leaf blower, using it for up to six hours at a time to try to create the perfect, leaf-free yard—but this was understandably considered a less pressing problem to his family and doctors.

enough to keep us hooked. If you're a lab rat, you press a lever again and again until you collapse or starve to death. If you're a human, this leaves you with a lighter wallet and a fuller stomach, at best. At worst, you may find yourself spiraling into obsession and compulsion.

THIS IS YOUR BRAIN ON DOPAMINE: THE RISE OF NEUROMARKETING

When dopamine is released by one promise of reward, it also makes you more susceptible to any other kind of temptation. For example, erotic images make men more likely to take financial risks, and fantasizing about winning the lottery leads people to overeat—two ways daydreaming about unattainable rewards can get you into trouble. High levels of dopamine amplify the lure of immediate gratification, while making you less concerned about long-term consequences.

Do you know who has figured this out? People who want your money. Many aspects of our retail environment have been designed to keep us always wanting more, from big food companies packing their recipes with just the right combination of sugar, salt, and fat to drive your dopamine neurons crazy to lotto commercials that encourage you to imagine what you would do with a million dollars if you hit the jackpot.

Grocery stores are no fools, either. They want you shopping under the influence of maximum dopamine, so they put their most tempting merchandise front and center. When I walk into my neighborhood store, the very first thing I'm hit with is the free samples in the bakery section. This is no accident. Marketing researchers at Stanford University have shown that food and drink samples make shoppers hungrier and thirstier, and put shoppers in a reward-seeking state of mind. Why? Because samples combine two of the biggest promises of reward: *Free* and *Food*. (If there's an attractive spokesperson handing out the samples, you can throw in a third *F*, and then you're really in trouble.) In one study, participants who sampled something sweet were more likely to purchase indulgent foods such as a steak or cake, as well as items that were on sale. The food and drink samples amplified the appeal of products that would typically activate the reward system. (Nothing triggers a budget-minded mom's promise of reward more than the opportunity to save money!) There was no effect, however, on utilitarian items like oatmeal and dishwasher liquid, demonstrating that even a hit of dopamine cannot make toilet paper irresistible to the average consumer (sorry, Charmin).* But take a bite of the store's new cinnamon strudel, and you may find yourself with a few more items in your cart than you planned. And even if you resist the temptation of the sample, your brain—hopped up on dopamine—will be looking for something to satisfy the promise of reward.

The Stanford researchers who ran this study asked twenty-one food and nutrition experts to predict the results, and shockingly, 81 percent believed that the opposite would be true—that samples would decrease a shopper's hunger and thirst, and satiate their reward seeking. This just goes to show how unaware most of us—experts included—are of the many environmental factors that influence our inner desires and behavior. For example, most people also believe that they are immune to advertisements, despite ample evidence that TV ads for snack foods make you more likely to hit the fridge—especially if you're a dieter trying to cut back on snacks.

The reward system of the brain also responds to novelty and variety. Your dopamine neurons eventually become less responsive to familiar rewards, even ones you really enjoy, whether it's a daily mocha latte or the same old lunch special. It's not a coincidence that places like Starbucks and Jack in the Box are constantly introducing new variations of the standard fare, and clothing retailers roll out new color choices for their wardrobe basics. Regular cup of joe? Been there, done that. Ah, but what's this on the menu—a white chocolate latte? The thrill is back! Cable-knit sweater in

---

*Sampling something sweet also made participants more interested in rewards that had nothing to do with the shopping experience, including a vacation in Bora Bora, a romantic movie, and a spa experience, suggesting that marketers trying to sell anything from real estate to luxury cars would be smart to serve cookies and punch at their sales pitch.

your favorite clothing catalog? Boring. But wait, it's now available in salted-caramel brown and melted-butter yellow? Dopamine days are here again!

Then there are the price tricks guaranteed to make the primitive part of your brain want to hoard scarce resources. Anything that makes you feel like you're getting a bargain is going to open the dopamine floodgates, from "Buy 1 Get 1 Free!" deals to signs that shout "60 Percent Off!" Especially potent are the price tags at discount retailers that list some ridiculously high "suggested retail price" next to the retailer's lower price. As Amazon.com knows and ruthlessly exploits, your brain quickly calculates the savings and (illogically) treats the difference as money earned. $999 marked down to $44.99? What a steal! I don't even know what it's for, but add to cart immediately! Throw in any kind of time pressure or scarcity cue (door-busters savings that end at noon, one-day sales, the ominous-sounding "while supplies last"), and you'll be hunting and gathering like you've found the last dwindling food supply on the savannah.

Businesses also use smells to manufacture desire where none existed. An appetizing odor is one of the fastest ways to trigger the promise of reward, and as soon as the scented molecules land on your olfactory receptors, the brain will begin searching for the source. The next time you walk by a fast-food restaurant and are tempted by the smell of french fries and burgers, it's a safe bet you're not smelling the food inside, but a carefully manufactured Eau de Eat More being piped onto the sidewalk through special vents. The website of Scent Air, a leader in the field of scent marketing,* brags about how it lured visitors into an ice cream parlor on the lower level of a hotel. With a strategically placed aroma-delivery system, they released the scent of sugar cookies to the top of the stairs and waffle cones to the bottom. The average passerby will think she is inhaling the authentic smell of the sweet treats. Instead, she is breathing in enhanced chemicals designed to maximize the firing of her dopamine neurons and lead her—and her

---

*Scent Air's list of available scents (scentair.com) runs the gamut from Fresh Linen to Birthday Cake and Mistletoe. It's easy to imagine the retailers who would want these appealing odors wafting around their merchandise. I'm left wondering, though, who the market is for Scent Air's Skunk, Dinosaur Breath, and Burning Rubber aromas.

wallet—straight down the stairs.* For Bloomingdale's, the company varied the scents by department: Baby Powder to trigger warm and fuzzy feelings in the maternity department, Coconut in the swimsuit department to inspire fantasies of cocktails on the beach, and the "soothing scent of Lilac" for the intimate apparel department, presumably to calm down women standing naked under fluorescent lighting in front of a three-way dressing-room mirror. You may not even consciously notice these scents, but they can influence your brain and your shopping all the same.

Of course, science can be used for good as well as profit, and to be fair, the field of scent marketing has done more for the world than sell ice cream cones and bikinis. A Florida hospital's MRI department reduced its last-minute appointment-cancellation rates by introducing Coconut Beach and Ocean fragrances into the waiting areas. A little promise of reward can be a powerful antidote to anxiety, and help people approach things they would rather avoid. Other industries and service providers might benefit from a similar strategy—perhaps dentists could infuse their offices with the scent of Halloween Candy, and tax advisers might choose Stiff Martini.

Become a Dopamine Detective

Once I introduce these neuromarketing and sales tricks to my students, it ignites a hunt for evidence. They start to see how many of their willpower failures are hastened by dopamine triggers in their everyday environments. Students return the next week with stories of how their favorite stores are manipulating them, from the scented candles burning in the cookware store to the scratch-and-win discount cards handed out to shoppers at the mall. They recognize why a clothing store company has pictures of naked models on its walls, and why auctioneers open the bidding at bargain

---

*While this approach might seem brazen, it's nothing compared with the motion-detecting ice-cream vending machine developed by Unilever. When it senses potential customers walking by, it calls out to them and encourages them to come over for ice cream.

prices. Once you start looking, it's impossible not to see the many traps that have been laid to ensnare you, your dopamine neurons, and your money.

Almost universally, students report feeling empowered by these observations. They have fun spotting the tricks. It also helps make sense of some shopping mysteries, like why something that seemed irresistible in the store seems so disappointing at home, far away from the dopamine that clouded your judgment. One woman finally understood why she always heads to the gourmet grocery store when she's bored—not for food, but just to wander around looking at things. Her brain is directing her to a reliable trigger of a dopamine rush. Another student canceled her catalog subscriptions when she recognized that she was essentially getting a dopamine delivery in the mail, each colorful page creating desires that could only be filled by that company's products. A student at a professional conference in Las Vegas was able to hold on to more of his money because he saw through the casino's strategies to overstimulate his dopamine neurons: nearly naked showgirls, all-you-can-eat buffets, lights and buzzers signaling every win in the house.

Although we live in a world engineered to make us want, we can—just by paying attention—start to see through some of it. Knowing what's going on won't eliminate all your wants, but it will give you at least a fighting chance to exercise your "I won't" power.

UNDER THE MICROSCOPE: WHO'S MANIPULATING YOUR DOPAMINE NEURONS?

Look for how retailers and marketers try to trigger the promise of reward. Make it a game when you go to the grocery store or watch advertisements. What do you smell? What do you see? What do you hear? Knowing that cues have been carefully chosen to tempt you can help you see them for what they are and resist them.

PUTTING DOPAMINE TO WORK

When I discuss neuromarketing in class, some student will inevitably propose that we make certain kinds of advertising and undisclosed retail manipulation illegal. This impulse is understandable, but almost certainly impossible. The number of restrictions that would have to be put in place to create a "safe" environment is not only implausible, but to the vast majority of people, unappealing. We want to *feel* our desires, and—for better or worse—we delight in a world that puts them on constant display for us to dream about. That's why people love window-shopping, flipping through luxury magazines, and touring open houses. It's difficult to imagine a world where our dopamine neurons aren't being constantly courted. And even if we were "protected" from dopamine stimulants, we'd most likely start looking for something to stimulate our desires.

Since it's unlikely we'll ever outlaw the promise of reward, we might as well put it to good use. We can take a lesson from neuromarketers and try to "dopaminize" our least favorite tasks. An unpleasant chore can be made more appealing by introducing a reward. And when the rewards of our actions are far off in the future, we can try to squeeze a little extra dopamine out of neurons by fantasizing about the eventual payoff (not unlike those lotto commercials).

Some economists have even proposed dopaminizing "boring" things like saving for retirement and filing your taxes on time. For example, imagine a savings account where your money is protected, and you can take it out whenever you want—but instead of getting a guaranteed low interest rate, you are entered in lotteries for large cash prizes. People who buy lottery tickets but don't have a dollar in the bank might be much more enthusiastic about saving their money if every deposit they made gave them another chance to win $100,000. Or imagine if by filing your taxes on time and honestly reporting all income and deductions, you had a shot at winning back the entire year's taxes. Wouldn't this motivate you to beat the April 15 deadline? While the IRS may be a little slow to move on this proposal, it's something that a business could easily implement to motivate on-time expense reports.

The promise of reward has even been used to help people overcome addiction. One of the most effective intervention strategies in alcohol and drug recovery is something called the fish bowl. Patients who pass their drug tests win the opportunity to draw a slip of paper out of a bowl. About half of these slips have a prize listed on them, ranging in value from $1 to $20. Only one slip has a big prize, worth $100. Half of the slips have no prize value at all—instead, they say, "Keep up the good work." This means that when you reach your hand into the fish bowl, the odds are you're going to end up with a prize worth $1 or a few kind words. This shouldn't be motivating—but it is. In one study, 83 percent of patients who had access to fish bowl rewards stayed in treatment for the whole twelve weeks, compared with only 20 percent of patients receiving standard treatment without the promise of reward. Eighty percent of the fish bowl patients passed all their drug tests, compared with only 40 percent of the standard treatment group. When the intervention was over, the fish bowl group was also far less likely to relapse than patients who received standard treatment—even without the continued promise of reward.

Amazingly, the fish bowl technique works even better than paying patients for passing their drug tests—despite the fact that patients end up with far less "reward" from the fish bowl than they would from guaranteed payments. This highlights the power of an unpredictable reward. Our reward system gets much more excited about a possible big win than a guaranteed smaller reward, and it will motivate us to do whatever provides the chance to win. This is why people would rather play the lottery than earn a guaranteed 2 percent interest in a savings account, and why even the lowest employee in a company should be made to believe he could someday be the CEO.

WILLPOWER EXPERIMENT: DOPAMINIZE
YOUR "I WILL" POWER CHALLENGE

My students have dopaminized tasks they typically put off by using music, fashion magazines, and television to help them work out; bringing dreaded paperwork to a favorite café and finishing it over hot chocolate; and, in a truly creative gesture, buying a bunch of scratch-off lottery tickets and placing them next to procrastinated projects around the house. Others visualize the best-possible outcome of their hard work, to make the faraway rewards seem more real. If there's something you've been putting off because it's so unpleasant, can you motivate yourself by linking it to something that gets your dopamine neurons firing?

A Procrastinator Dopaminizes Her "I Will" Power Challenge

Nancy, whose youngest son had graduated from college nearly a decade earlier, had a problem with her empty nest. It wasn't empty. She had turned her son's old bedroom into the "spare" room, and over the years, it had become more like a salvage yard. Anytime she didn't know where to put something, into the spare room it went. She wanted to clean it out and turn it into a guest room, not a room she had to hide from visitors. And yet every time she opened the door, she was overwhelmed. Cleaning out the room became her class willpower challenge, but it wasn't until we hit on the promise of reward that Nancy found her way in. She was inspired by a study that combined Christmas music with holiday scents to increase shoppers' enjoyment and desire to stay in a store. For many people, a little Ho-Ho-Ho plus the smell of fresh fir trees brings up memories of the most wonderful "promise of reward" we have ever experienced: waking up on Christmas morning to a pile of presents. Nancy decided to bring out her holiday music and candles (conveniently enough, stored in the spare room!) to get her through the task of cleaning. Though she'd been dreading it, she actually enjoyed working on the room in small bursts. The overwhelm was worse than the actual process, and the holly, jolly dopamine helped her find the motivation to get started.

THE DARK SIDE OF DOPAMINE

Dopamine can be a great motivator, and even when it's tempting us to order dessert or max out our credit cards, it's hard to describe this tiny neurotransmitter as evil. But dopamine does have a dark side, one that's not hard to see if we pay close attention. If we pause and notice what's really going on in our brains and bodies when we're in that state of wanting, we will find that the promise of reward can be as stressful as it is delightful. Desire doesn't always make us feel good—sometimes it makes us feel downright rotten. That's because dopamine's primary function is to make us *pursue* happiness, not to make us happy. It doesn't mind putting a little pressure on us—even if that means making us unhappy in the process.

To motivate you to seek the object of your craving, the reward system actually has two weapons: a carrot and a stick. The first weapon is, of course, the promise of reward. Dopamine-releasing neurons create this feeling by talking to the areas of your brain that anticipate pleasure and plan action. When these areas are bathed in dopamine, the result is desire—the carrot that makes the horse run forward. But the reward system has a second weapon that functions more like the proverbial stick. When your reward center releases dopamine, it also sends a message to the brain's stress center. In this area of the brain, dopamine triggers the release of stress hormones. The result: You feel anxious as you anticipate your object of desire. The need to get what you want starts to feel like a life-or-death emergency, a matter of survival.

Researchers have observed this mixed inner experience of desire and stress in women who crave chocolate. When they see images of chocolate, the women show a startle response—a physiological reflex associated with alarm and arousal, as if spotting a predator in the wild. When asked what they were feeling, the women reported both pleasure and anxiety, along with the feeling of being out of control. When we find ourselves in a similar state, we attribute the pleasure to whatever triggered the response, and the stress to not yet having it. We fail to recognize that the object of our desire is causing both the anticipated pleasure and the stress.

UNDER THE MICROSCOPE: THE STRESS OF DESIRE

Most of us pay far more attention to the *promise* of feeling good than the *actual* feeling bad that accompanies dopamine-drive desire. This week, see if you can notice when wanting triggers stress and anxiety. If you give in to temptation, do you feel like you are responding to the promise of reward? Or are you trying to relieve the anxiety?

A SHOPPER FEELS THE ANXIETY, BUT KEEPS THE PROMISE

Whenever Yvonne wanted to feel good, she hit the mall. She was sure that shopping made her happy, because whenever she was bored or upset, it's what she wanted to do. She had never really noticed the complex feelings that went along with shopping, but took the assignment of paying closer attention. She discovered that she was most happy on the way to the mall. Driving there, she felt hopeful and excited. Once she arrived, as long as she was window-shopping from the center of the mall, she felt good. But when she was in a store, the feelings shifted. She felt tense, especially if the store was crowded. She felt an urge to get all the way through the store, and a sense of time pressure. When she waited in line to buy something, she noticed that she felt impatient and anxious. If the customer in front of her had too many things or was making a return, she found herself getting angry. Getting to the register and handing over her credit card felt like a relief, not like the happiness she had felt before the purchase. Yvonne realized that the hope and excitement she felt while driving to the mall was the carrot to *get* her there; the anxiety and anger was the stick keeping her in line. She never felt as good going home as she did driving over.

For many people, this kind of realization leads to turning away from the unsatisfying reward. The potato chip junkie eyes the bag of chips with newfound suspicion, and the late-night TV addict turns the tube off. But Yvonne settled on a different strategy: window-shopping for maximum happiness. The feeling of being in the mall produced the feeling that she liked best; spending was stressful. Surprisingly, when she went with the mind-set of not buying, and left her credit cards at home so she couldn't overspend, she went home happier than if she had spent a lot of money.

When you really understand how a so-called reward makes you feel, you will be best able to make smart decisions about whether and how to "reward" yourself.

WE MISTAKE THE PROMISE OF REWARD FOR HAPPINESS

When Olds and Milner watched their rats refuse food and run back and forth across an electrified grid, they made the same mistake each of us makes when we interpret our own dopamine-driven behavior. We observe our intense focus, the consistent seeking of what we crave, and the willingness to work—even suffer—for what we want as evidence that the object of our desire must make us happy. We watch ourselves buy the one thousandth candy bar, the new kitchen gadget, the next drink; we wear ourselves out chasing the new partner, the better job, the highest stock return. We mistake the experience of wanting for a guarantee of happiness. It's no wonder Olds and Milner looked at those rats shocking themselves to exhaustion and assumed that they were happy. We humans find it nearly impossible to distinguish the promise of reward from whatever pleasure or payoff we are seeking.

The promise of reward is so powerful that we continue to pursue things that don't make us happy, and consume things that bring us more misery than satisfaction. Because the pursuit of reward is dopamine's main goal, it is never going to give you a "stop" signal—even when the experience does not live up to the promise. Brian Wansink, director of the Cornell University Food and Brand Laboratory, demonstrated this with a trick he played on moviegoers at a Philadelphia theater. The sight and smell of movie theater popcorn is a reliable way to get most people's dopamine neurons dancing—customers stand in line like Pavlov's dogs, tongues hanging out and drooling in anticipation of the first mouthful. Wansink arranged to have the theater's concession stand sell fourteen-day-old popcorn to the moviegoers. He wanted to find out whether the moviegoers would keep eating, listening to the brain's belief that movie theater popcorn is always delicious, or whether they would notice the actual taste of the treat, and refuse to eat it.

After the film, the moviegoers confirmed that the two-week-old popcorn was indeed nasty stuff: stale, soggy, verging on disgusting. But did they storm the popcorn stand demanding refunds? No, they ate it up. They even ate 60 percent as much popcorn as moviegoers who received a fresh batch! They believed their dopamine neurons, not their taste buds.

We may scratch our heads and wonder how this is possible, but it's something few of us are immune to. Just think of your own biggest "I won't" power challenge. Chances are this is something you believe makes you happy—or would make you happy, if you could just get enough of it. But a careful analysis of the experience and its consequences often reveals the opposite. At best, giving in takes away the anxiety that the promise of reward produces to make you want it more. But ultimately, you're left frustrated, unsatisfied, disappointed, ashamed, tired, sick, or simply no happier than when you started. There is growing evidence that when people pay close attention to the experience of their false rewards, the magical spell wears off. If you force your brain to reconcile what it expects from a reward—happiness, bliss, satisfaction, an end to sadness or stress—with what it actually experiences, your brain will eventually adjust its expectations. For example, when overeaters slow down and really experience a food that usually triggers cravings and bingeing, they typically notice that the food looks and smells better than it tastes; even with the mouth and stomach full, the brain begs for more; their feelings of anxiety only increase as they eat more; sometimes they don't even *taste* the food when they're bingeing, because they're eating so fast; and they feel worse physically and emotionally afterward than they did before. At first, this can be disturbing—after all, they had really believed that food was a source of happiness. However, the research shows that people who practice this mindful-eating exercise develop greater self-control around food and have fewer episodes of binge-eating. Over time, they not only lose weight, but they also experience less stress, anxiety, and depression. When we free ourselves from the false promise of reward, we often find that the thing we were seeking happiness from was the main source of our misery.

WILLPOWER EXPERIMENT: TEST THE PROMISE OF REWARD

Test the promise of reward with a temptation that you regularly indulge in because your brain tells you it will make you happy. The most common choices in my class are snack foods, shopping, television, and online time-wasters from e-mail to poker. Mindfully indulge, but don't rush through the experience. Notice what the promise of reward feels like: the antici-pation, the hope, the excitement, the anxiety, the salivation—whatever is going on in your brain and body. Then give yourself permission to give in. How does the experience compare with the expectation? Does the feeling of the promise of reward ever go away—or does it continue to drive you to eat more, spend more, or stay longer? When, if ever, do you become satis-fied? Or do you simply reach the point of being unable to continue, because you're stuffed, exhausted, frustrated, out of time, or out of the "reward"?

People who try this exercise commonly have one of two results. Some people find that when they really pay attention to the experience of indulg-ing, they need far less than they thought they would to feel satisfied. Others find that the experience is completely unsatisfying, revealing a huge gap between the promise of reward and the reality of their experience. Both observations can give you greater control over what has felt like an out-of-control behavior.

THE IMPORTANCE OF DESIRE

Before you ask your doctor for dopamine-suppressing drugs, it's worth contemplating the upside of the promise of reward. While we get into trouble when we mistake wanting for happiness, the solution is not to eliminate wanting. A life without wants may not require as much self-control—but it's also not a life worth living.

AN ADDICT LOSES HIS CRAVINGS

Adam was not a man of self-restraint. At age thirty-three, a typical day included up to ten drinks, a hit of crack cocaine, and sometimes a bonus round of Ecstasy. His substance abuse had a long history, starting with alcohol at age nine and cocaine at thirteen, and by the time he was an adult, he was hooked on marijuana, cocaine, opiates, and Ecstasy.

All that changed the day he was taken from a party to the emergency room, where he promptly ingested all the drugs in his possession to avoid being caught with illegal substances (not a smart move, but to be fair, he wasn't in the clearest state of mind). The dangerous drug combination of cocaine, Ecstasy, oxycodone, and methadone led to a near-fatal drop in blood pressure and reduced oxygen to his brain.

Although he was resuscitated and eventually released from intensive care, the temporary oxygen deprivation would prove to have profound consequences. Adam lost all of his cravings for drugs and alcohol. His daily drug use dropped to complete abstinence, confirmed by drug tests over the following six months. This miraculous change was not a spiritual revelation or some kind of wake-up call inspired by his brush with death. According to Adam, he simply had no desire to consume the substances.

This might sound like a positive turn of events, but the loss of desire went beyond cocaine and alcohol. Adam lost desire, period. He could not imagine that anything would make him happy. His physical energy and ability to concentrate disappeared, and he became increasingly isolated from others.

Without the ability to expect pleasure, he lost hope and spiraled into a severe depression.

What triggered this loss of desire? The psychiatrists at Columbia University who treated Adam discovered the answer in scans of his brain. The oxygen deprivation during his drug overdose had left Adam with lesions in the brain's reward system.

Adam's case, reported in the *American Journal of Psychiatry*, is extraordinary because of the dramatic change from addict to absolute loss of "I want." But there are many other cases of people who lose desire and the ability to expect happiness. Psychologists call it anhedonia—literally, "without pleasure." People with anhedonia describe life as a series of habits with no expectation of satisfaction. They may eat, shop, socialize, and have sex, but they don't anticipate pleasure from these activities. Without the possibility of pleasure, they lose motivation. It's hard to get out of bed when you can't imagine that anything you do will make you feel good. This complete disconnect from desire drains hope and, for many, the will to live.

When our reward system is quiet, the result isn't so much total contentment as it is apathy. It's why many Parkinson's patients—whose brains aren't producing enough dopamine—are depressed, not peaceful. In fact, neuroscientists now suspect that an underactive reward system contributes to the biological basis of depression. When scientists have watched the activity of depressed people's brains, they've seen that the reward system can't sustain activation, even in the face of immediate reward. There's a little burst of activity, but not enough to create the full feeling of "I want" and "I'm willing to work for it." This produces the loss of desire and motivation that many people who are depressed experience.

THE PARADOX OF REWARD

If you're like most of my students, you're probably wondering where all this leaves us. The promise of reward doesn't guarantee happiness, but *no* promise of reward guarantees unhappiness. Listen to the promise of reward, and we give in to temptation. Without the promise of reward, we have no motivation.

To this dilemma, there's no easy answer. It's clear that we need the promise of reward to keep us interested and engaged in life. If we're lucky, our reward systems won't stop serving us in this way—but hopefully, they also won't turn against us either. We live in a world of technology, advertisements, and twenty-four-hour opportunities that leave us always wanting and rarely satisfied. If we are to have any self-control, we need to separate the real rewards that give our lives meaning from the false rewards that keep us distracted and addicted. Learning to make this distinction may be the best we can do. This isn't always easy, but understanding what's happening in the brain can make it a little easier. If we can remember Olds and Milner's rat pressing that lever, we may find just enough clarity in moments of temptation to not believe the brain's big lie.

THE LAST WORD

Desire is the brain's strategy for action. As we've seen, it can be both a threat to self-control and a source of willpower. When dopamine points us to temptation, we must distinguish wanting from happiness. But we can also recruit dopamine and the promise of reward to motivate ourselves and others. In the end, desire is neither good nor bad—what matters is where we let it point us, and whether we have the wisdom to know when to follow.

CHAPTER SUMMARY

The Idea: Our brains mistake the promise of reward for a guarantee of happiness, so we chase satisfaction from things that do not deliver.

Under the Microscope

- *What gets your dopamine neurons firing?* What unleashes that promise of reward that compels you to seek satisfaction?

- *Neuromarketing and environmental triggers.* Look for how retailers and marketers try to trigger the promise of reward.
- *The stress of desire.* Notice when wanting triggers stress and anxiety.

Willpower Experiments

- *Dopaminize your "I will" power challenge.* If there's something you've been putting off, motivate yourself by linking it with something that gets your dopamine neurons firing.
- *Test the promise of reward.* Mindfully indulge in something your brain tells you will make you happy but that never seems to satisfy (e.g., snack food, shopping, television, and online time-wasters). Does reality match the brain's promises?

SIX

What the Hell: How Feeling Bad Leads to Giving In

When you're feeling down, what do you do to feel better? If you're like most people, you turn to the promise of reward. According to the American Psychological Association (APA), the most commonly used strategies for dealing with stress are those that activate the brain's reward system: eating, drinking, shopping, watching television, surfing the Web, and playing video games. And why not? Dopamine promises us that we're going to feel good. It's only natural that we turn to the biggest dopamine releasers when we want to feel better. Call it the promise of relief.

Wanting to feel better is a healthy survival mechanism, as built into our human nature as the instinct to flee danger. But where we turn for relief matters. The promise of reward—as we've seen—does not always mean that we *will* feel good. More often, the things we turn to for relief end up turning on us. The APA's national survey on stress found that the most commonly used strategies were also rated as highly *ineffective* by the same people who reported using them. For example, only 16 percent of people who eat to reduce stress report that it actually helps them. Another study found that women are most likely to eat chocolate when they are feeling anxious or depressed, but the only reliable change in mood they experience from their drug of choice is an increase in guilt. Certainly not what most of us are looking for when we reach for our favorite comfort food!

As we explore the effects of stress, anxiety, and guilt on self-control, we'll see that feeling bad leads to giving in, and often in surprising ways. Frightening cigarette warnings can make smokers crave a cigarette, economic crises can make people shop, and the nightly news can make you fat. No, it's not logical, but it's utterly human. If we want to avoid such stress-induced willpower failures, we'll need to find a way to feel better that doesn't require turning to temptation. We'll also need to give up the self-control strategies—like guilt and self-criticism—that only make us feel worse.

WHY STRESS MAKES US WANT

The brain, it turns out, is especially susceptible to temptation when we're feeling bad. Scientists have come up with clever ways to stress out their laboratory subjects, and the results are always the same. When smokers imagine a trip to the dentist, they experience off-the-chart cravings for a cigarette. When binge-eaters are told they will have to give a speech in public, they crave high-fat, sugary foods. Stressing out lab rats with unpredictable electric shocks (to the body, not the brain's reward center!) will make them run for sugar, alcohol, heroin, or whatever reward researchers have made available in their cage. Outside the laboratory, real-world stress increases the risk of relapse among smokers, recovering alcoholics, drug addicts, and dieters.

Why does stress lead to cravings? It's part of the brain's rescue mission. Previously, we saw how stress prompts a fight-or-flight response, a coordinated set of changes in the body that allows you to defend yourself against danger. But your brain isn't just motivated to protect your life—it wants to protect your mood, too. So whenever you are under stress, your brain is going to point you toward whatever it thinks will make you happy. Neuroscientists have shown that stress—including negative emotions like anger, sadness, self-doubt, and anxiety—shifts the brain into a reward-seeking state. You end up craving whatever substance or activity your brain associates with the promise of reward, and you become convinced that the "reward" is the only way to feel better. For example, when a cocaine addict remembers a fight with a family member or being criticized at work, his brain's reward system becomes activated, and he experiences intense cravings for cocaine. The stress hormones released during a fight-or-flight response also increase the excitability of your dopamine neurons. That means that when you're under stress, any temptations you run into will be even more tempting. For example, one study compared the appeal of chocolate cake to participants before and after they were made to feel bad about themselves by thinking about their personal failures. Feeling bad made the cake look better to everyone, but *even people who had said they did not like chocolate cake at all* suddenly expected that the cake would make them happy.

In moments far away from stress, we may know that food doesn't really make us feel better, but this clarity flies out the window when we're stressed out and the brain's reward system is screaming at us, "There's a pint of Ben and Jerry's in the freezer!" Stress points us in the wrong direction, away from our clear-headed wisdom and toward our least helpful instincts. That's the power of the one-two punch of stress and dopamine: We are drawn back again and again to coping strategies that don't work, but that our primitive brains persistently believe are the gateway to bliss.

The promise of reward combined with the promise of relief can lead to all sorts of illogical behavior. For example, one economic survey found that women worried about their finances shop to cope with their anxiety and depression. Yes, you read that right: *shop*. It defies reason—they're just adding to their credit card debt, which will make them feel even more overwhelmed down the road. But it makes perfect sense to a brain that just wants to feel better now. If you believe at some level that buying things makes you feel better, you will shop to relieve debt-induced stress.

Binge-eaters who feel ashamed of their weight and lack of control around food turn to—what else?—more food to fix their feelings. Procrastinators who are stressed out about how behind they are on a project will put it off even longer to avoid having to think about it. In each of these cases, the goal to feel better trumps the goal of self-control.

UNDER THE MICROSCOPE: THE PROMISE OF RELIEF

What do you turn to when you're feeling stressed, anxious, or down? Are you more susceptible to temptation when you are upset? Are you more easily distracted, or more likely to procrastinate? How does feeling bad affect your willpower challenge?

WILLPOWER EXPERIMENT: TRY A STRESS-RELIEF STRATEGY THAT WORKS

While many of the most popular stress-relief strategies fail to make us feel better, some strategies really work. According to the American Psychological Association, the most effective stress-relief strategies are exercising or playing sports, praying or attending a religious service, reading, listening to music, spending time with friends or family, getting a massage, going outside for a walk, meditating or doing yoga, and spending time with a creative hobby. (The least effective strategies are gambling, shopping, smoking, drinking, eating, playing video games, surfing the Internet, and watching TV or movies for more than two hours.)

The main difference between the strategies that work and the strategies that don't? Rather than releasing dopamine and relying on the promise of reward, the real stress relievers boost mood-enhancing brain chemicals like serotonin and GABA, as well as the feel-good hormone oxytocin. They also help shut down the brain's stress response, reduce stress hormones in the

body, and induce the healing relaxation response. Because they aren't exciting like the dopamine releasers, we tend to *underestimate* how good they
will make us feel. And so we forget about these strategies not because they
don't work, but because when we're stressed, our brains persistently mis-
predict what will make us happy. This means that we'll often talk ourselves
out of doing the very thing that will actually make us feel better.

*The next time you're feeling stressed and about to reach for the promise of
relief, consider trying a more effective stress reliever instead.*

A LITTLE HELP REMEMBERING WHAT WORKS

Whenever Denise, who was in charge of new project development for a
high-tech start-up, had a difficult day at work, she rewarded herself with
a bottle of wine and a rendezvous with her favorite real estate website. She
clicked through the endless and mind-numbing options of living rooms,
kitchens, and backyards. Not limiting herself to her own neighborhood, she
would type in faraway cities to see what was for sale in Portland, Raleigh,
or Miami. After an hour or so, she felt not so much relaxed as numbed (not
to mention a little depressed about her own home's square footage and
decidedly non-granite countertops).

A few years earlier, when Denise had a less demanding job, she had
enjoyed going to a yoga class after work. It left her both relaxed and
refreshed. She knew that yoga would make her feel better than her wine-
fueled real estate voyeurism, but whenever she thought about going to a
class, it seemed like too much trouble. The pull to go home and uncork a
bottle was stronger. As part of our class experiment, Denise committed to
doing yoga at least once. When she did, she felt even better than she had
remembered and couldn't believe she had talked herself out of it for almost
three years. Knowing that she was likely to forget again and fall into her
old routine, she made a voice memo on her phone after class one evening,
describing how good she felt after doing yoga. When she was tempted to

skip yoga, she listened to the memo to remind herself, knowing that she could not trust her impulses when she was stressed.

> *Is there a way to remind your stressed-out self what actually makes you feel better? What encouragement can you create for yourself before you are stressed?*

IF YOU EAT THIS COOKIE, THE TERRORISTS WIN

Last night, I made the mistake of watching the evening news. The opening story was about a failed terrorist bomb plot in the United States, followed by reports of a missile attack overseas and the arrest of a young man for murdering his ex-girlfriend. Just before going to break, the anchor promised to tell me about "the surprising thing you eat every day that might give you cancer." Then the show cut to a car commercial.

It used to puzzle me: Why do companies advertise during such depressing programming? Do they really want viewers to associate their products with the horror stories that fill the nightly news? And who is going to be in the mood for a department store sale after hearing about a brutal murder or the threat of a terrorist attack? It turns out I might be, and you might be, too, thanks to a psychological phenomenon called *terror management*.

According to terror-management theory, human beings are—naturally—terrified when we think about our own deaths. It's the one threat we can try to avoid but will never escape. Whenever we are reminded of our mortality (say, every twenty-nine seconds on the nightly news), it triggers a panic response in the brain. We aren't always aware of it—the anxiety may be just below the surface, creating a free-floating sense of discomfort, without our knowing why. Even when it's outside our conscious awareness, this terror creates an immediate need to do something to counter our feelings of powerlessness. We will reach for our security blankets, whatever makes us feel safe, powerful, or comforted. (Barack Obama got in a lot of trouble for pointing this out in 2008, when he told a San Francisco crowd that in uncertain times, people "cling to guns or religion.") Politics aside, terror-management theory can teach us a lot about our own willpower failures. We don't just cling to guns and God when we're scared; many of us also cling to credit cards, cupcakes, and cigarettes. Studies show that being reminded of our mortality makes us more susceptible to all sorts of temptations, as we look for hope and security in the things that promise reward and relief.

For example, a study of grocery shoppers found that when people are asked to think about their own death, they make longer shopping lists, are willing to spend more on comfort food, and eat more chocolate and cookies. (I can see the retail strategy now: Supermarkets invite local funeral homes to hand out brochures by the shopping carts.) Another study found that reports of death on the news make viewers respond more positively to advertisements for status products, like luxury cars and Rolex watches. It's not that we think a Rolex will protect us from a missile attack—it's that these goods bolster our self-image and make us feel powerful. For many people, buying things is an immediate way to feel more optimistic and in control. This is surely one reason Americans were so receptive to President George W. Bush's request, "Mrs. Bush and I want to encourage Americans to go out shopping," following the attacks of September 11, 2001.

It doesn't take planes flying into buildings to press our inner panic buttons. In fact, it doesn't even take real deaths to set us spending—television dramas and movies can have the same effect. In one study, watching a death scene in the 1979 tearjerker film *The Champ* made people willing to pay three times as much for something they didn't need (and would later regret). Importantly, the participants in this study were oblivious to the fact that watching the film had influenced what they were willing to pay. When given the opportunity to buy an insulated water bottle, they just thought they wanted the water bottle. (In contrast, people who had watched a National Geographic special about the Great Barrier Reef were completely unimpressed by the bottle and held on to their money.) This, no doubt, is how we end up with half the purchases that clutter our homes and pad our credit card bills. We're feeling a little down, we come across an opportunity to purchase something, and a little voice—OK, a few dopamine neurons—in our head tell us, "Buy this—it's everything you never knew you wanted!"

Terror management strategies may take our minds off our inevitable demise, but when we turn to temptation for comfort, we may inadvertently be quickening our race to the grave. Case in point: Warnings on cigarette packages can *increase* a smoker's urge to light up. A 2009 study found that death warnings trigger stress and fear in smokers—exactly what public health officials hope for. Unfortunately, this anxiety then triggers smokers' default stress-relief strategy: smoking. Oops. It isn't logical, but it makes sense based on what we know about how stress influences the brain. Stress triggers cravings and makes dopamine neurons even more excited by any temptation in sight. It doesn't help that the smoker is—of course—staring at a pack of cigarettes as he reads the warning. So even as a smoker's brain encodes the words "WARNING: Cigarettes cause cancer" and grapples with awareness of his own mortality, another part of his brain starts screaming, "Don't worry, smoking a cigarette will make you feel better!"

There is a global trend of adding increasingly graphic and disturbing photos of tumors and dead bodies to cigarette warnings. This may or may not be a good idea. According to terror-management theory, the more horrifying the images, the more they will prompt smokers to relieve their anxiety by smoking. However, these images may be quite effective at preventing people from taking up the habit, or strengthening a smoker's intention to quit. The verdict is still out on whether these new warnings will reduce smoking, but we should keep an eye on the possibility that they will have unintended consequences.*

---

*We should also think twice before slapping similar warnings about life-threatening STDs onto condom packages—men reminded of their mortality are more interested in having casual sex, and less likely to use condoms.

UNDER THE MICROSCOPE: WHAT'S TERRIFYING YOU?

This week, pay attention to what might be triggering terror management in your own mind. What do you hear or see in the media or online? What new flesh-eating bacteria is going to infect you at your local playground? Where are the killer bees coming from this time? What building exploded, where was the fatal car crash, and who was found dead in their home? (For extra credit, check out what products are advertised in between or alongside the fright tactics. Do they have anything to do with your willpower challenges?) Are there any other scare tactics or warnings you're exposed to that might be triggering cravings for comfort?

Sometimes terror management leads us not into temptation, but procrastination. Many of the most put-off tasks have a whiff of mortality salience about them: making a doctor's appointment, filling a prescription and taking it when we're supposed to, taking care of legal documents such as wills, saving for retirement, even throwing out things we're never going to use again, or clothes we'll never fit into. If there's something you've been putting off or keep "forgetting" to do, is it possible that you are trying to avoid facing your vulnerability? If so, just seeing the fear can help you make a rational choice—the motivations we understand are always easier to change than the influences we cannot see.

A LATE-NIGHT SNACKER GOES ON A TV DIET

Valerie had the living room television on for an hour or two most evenings, as background for cleaning up or whatever needed to be organized for her kids' activities the next day. She usually kept it set to a news channel that specialized in missing people, unsolved mysteries, and true crime. The stories were fascinating, and even though she sometimes wished that she hadn't seen a particular crime photo, she couldn't look away. When we talked about terror-management theory in class, it was the first time she'd really thought about the effects of listening to so many horrifying stories day in and day out. She started to wonder if her evening cravings for salty and sweet snacks (one of her willpower challenges) had something to do with the tales of kidnapped girls and murdered wives.

Valerie started to pay attention to how she felt during the news stories, especially the tragedies involving children. In class the next week, she reported, "It's awful. I feel a pit in my stomach, but it's like I have to keep watching. It feels urgent, but it has nothing to do with me. I don't know why I do this to myself." She decided to turn the channel-of-doom off and find something less stressful to put on in the background—music, podcasts, or sitcom reruns. Within a week, she felt as if a dark cloud had lifted off of her mood at the end of the evening. Better yet, when she switched from terror-tainment to more uplifting media, she didn't find herself finishing a whole bag of trail mix that was supposed to be for school lunches.

Take a twenty-four-hour break from TV news, talk radio, magazines, or websites that profit from your fear. If the world doesn't end without you watching every private and global crisis unfold (prediction: It won't), consider cutting out mindless consumption of these media.

THE WHAT-THE-HELL EFFECT: WHY GUILT DOESN'T WORK

Before he ordered a Guinness from the bartender, a forty-year-old man pulled out his Palm Pilot. *First beer, 9:04 p.m.* His intention to drink? Two beers, tops. Several miles away, a young woman arrived at a fraternity house. Ten minutes later, she typed into her Palm Pilot: *One shot of vodka.* The party was just starting!

These drinkers were part of a study by psychologists and addiction researchers at the State University of New York and the University of Pittsburgh. A group of 144 adults, ages eighteen to fifty, had been given handheld personal computers to keep track of their drinking. Each morning at eight, the participants also logged on to report how they felt about the previous night's drinking. The researchers wanted to know: What happened when the drinkers drank more than they intended to?

Not surprisingly, people who drank too much the previous night felt worse in the morning—headaches, nausea, fatigue. But their misery wasn't limited to hangovers. Many also felt guilty and ashamed. That's where things get disturbing. The worse a person felt about how much they drank the night before, the *more* they drank that night and the next. The guilt was driving them back to the bottle.

Welcome to one of the biggest threats to willpower worldwide: the "what-the-hell effect." First coined by dieting researchers Janet Polivy and C. Peter Herman, the what-the-hell effect describes a cycle of indulgence, regret, and greater indulgence. These researchers noticed that many dieters would feel so bad about any lapse—a piece of pizza, a bite of cake*— that they felt as if their whole diet was blown. Instead of minimizing the harm by not taking another bite, they would say, "What the hell, I already blew my diet. I might as well eat the whole thing."

It's not just eating the wrong thing that triggers the what-the-hell effect in dieters. Eating more than other people can create the same feelings of guilt, and lead to eating even more (or bingeing later in private). Any setback can create the same downward spiral. In one not-so-nice study, Polivy and Herman rigged a scale to make dieters think they had gained five pounds. The dieters felt depressed, guilty, and disappointed with themselves—but instead of resolving to lose the weight, they promptly turned to food to fix those feelings.

Dieters aren't the only ones susceptible to the what-the-hell effect. The cycle can happen with any willpower challenge. It's been observed in smokers trying to quit, alcoholics trying to stay sober, shoppers trying to stick to

---

*What foods are we most likely to regret? According to a 2009 survey published in *Appetite*, the most guilt-inducing foods are: 1. candy and ice cream, 2. potato chips, 3. cake, 4. pastries, and 5. fast food.

a budget, and even child molesters trying to control their sexual impulses. Whatever the willpower challenge, the pattern is the same. Giving in makes you feel bad about yourself, which motivates you to do something to feel better. And what's the cheapest, fastest strategy for feeling better? Often the very thing you feel bad about. That's how eating a few potato chips becomes looking for crumbs at the bottom of an empty, greasy bag. Or how losing $100 at the casino can trigger a gambling binge. You say to yourself, "I've already broken my [diet, budget, sobriety, resolution], so what the hell. I might as well really enjoy myself." Crucially, it's not the first giving-in that guarantees the bigger relapse. It's the feelings of shame, guilt, loss of control, and loss of hope that follow the first relapse. Once you're stuck in the cycle, it can seem like there is no way out except to keep going. This leads to even bigger willpower failures and more misery as you then berate yourself (again) for giving in (again). But the thing you're turning to for comfort can't stop the cycle, because it only generates more feelings of guilt.

UNDER THE MICROSCOPE: WHEN SETBACKS HAPPEN

This week, pay special attention to how you handle any willpower failure. Do you criticize yourself and tell yourself that you'll never change? Do you feel like this setback reveals what is wrong with you—that you're lazy, stupid, greedy, or incompetent? Do you feel hopeless, guilty, ashamed, angry, or overwhelmed? Do you use the setback as an excuse to indulge further?

BREAKING THE WHAT-THE-HELL CYCLE

Two psychologists—Claire Adams at Louisiana State University and Mark Leary at Duke University—set up a study guaranteed to trigger the what-the-hell effect. They invited weight-watching young women into the laboratory, then encouraged them to eat doughnuts and candy in the name of science. These researchers had an intriguing hypothesis about how to break the what-the-hell cycle. If guilt sabotages self-control, they thought, then maybe the opposite of guilt would support self-control. Their unlikely strategy: Make half these doughnut-eating dieters feel *better* about giving in.

The women were told that they would be participating in two separate studies: one on the effect of food on mood, and a taste test of several different candies. In the first study, all of the women were asked to choose either a glazed or chocolate doughnut and finish the whole thing within four minutes. They were also asked to drink an entire glass of water—the researchers' trick to make sure they felt uncomfortably full (a tighter waistband is good for inducing guilt). Then the women filled out surveys about how they felt.

Before the candy taste test, half of the women received a special message designed to relieve their guilt. The experimenter mentioned that participants sometimes felt guilty about eating a whole doughnut. The experimenter then encouraged each participant not to be too hard on herself, and to remember that everyone indulges sometimes. The other women got no such message.

Then came the test of whether self-forgiveness would break the what-the-hell cycle. The experimenter served each dieter three large bowls of candy—peanut-butter-and-chocolate Reese's Poppers, fruit-flavored Skittles, and York Peppermint Patties—chosen to appeal to any sweet tooth. The women were asked to sample each candy in order to rate it, and were invited to eat as much or as little as they liked. If the women still felt guilty about eating the doughnut, they should say to themselves, "I already broke the diet, so what does it matter if I inhale these Skittles?"

After the taste test, the experimenter weighed the candy bowls to find out how much each participant had eaten. The self-forgiveness intervention was a clear success: The women who received the special message ate only 28 grams of candy, compared with almost 70 grams by women who were not encouraged to forgive themselves. (For reference, a single Hershey's Kiss is 4.5 grams.) Most people are surprised by this finding. Common sense says that the message "Everyone indulges sometimes; don't be too hard on yourself" will only give dieters permission to eat more. And yet getting rid of guilt kept the women from overindulging in the taste test. We may think that guilt motivates us to correct our mistakes, but it's just one more way that feeling bad leads to giving in.

ANYTHING BUT SELF-FORGIVENESS!

As soon as I mention self-forgiveness in class, the arguments start pouring in. You would think I had just suggested that the secret to more willpower was throwing kittens in front of speeding buses. "If I'm not hard on myself, I'll never get anything done." "If I forgive myself, I'll just do it again." "My problem isn't that I'm too hard on myself—my problem is that I'm not self-critical enough!" To many people, self-forgiveness sounds like excuse-making that will only lead to greater self-indulgence. My students commonly argue that if they are easy on themselves—that is, if they don't focus on their failures, criticize themselves when they don't live up to their high standards, or threaten themselves with horrible consequences if they don't improve—they will slide into sloth. They believe that they need a stern voice in their head controlling their appetites, their instincts, and their weaknesses. They fear that if they give up this inner dictator and critic, they will have no self-control at all.

Most of us believe this at some level—after all, we first learned to control ourselves as children through parental commands and punishment. This approach is necessary during childhood because, let's face it, children are wild animals. The brain's self-control system does not fully develop until young adulthood, and kids need some external support while their prefrontal cortices fill out. However, many people treat themselves like they are still children—and frankly, they act more like abusive parents than supportive caregivers. They criticize themselves whenever they give in to temptation or fail in their own eyes: "You're so lazy! What's the matter with you?" Each failure is used as evidence that they need to be even stricter with themselves. "You can't be trusted to do anything you say you will."

If you think that the key to greater willpower is being harder on yourself, you are not alone. But you are wrong. Study after study shows that self-criticism is consistently associated with less motivation and worse self-control. It is also one of the single biggest predictors of depression, which drains both "I will" power and "I want" power. In contrast, self-compassion—being supportive and kind to yourself, especially in the face of stress and failure—is associated with more motivation and better self-control. Consider, for example, a study at Carleton University in Ottawa, Canada, that tracked the procrastination of students over an entire semester. Lots of students put off studying for the first exam, but not every student made it a habit. Students who were harder on themselves for procrastinating on their first exam were more likely to procrastinate on later exams than students who forgave themselves. The harder they were on themselves about procrastinating the first time, the longer they procrastinated for the next exam! Forgiveness—not guilt—helped them get back on track.

These findings fly in the face of our instincts. How can this be, when so many of us have a strong intuition that self-criticism is the cornerstone of self-control, and self-compassion is a slippery slope to self-indulgence? What would motivate these students if not feeling bad for procrastinating the last time? And what would keep *us* in check if we didn't feel guilty for giving in?

Surprisingly, it's forgiveness, not guilt, that increases accountability. Researchers have found that taking a self-compassionate point of view on a personal failure makes people *more* likely to take personal responsibility for the failure than when they take a self-critical point of view. They also are more willing to receive feedback and advice from others, and more likely to learn from the experience.

One reason forgiveness helps people recover from mistakes is that it takes away the shame and pain of thinking about what happened. The what-the-hell effect is an attempt to escape the bad feelings that follow a setback. Without the guilt and self-criticism, there's nothing to escape. This means it's easier to reflect on how the failure happened, and less tempting to repeat it.

On the other hand, if you view your setbacks as evidence that you are a hopeless loser who screws everything up, thinking about your failure is a miserable exercise in self-hate. Your most urgent goal will be to soothe those feelings, not learn from your experience. This is why self-criticism backfires as a strategy for self-control. Like other forms of stress, it drives you straight to comfort coping, whether that's drowning your sorrows at the nearest dive bar, or lifting your spirits with a Visa-sponsored shopping spree.

WILLPOWER EXPERIMENT: FORGIVENESS WHEN YOU FAIL

Everybody makes mistakes and experiences setbacks. How we handle these setbacks matters more than the fact that they happened. Below is an exercise that psychologists use to help people find a more self-compassionate response to failure. Research shows that taking this point of view reduces guilt but increases personal accountability—the perfect combination to get you back on track with your willpower challenge. Bring to mind a specific time when you gave in to temptation or procrastination, and experiment with taking the following three points of view on that failure. When you experience a setback, you can bring these perspectives to mind to help you avoid a downward spiral of guilt, shame, and giving in again.

1. **What are you feeling?** As you think about this failure, take a moment to notice and describe how you are feeling. What emotions are present? What are you are feeling in your body? Can you remember how you felt immediately after the failure? How would you describe that? Notice if self-criticism comes up, and if it does, what you say to yourself. The perspective of mindfulness allows you to see what you are feeling without rushing to escape.

2. **You're only human.** Everyone struggles with willpower challenges and everyone sometimes loses control. This is just a part of the human condition, and your setback does not mean there is something wrong with you. Consider the truth of these statements. Can you think of other people

you respect and care about who have experienced similar struggles and setbacks? This perspective can soften the usual voice of self-criticism and self-doubt.

3. **What would you say to a friend?** Consider how you would comfort a close friend who experienced the same setback. What words of support would you offer? How would you encourage them to continue pursuing their goal? This perspective will point the way to getting back on track.

A WRITER CHALLENGES THE VOICE OF SELF-CRITICISM

Ben, a twenty-four-year-old middle-school social studies teacher with literary aspirations, had set the goal to finish writing his novel by the end of summer vacation. This deadline required him to write ten pages a day, every day. In reality, he would write two to three pages one day, then feel so overwhelmed by how far behind he was that he skipped the next day completely. Realizing that he wasn't going to finish the book by the start of the school year, he felt like a fraud. If he couldn't make the effort now, when he had so much free time, how was he going to make any progress when he had homework to grade and lessons to plan? Ben started to doubt whether he should even bother with the goal, since he wasn't making the progress he thought he should be. "A real writer would be able to churn those pages out," he told himself. "A real writer would never play computer games instead of writing." In this state of mind, he turned a critical eye to his writing and convinced himself it was garbage.

Ben had actually abandoned his goal when he found himself in my class that fall. He had enrolled in the class to learn how to motivate his students, but he recognized himself in the discussion about self-criticism. When he did the self-forgiveness exercise for his abandoned novel, the first thing he noticed was the fear and self-doubt behind his giving up. Not meeting his small goal to write ten pages a day made him afraid that he did not have the talent or dedication to realize his big goal of becoming a novelist. He took comfort in the idea that his setbacks were just part of being human, and not proof that he would never succeed. He remembered stories he had read about other writers who had struggled early in their careers. To find a more compassionate response to himself, he imagined how he would mentor a student who wanted to give up on a goal. Ben realized he would encourage the student to keep going if the goal was important. He would say that any effort made now would take the student closer to the goal. He certainly would *not* say to the student, "Who are you kidding? Your work is garbage."

From this exercise, Ben found renewed energy for writing and returned to his work-in-progress. He made a commitment to write once a week, a more reasonable goal for the school year, and one he felt comfortable holding himself accountable to.

We all have the tendency to believe self-doubt and self-criticism, but listening to this voice never gets us closer to our goals. Instead, try on the point of view of a mentor or good friend who believes in you, wants the best for you, and will encourage you when you feel discouraged.

RESOLVING TO FEEL GOOD

So far, we've seen the many ways that feeling bad can lead to giving in. Stress sets off cravings and makes our brains even more attracted to temptation. Reminders of our mortality can send us searching for the comfort of food, shopping, or cigarettes. Guilt and self-criticism? That's a quick path to "What the hell, I might as well indulge some more."

Sometimes, though, feeling bad pushes us in a very different direction. Overwhelmed by guilt, anxiety, and stress, we turn to the one thing that really does feel good: resolving to change. University of Toronto psychologists Janet Polivy and C. Peter Herman—the researchers who first identified the what-the-hell effect—have discovered that we are most likely to decide to change when we are at a low point: feeling guilty about a binge, staring at a credit card bill, waking up hung over, or worried about our health. Setting a resolution offers an immediate sense of relief and control. We don't have to believe that we are the person who made that mistake; we can become a completely different person.

Vowing to change fills us with hope. We love to imagine how making the change will transform our lives, and we fantasize about the person we will become. Research shows that deciding to start a diet makes people feel stronger, and planning to exercise makes people feel taller. (Nobody said these fantasies were realistic.) People will treat us differently, we tell ourselves. *Everything* will be different. The bigger the goal, the bigger the burst of hope. And so when we decide to change, it's tempting to give ourselves some very large assignments. Why set a modest goal when setting a gigantic goal will make us feel even better? Why start small when you can dream big?

Unfortunately, the promise of change—like the promise of reward and the promise of relief—rarely delivers what we're expecting. Unrealistic optimism may make us feel good in the moment, but it sets us up to feel much worse later on. The *decision* to change is the ultimate in instant gratification—you get all the good feelings before anything's been done. But the challenge of actually making a change can be a rude awakening, and the initial rewards are rarely as transformative as our most hopeful fantasies ("I lost five pounds, and I still have a crappy job!"). As we face our first setbacks, the initial feel-good rush of deciding to change is replaced with disappointment and frustration. Failing to meet our expectations triggers the same old guilt, depression, and self-doubt, and the emotional payoff of vowing to change is gone. At this point, most people will abandon their efforts altogether. It's only when we are feeling out of control and in need of another hit of hope that we'll once again vow to change—and start the cycle all over.

Polivy and Herman call this cycle the "false hope syndrome." As a strategy for change, it fails. But that's because it was never meant to be a strategy for change. It's a strategy for feeling better, and these are not the same thing. If all you care about is the feeling of hope, this is not an irrational strategy. Resolving to change is, for most people, the best part of the change process. It's all downhill after that: having to exert self-control, saying no when you want to say yes, saying yes when you want to say no. The effort of actually making the change cannot compare, from a happiness point of view, to the rush of imagining that you will change. And so it's not only easier, but also much more fun, to milk the *promise* of change for all it's worth, without the messy business of following through. That is why so many people are happier giving up and starting again, over and over, rather than finding a way to make a change for good. The high we get from imagining our own extreme makeovers is a difficult drug to quit.

False hope syndrome is especially sneaky because it masquerades as self-control. In fact, it does such a good job fooling us, I'd wager that while you were reading this very section, it took you a moment to realize that I was describing another willpower trap, not the silver lining of feeling bad. And that's exactly why the promise of change is worth looking at. There is a fine line between the motivation we need to make a change, and the kind of unrealistic optimism that can sabotage our goals. We need to believe that change is possible; without hope, we'd resign ourselves to the way things are. But we must avoid the common trap of using the promise of change to fix our feelings, not to fix our behaviors. Otherwise, we can turn what looks like willpower into just another version of a rat pressing a lever, hoping this is the time we get the reward.

UNDER THE MICROSCOPE: RESOLVING TO FEEL GOOD

Take a moment to think about your own motivations and expectations for change. Do you only feel motivated to change when you are feeling bad? Is the best part of setting goals the pleasure of imagining how succeeding will change your life? Do you use fantasies of your future self to fix your feelings now, more than you take concrete steps to fix your behavior?

WILLPOWER EXPERIMENT: OPTIMISTIC PESSIMISM FOR SUCCESSFUL RESOLUTIONS

Optimism can make us motivated, but a dash of pessimism can help us succeed. Research shows that predicting how and when you might be tempted to break your vow increases the chances that you will keep a resolution.

For your own willpower challenge, ask yourself: When am I most likely to be tempted to give in? How am I most likely to let myself get distracted from my goal? What will I say to myself to give myself permission to procrastinate? When you have such a scenario in mind, imagine yourself in that situation, what it will feel like, and what you might be thinking. Let yourself see how a typical willpower failure unfolds.

Then turn this imaginary failure into a willpower success. Consider what specific actions you could take to stick to your resolution. Do you need to remember your motivation? Get yourself away from the temptation? Call a friend for support? Use one of the other willpower strategies you've learned? When you have a specific strategy in mind, imagine yourself doing it. Visualize what it will feel like. See yourself succeed. Let this vision of yourself give you the confidence that you will do what it takes to reach your goal.

Planning for failure in this way is an act of self-compassion, not self-doubt. When that moment of possible willpower failure hits, you will be ready to put your plan into action.

THE LAST WORD

To avoid stress-induced willpower failures, we need to discover what really makes us feel better—not the false promise of reward, and not empty promises to change. We need to give ourselves permission to do these things, and to protect ourselves from sources of stress that have nothing to do with our lives. When we do experience setbacks—which we will—we need to forgive those failures, and not use them as an excuse to give in or give up. When it comes to increasing self-control, self-compassion is a far better strategy than beating ourselves up.

CHAPTER SUMMARY

The Idea: Feeling bad leads to giving in, and dropping guilt makes you stronger.

Under the Microscope

- *The promise of relief.* What do you turn to when you're feeling stressed, anxious, or down?
- *What's terrifying you?* Pay attention to the stress of what you hear or see in the media, online, or from other sources.
- *When setbacks happen.* Do you respond to a willpower failure with guilt and self-criticism?
- *Resolving to feel good.* Do you use fantasies of your future self to fix your feelings now, more than you take concrete steps to fix your behavior?

Willpower Experiments

- *Stress-relief strategies that work.* The next time you're stressed out, try one of the stress-relief strategies that really work, such as exercising or playing sports, praying or attending a religious service, reading, listening to music, spending time with friends or family, getting a massage, going outside for a walk, meditating or doing yoga, and spending time with a creative hobby.
- *Forgiveness when you fail.* Take a more compassionate perspective on your setbacks to avoid the guilt that leads to giving in again.
- *Optimistic pessimism for successful resolutions.* Predict how and when you might be tempted to break your vow, and imagine a specific plan of action for not giving in.

SEVEN

Putting the Future on Sale:
The Economics of
Instant Gratification

I t was a competition you don't see every day: nineteen chimpanzees versus forty humans. And not just any humans—students from Harvard University and the Max Planck Institute in Leipzig, Germany. The chimps were from the equally prestigious Wolfgang Koehler Primate Research Center in Leipzig. After all, in a match-up with Harvard and Max Planck, you can't throw just any old circus chimps into the ring.

The challenge: Delay the gratification of an immediate snack to win more food. The temptation: grapes for the chimps, and raisins, peanuts, M&M's, Goldfish crackers, and popcorn for the humans. First, all the competitors were offered a choice between two and six of their favorite edible rewards. This was an easy choice—both humans and chimps agreed that six was indeed better than two. Then the researchers complicated the choice. Each competitor was given the opportunity to eat two treats immediately, *or* wait two minutes for six. The researchers knew the participants preferred six to two. But would they wait for it?

This study, published in 2007, was the first to directly compare the self-control of chimpanzees and humans. What the researchers found, however, says as much about human nature as about the evolutionary basis of patience. Although both chimps and humans preferred six treats to two if they *didn't* have to wait, the species made very different decisions when they had to wait. Chimpanzees chose to wait for the larger reward an impressive 72 percent of the time. The Harvard and Max Planck Institute students? Only 19 percent of the time.

How are we to interpret this crushing defeat of humans by incredibly patient primates? Are we to believe that chimpanzees have been blessed with a secret source of self-control? Or that we humans at some point in our evolutionary history *lost* the capacity to wait two minutes for peanuts?

Of course not. When we're on our best behavior, humans' ability to control our impulses puts other species to shame. But all too often, we use our fancy brains not to make the most strategic decisions, but to give ourselves permission to act *more* irrationally. That's because a big prefrontal cortex is good at more than self-control. It can also rationalize bad decisions and promise we'll be better tomorrow. You can bet those chimpanzees weren't telling themselves, "I'll take the two grapes now, because I can always wait for the six grapes next time." But we humans have all sorts of mental tricks for convincing ourselves that the time to resist temptation is tomorrow— and so we of the gigantic prefrontal cortices find ourselves giving in again and again to immediate gratification.

Whether we look to economics, psychology, or neuroscience for an explanation, many of our problems with temptation and procrastination come back to one uniquely human problem: how we think about the future. Harvard psychologist Daniel Gilbert has made the bold claim that humans are the only species to think in any meaningful way about the future. And while this ability has led to all sorts of wonderful contributions to the world, such as psychic hotlines and sports betting, it also gets our present selves into trouble. The problem is not so much that we can foresee a future, but that we cannot see it clearly.

PUTTING THE FUTURE ON SALE

One way to look at the results of the chimpanzee-human matchup is like an economist. The chimpanzees acted much more rationally, despite having brains one-third the size of their human competitors'. The chimpanzees expressed a preference (six is better than two) and then acted on it. They maximized their gains with very little personal cost (a mere 120 seconds' delay). The humans' choices, on the other hand, were irrational. Before the challenge began, they clearly stated that they preferred six treats to two. But as soon as they had to wait two minutes to triple their snacks, their preferences reversed more than 80 percent of the time. They deprived themselves of what they really wanted for the fleeting satisfaction of a quick fix.

Economists call this *delay discounting*—the longer you have to wait for a reward, the less it is worth to you. Even small delays can dramatically lower the perceived value. With a delay of just two minutes, six M&M's became worth less than two immediate M&M's. The value of each M&M shrank as it became more distant.

Delay discounting explains not just why some college kids took two M&M's instead of six, but why we choose immediate satisfaction at the cost of future happiness. It's why we put off paying our taxes, choosing peace of mind today at the price of panic on April 14 or financial penalties on April 16. It's why we use today's fossil fuels without regard to tomorrow's energy crisis, and load up our credit cards without giving a thought to the crushing interest rates. We take what we want when we want it (*now*), and we put off until tomorrow whatever we don't want to face today.

UNDER THE MICROSCOPE: HOW ARE YOU DISCOUNTING FUTURE REWARDS?

For your willpower challenge, ask yourself what future rewards do you put on sale each time you give in to temptation or procrastination. What is the *immediate* payoff for giving in? What is the long-term cost? Is this a fair trade? If the rational you says, "No, it's a lousy deal!" try to catch the moment you reverse your preferences. What are you thinking and feeling that lets you put the future on sale?

BLINDED BY REWARD

In our opening competition of self-control, the humans agreed that six snacks were worth more than two. It wasn't until the experimenter put the two snacks on the table and said, "Do you want these now, or do you want to wait?" that 80 percent of the Harvard and Max Planck students changed their minds. They weren't bad at math; they were blinded by the promise of reward. Behavioral economists call this the problem of *bounded rationality*—we're rational until we aren't. We will be perfectly rational when everything is in theory, but when the temptation is real, the brain shifts into reward-seeking mode to make sure we don't miss out.

Influential behavioral economist George Ainslie has argued that this type of reversal is behind most failures of self-control, from alcoholism and addiction to weight gain and debt. Most people, deep down, want to resist temptation. We *want* to make the choice that will lead to long-term happiness. Not the drink, but sobriety. Not the deep-fried doughnut, but the tight derrière. Not the fancy new toy, but financial security. We only prefer the short-term, immediate reward when it is right there staring us in the face, and the want becomes overwhelming. This leads to *bounded willpower*—we have self-control until we need it.

One reason we're so susceptible to immediate gratification is that our brain's reward system did not evolve to respond to future rewards. Food was the reward system's original target, which is why humans are still exceptionally responsive to the smell or sight of anything yummy. When dopamine was first perfecting its effects in the human brain, a reward that was far off—whether by sixty miles or sixty days—was irrelevant to daily survival. The system we needed was the one that ensured that we snapped up rewards when they were available. At most, we needed the motivation to pursue a *near* reward—the fruit you had to climb a tree or cross a river to get your hungry hands on. A reward you had to work five, ten, twenty years to obtain? In the millennia before college degrees, Olympic medals, and retirement accounts, such delay of gratification would have been literally unthinkable. Saving for tomorrow, maybe. Saving for ten thousand tomorrows from now, not so much.

When our modern selves contemplate immediate versus future rewards, the brain processes these two options very differently. The immediate reward triggers the older, more primitive reward system and its dopamine-induced desire. Future rewards don't interest this reward system so much. Their value is encoded by the more recently evolved prefrontal cortex. To delay gratification, the prefrontal cortex has to cool off the promise of reward. It's not an impossible feat—after all, that's what the prefrontal cortex is there for. But it has to fight a feeling that's been known to make rats run across electrified grids and men blow their life savings on a slot machine. In other words, it's not easy.

The good news is, temptation has a narrow window of opportunity. To really overwhelm our prefrontal cortex, the reward must be available now, and—for maximum effect—you need to see it. As soon as there is any distance between you and the temptation, the power of balance shifts back to the brain's system of self-control. Take, for example, the Harvard and Max Planck students whose self-control collapsed at the sight of two M&M's. In another version of the study, experimenters asked the students to make the choice *without* putting the rewards on the table. This time, the students were much more likely to choose the larger, delayed reward. Not being able to see the immediate reward made it more abstract and less exciting to the reward system. This helped the students make a rational choice based on mental calculations, not primal feelings.

This is good news for those who want to delay gratification. Anything you can do to create that distance will make it easier to say no. For example, one study found that just putting a candy jar inside a desk drawer instead of on top of the desk reduced office workers' candy consumption by one third. It isn't any more difficult to open a drawer than to reach across a desk, but putting the candy away reduced the constant stimulation of desire. When you know your own triggers, putting them out of sight can keep them from tempting your mind.

WILLPOWER EXPERIMENT: WAIT TEN MINUTES

Ten minutes might not seem like much time to wait for something you want, but neuroscientists have discovered that it makes a big difference in how the brain processes a reward. When immediate gratification comes with a mandatory ten-minute delay, the brain treats it like a future reward. The promise-of-reward system is less activated, taking away the powerful biological impulse to choose immediate gratification. When the brain compares a cookie you have to wait ten minutes for to a longer-term reward, like losing weight, it no longer shows the same lopsided bias toward the sooner reward. It's the "immediate" in immediate gratification that hijacks your brain and reverses your preferences.

For a cooler, wiser brain, institute a mandatory ten-minute wait for any temptation. If, in ten minutes, you still want it, you can have it—but before the ten minutes are up, bring to mind the competing long-term reward that will come with resisting temptation. If possible, create some physical (or visual) distance as well.

If your willpower challenge requires "I will" power, you can still use the ten-minute rule to help you overcome the temptation to procrastinate. Flip the rule to "Do ten minutes, then you can quit." When your ten minutes are up, give yourself permission to stop—although you may find that once you get started, you'll want to keep going.

THE TEN-MINUTE RULE HELPS
A SMOKER CUT BACK

Keith had smoked his first cigarette almost twenty years earlier as a college freshman, and had been wishing he could quit for almost as long. Sometimes he wondered what the point of quitting would be. He had been smoking for so many years, surely the damage had been done. But then he'd hear some report that quitting could reverse damage to a smoker's heart and lungs, even in smokers who—like Keith—had maintained a pack-a-day habit for decades. He wasn't ready to quit cold turkey—he couldn't quite imagine himself *never* smoking, even though part of him wanted to stop. He decided to cut back as a first step.

The ten-minute rule was a perfect match for Keith. Realistically, he knew that he was going to give in sometimes. The ten-minute delay helped him practice dealing with the urge to smoke, and forced him to remember his desire to lower his risk of cardiovascular disease and cancer. Sometimes Keith waited the full ten minutes and smoked, and sometimes he didn't even last the full ten minutes before he lit up. But the delay was strengthening his intention to quit. He also noticed that saying "yes, but in ten minutes" reduced some of the panic and stress that kicked in when he said a flat-out "no" to his urge. This made it easier to wait, and a few times he even got distracted and forgot the impulse.

After a few weeks of this practice, Keith took it up a notch. Whenever possible, he used his ten-minute wait period to get himself somewhere he couldn't light up—like a coworker's office or inside a store. That bought him some extra time to cool off or at least make it more difficult to give in. Other times, he called his wife to seek moral support. Eventually, he decided to make the ten-minute rule renewable. "If I made it through the first ten minutes, I can wait another ten minutes, and then smoke if I still really want to." Pretty soon, he was down to a pack every other day. More important, he was starting to see himself as someone who *could* quit, and was strengthening the self-control he'd need to do it.

When "never again" seems too overwhelming a willpower challenge to tackle, use the ten-minute delay rule to start strengthening your self-control.

What's Your Discount Rate?

While it's human nature to discount future rewards, everyone has a different discount rate. Some people have a very low discount rate, like a high-end store that never puts its best merchandise on sale. These folks are able to keep the big reward in mind and wait for it. Others have a very high discount rate. They cannot resist the promise of immediate gratification, like a going-out-of-business sale that slashes prices up to 90 percent just to get some quick cash. How big your discount rate is turns out to be a major determinant of your long-term health and success.

The first study to look at the long-term consequences of a person's discount rate was a classic psychology experiment best known as "The Marshmallow Test." In the late 1960s, Stanford psychologist Walter Mischel gave a bunch of four-year-olds the choice between one treat now or two treats in fifteen minutes. After explaining the choice, the experimenter left the child alone in a room with both treats and a bell. If the child could wait until the experimenter returned, he could have both treats. But if the child couldn't wait, he could ring the bell at any time and eat one treat immediately.

Most of the four-year-olds took what you and I would now recognize as the least effective strategy for delaying gratification: staring at the reward and imagining how it would taste. These kids folded in a matter of seconds. The four-year-olds who waited successfully tended to get their eyeballs off the promise of reward. There is delightful video footage of the kids struggling to wait, and watching it is a surprisingly good lesson in self-control. One girl covers her face with her hair so she can't see the treats; one boy keeps an eye on the treats but moves the bell far away so he can't reach it; another boy decides to compromise by licking the treats without actually eating them, portending an excellent future in politics.

Although the study taught the researchers a lot about how four-year-olds delay gratification, it also provided a shockingly good way to predict a child's future. How long a four-year-old waited in the marshmallow test predicted that child's academic and social success ten years later. The kids who waited the longest were more popular, had higher GPAs, and were better able to handle stress. They also had higher SAT scores and performed better on a neuropsychological test of prefrontal cortex function. Being able to wait fifteen minutes for two marshmallows was the perfect measure of something far more important: How well could a child handle temporary discomfort to accomplish a long-term goal? And did the child know how to turn the mind away from the promise of immediate reward?

This individual difference—whether measured in childhood or later years—plays a major role in how our lives turn out. Behavioral economists and psychologists have come up with complex formulas for determining people's discount rates—basically, how much more is your happiness today worth than your happiness tomorrow? People with higher future-reward discount rates are more susceptible to a wide range of self-control problems. They are more likely to smoke and drink to excess, and they have a greater risk of drug use, gambling, and other addictions. They are less likely to save for retirement, and more likely to drive drunk and have unprotected sex. They procrastinate more. They're even less likely to wear a watch—it's as if they are so focused on the present, time itself doesn't matter. And if the present is more important than the future, there is no reason to delay gratification. To escape this mind-set, we must find a way to make the future matter.

WILLPOWER EXPERIMENT: LOWER YOUR DISCOUNT RATE

Fortunately, a person's discount rate is not an immutable law of physics. It can be lowered just by changing how you think about your choices.

Imagine I give you a $100 check that is good in ninety days. Then I try to bargain you down: Would you be willing to trade it in for a $50 check that is good today? Most people would not. However, if people are first given the $50 check, and then asked if they'd be willing to exchange it for a $100 delayed reward, most will not. The reward you start with is the one you want to keep.

One reason is that most people are loss-averse—that is, we really don't like to lose something we already have. Losing $50 makes people more *unhappy* than getting $50 makes them happy. When you think about a larger, future reward first and consider trading it in for a smaller, immediate reward, it registers as a loss. But when you start with the immediate reward (the $50 check in your hand) and consider the benefits of delaying gratification for a larger reward, it also feels like a loss.

Economists have found that you will come up with more reasons to justify choosing whichever reward you think about first. People who start by asking themselves, "Why should I take the check for $50?" will think of more reasons to support immediate gratification ("I can really use the money," "Who knows if the $100 check will even be good in ninety days?"). People who start by asking themselves, "Why should I take the check for $100?" will think of more reasons to support delaying gratification ("That will buy twice as many groceries," "I'm going to need money just as much in ninety days as I do now"). Future-reward discounting drops dramatically when people think about the future reward first.

You can use this quirk of decision making to resist immediate gratification, whatever the temptation:

1. When you are tempted to act against your long-term interests, frame the choice as giving up the best possible long-term reward for whatever the immediate gratification is.
2. Imagine that long-term reward as already yours. Imagine your future self enjoying the fruits of your self-control.
3. Then ask yourself: Are you willing to give that up in exchange for whatever fleeting pleasure is tempting you now?

NO WEBSITE IS WORTH A DREAM

Amina, a sophomore at Stanford, was an ambitious human biology major with her sights on med school. She was also a self-confessed Facebook addict. She had a hard time staying off the website during classes, which meant she missed important lecture information. She also spent hours on Facebook when she should have been studying. Because there was always something more to do on Facebook—reading updates about her friends, looking at photo albums, following links—the temptation was endless. The site was never going to stop for her, so she had to find a way to stop herself.

To help her resist the immediate gratification of the site, Amina framed it as a threat to her biggest goal: becoming a doctor. When she was tempted to spend time on Facebook, she asked herself, "Is this worth not becoming a doctor?" Framed that way, she could no longer deny how much time she was wasting. She even Photoshopped her head onto the body of a surgeon and made the photo the background of her laptop. She looked at it whenever she needed to remember how much the future reward meant to her, or to make the future reward seem real.

NO WAY OUT: THE VALUE OF PRECOMMITMENT

In 1519, Hernán Cortés de Monroy y Pizarro, a Spanish *conquistador* searching for gold and silver, led an expedition from Cuba to the Yucatán Peninsula in southeastern Mexico. He brought with him five hundred soldiers and three hundred civilians on eleven ships. Cortés's goal was to head inland, conquer the natives, claim the land, and steal whatever gold and silver they could get their hands on.

The natives, however, were not going to surrender meekly. Central Mexico was the homeland of the Aztecs, led by the powerful god-king Moctezuma and known for their bloody human sacrifices. Cortés's crew had only a few horses and pieces of artillery. They were hardly a powerful military, and when the men landed on the coast of Mexico, they hesitated about marching inland. They were reluctant to leave the safety of the coast, where they could escape by ship. Cortés knew that when they faced their first battle, the crew would be tempted to retreat if they knew they had the option to sail away. So according to legend, he ordered his officers to set the ships on fire. The ships—Spanish galleons and caravels—were made entirely of wood and waterproofed with an extremely flammable pitch. Cortés lit the first torch, and as his men destroyed the ships, they burned to the water line and sank.

This is one of history's most notorious examples of committing one's future self to a desired course of action. In sinking his ships, Cortés demonstrated an important insight into human nature. While we may feel brave and tireless when we embark on an adventure, our future selves may be derailed by fear and exhaustion. Cortés burned those ships to guarantee that his men didn't act on their fear. He left the crew—and all their future selves—with no choice but to go forward.

This is a favorite story of behavioral economists who believe that the best strategy for self-control is, essentially, to burn your ships. One of the first proponents of this strategy was Thomas Schelling, a behavioral economist who won the 2005 Nobel Prize in Economic Sciences for his Cold War theory of how nuclear powers can manage conflict. Schelling believed that to reach our goals, we must limit our options. He called this *precommitment*. Schelling borrowed the idea of *precommitment* from his work on nuclear deterrence. A nation that precommits itself—say, by adopting a policy of immediate and escalated retaliation—makes its threats more credible than a nation that expresses reluctance to retaliate. Schelling viewed the rational self and the tempted self as engaged in a war, each with very different goals. Your rational self sets a course of action for you to follow, but often the tempted self decides to change course at the last minute. If the tempted self, with its reversed preferences, is allowed to do what it wants, the result will ultimately be self-sabotage.

From this point of view, the tempted self is an unpredictable and unreliable enemy. As behavioral economist George Ainslie puts it, we need to "take steps to predict and constrain that self as if it were another person." This requires cunning, courage, and creativity. We must study our tempted selves, see their weaknesses, and find a way to bind them to our rational preferences. Celebrated author Jonathan Franzen has publicly shared his own version of burning his ships to keep his writing on track. Like many writers and office workers, he is easily distracted by computer games and the Internet. Talking to a *Time* magazine reporter, he explained how he dismantled his laptop to prevent his tempted self from procrastinating. He took every time-wasting program off the hard drive (including every writer's nemesis, solitaire). He removed the computer's wireless card and destroyed its Ethernet port. "What you have to do," he explained, "is you plug in an Ethernet cable with superglue, and then you saw the little head off it."

You may not want to go so far as to destroy your computer to prevent distraction, but you can make good use of technology to keep your future self on course. For example, a program called "Freedom" (macfreedom. com) allows you to turn your computer's Internet access off for a predetermined period of time, while "Anti-Social" (anti-social.cc) will selectively keep you off social networks and e-mail. I myself prefer "ProcrasDonate" (procrasdonate.com), which bills you for every hour you spend on time-wasting websites and donates the money to charity. And if your temptation takes a more tangible form—say, chocolate or cigarettes—you can try a product like CapturedDiscipline, a solid-steel safe that can be locked for anywhere from two minutes to ninety-nine hours. If you want to buy a box of Girl Scout cookies but not finish them in one sitting, lock 'em up. If you want to impose a moratorium on credit card use, they can go in the safe, too, where your future tempted self cannot get to them without a stick of dynamite. If it's action you need to commit to, try putting your money where your goals are. For example, if you want to coerce yourself to exercise, you could precommit by buying an expensive annual gym membership.* As Schelling argues, this strategy is not unlike a country that invests in expanding its nuclear weapons arsenal. Your future tempted self will know you mean business, and think twice before threatening your rational self's goals.

---

*In some markets, you can even join a gym that will charge you more for not showing up than for regular attendance—a nice way to pressure the self who is tempted to skip today's workout.

WILLPOWER EXPERIMENT: PRECOMMIT YOUR FUTURE SELF

Ready to put the squeeze on your future tempted self? This week, commit yourself from a clear distance. Pick one of the following strategies and apply it to your willpower challenge.

1. Create a new default. Make choices in advance and from a clear distance, before your future self is blinded by temptation. For example, you can pack a healthy lunch before you're hungry and salivating over take-out menus. You can schedule and prepay for anything from personal training sessions to dental visits. For your willpower challenge, what can you do to make it easier for your future self to act on your rational preferences?

2. Make it more difficult to reverse your preferences. Like Cortés sinking his ships, find a way to eliminate the easiest route to giving in. Get rid of temptation in your home or office. Don't carry your credit cards when you go shopping, and only bring as much cash as you want to spend. Put your alarm clock across the room so you'll have to get out of bed to turn it off. None of these things make it impossible to change your mind—but they will at least make it damn inconvenient. What can you do that would put a delay or roadblock between your feelings of temptation and your ability to act on them?

3. Motivate your future self. There is no shame in using a carrot or a stick to nudge yourself toward long-term health and happiness. So argues Yale economist Ian Ayres, who created the innovative website stickk .com to help people precommit their future selves to change. His site emphasizes the stick—finding a way to make immediate gratification more painful if you give in. Whether it's taking bets on whether you'll gain weight (something Ayres did, to great success) or donating money to a charity if you don't meet your predetermined goals, you can add a "tax" to the immediate reward. (Ayres even recommends choosing an "anti-charity"—an organization you don't support—so the cost of failure is more painful.) The reward's value may stay the same, but the cost of giving in makes immediate gratification far less tempting.

MONEY MANAGEMENT FOR TEMPTED SELVES

One of the biggest challenges for recovering drug addicts is holding on to their money. Many don't have bank accounts and so must rely on check-cashing businesses to cash a paycheck or social services payment. That lump of cash burns a hole in their pockets, and they can easily blow a two-week paycheck on a single night's entertainment—leaving them unable to buy food, pay the rent, or send child support. Marc Rosen and Robert Rosen-heck, psychiatrists at Yale University School of Medicine, have created a money-management program for recovering addicts that both Cortés and Schelling would approve of. It's called ATM—short for Advisor-Teller Money Manager Intervention. The program uses a combination of rewards and precommitments to make it more appealing to spend wisely, and more difficult to spend foolishly.

Recovering addicts who enroll in the program are assigned a money manager. They agree to deposit their money in an account that only the money manager can access, and the manager holds on to the client's checkbook and ATM card. The money manager talks each "client" through a goal-setting process, helping them identify what they want to do with their money, and how saving money could support their long-term goals. Together, they create a budget for the month, deciding what to spend on food, rent, and other expenses, and write checks to pay any bills that are due. They also set weekly spending plans consistent with the client's long-term goals.

The money manager gives each client only enough money to cover his or her planned expenses. To make an unplanned purchase, the client has to meet with the money manager to fill out a formal request. The manager can put a forty-eight-hour hold on any request that is not consistent with the client's stated goals and budget, or if the manager suspects the client is intoxicated or high. In this way, the client is held to his or her rational preferences, and cannot act on a tempted self's impulses. The manager can also "reward" clients with access to their own money when they take steps to support their recovery, such as looking for a job, attending rehabilitation meetings, and passing weekly drug tests.

The intervention has proved successful not just in helping recovering addicts manage their money, but also at reducing substance use. Importantly, it's not just the precommitment that helps. The program changes the way the recovering addicts think about time and rewards. Research shows that the program lowers their discount rates and increases the value they place on future rewards. The recovering addicts who show the biggest decrease in their discount rates are the most likely to avoid future drug relapse.

> *One reason this intervention works is that the participants are held accountable by someone who supports their goals. Is there someone you can share your goals with and call on for support when you're feeling tempted?*

MEET YOUR FUTURE SELF

I'd like to introduce you to two people I think you'll really get along with. This first is You. You is prone to procrastination, has trouble controlling impulses, and doesn't really like to exercise, finish up paperwork, or do the laundry. The second is, um, also named You. For convenience, let's call this person You 2.0. You 2.0 has no trouble with procrastination because You 2.0 has boundless energy for all tasks, no matter how boring or difficult. You 2.0 also has amazing self-control, and is able to face down potato chips, the Home Shopping Network, and inappropriate sexual advances with nary a craving nor a tremble.

Who are You and You 2.0? *You* is the person reading this chapter, perhaps feeling a little tired and cranky from lack of sleep and overwhelmed by the ten other things you need to do today. You 2.0 is future you. No, not the person you'll magically become when you finish the last page of this book. Future you is the person you imagine when you wonder whether you should clean the closet today or leave it to your future self. Future you is the person who will be much more enthusiastic about exercising than you are right now. Future you is the person who will order the healthiest item on the fast-food menu, so that present you can enjoy the burger so artery-clogging, you must sign a legal waiver to order it. *

Future you always has more time, more energy, and more willpower than present you. At least, that's the story we tell ourselves when we think about our future selves. Future you is free from anxiety and has a higher pain tolerance than present you—making future you the perfect person to get that colonoscopy. Future you is better organized and more motivated than present you, making it only logical to let future you handle the hard stuff.

It is one of the most puzzling but predictable mental errors humans make: We think about our future selves like different people. We often idealize them, expecting our future selves to do what our present selves cannot manage. Sometimes we mistreat them, burdening them with the consequences of our present selves' decisions. Sometimes we simply misunderstand them, failing to realize that they will have the same thoughts and feelings as our present selves. However we think of our future selves, rarely do we see them as fully *us*.

Princeton University psychologist Emily Pronin has shown that this failure of imagination leads us to treat our future selves like strangers. In her experiments, students are asked to make a series of self-control choices. Some are choosing what they are willing to do today, while others are choosing for themselves in the future. Still others get to decide what another student—the next person to show up for the study—will have to do. And though you might think we would naturally form an alliance between our present selves and future selves, it turns out that we are more likely to save our present selves from anything too stressful, but burden our future selves like we would a stranger.

In one experiment, students were asked to drink a revolting liquid made from ketchup and soy sauce. The students got to choose how much of the drink

---

*Yes, this actually exists—at the time of this writing, you had to sign a legal waiver to order El Jefe Grande, which clocks in at seven pounds and 7,000 calories, at Kenny's Burger Joint in Frisco, Texas.

they were willing to consume in the name of science. The more they drank, the more helpful it would be to the researchers—a perfect "I will" power challenge. Some students were told that the drinking part of the study would take place in a matter of minutes. Other students were told that the drinking part of the study would be scheduled for *next* semester. Their present selves were off the hook, and their future selves would be the ones choking down the concoction. Still other students were asked to choose how much of the ketchup cocktail the next participant in the study would be required to drink. What would you do? What would future you do? What would you expect of a stranger?

If you're like most people, your future self has more of an appetite for science (and soy sauce) than present you. The students assigned their future selves, and the next participant, more than twice as much of the disgusting liquid (almost half a cup) as they were willing to drink in the present (two tablespoons). Students showed the same bias when asked to donate time for a good cause. They signed up their future selves for 85 minutes of tutoring fellow students in the next semester. They were even more generous with other students' time, signing them up for 120 minutes of tutoring. But when asked to commit for the present semester, their present selves had only 27 minutes to spare. In a third study, students were given the choice between a small amount of money now, or a larger delayed payment. When choosing for their present selves, they took the immediate reward. But they expected their future selves—and other students—to delay gratification.

Thinking so highly of our future selves would be fine if we could really count on our future selves to behave so nobly. But more typically, when we get to the future, our ideal future self is nowhere to be found, and our same old self is left making the decisions. Even as we're in the middle of a self-control conflict, we foolishly expect that our future selves will be unconflicted. The future self keeps being pushed into the future, like a deus ex machina* that will emerge to save us from our present selves in the very

---

*A favorite Greek tragedy plot device in which a god shows up out of nowhere (typically, lowered onto the stage by a mechanical crane) to solve what seemed like an unsolvable problem for the characters. Would that we all had such convenient conflict-resolution strategies for our own lives.

last act. We put off what we need to do because we are waiting for someone else to show up who will find the change effortless.

UNDER THE MICROSCOPE: ARE YOU WAITING FOR FUTURE YOU?

Is there an important change or task you're putting off, hoping that a future you with more willpower will show up? Do you optimistically overcommit yourself to responsibilities, only to find yourself overwhelmed by impossible demands? Do you talk yourself out of something today, telling yourself that you'll feel more like it tomorrow?

A DENTAL PHOBIC STOPS WAITING FOR A FUTURE DENTIST-LOVING SELF TO SHOW UP

It had been almost ten years since Paul, age forty-five, had been to the dentist. His gums were sensitive, and he had recurrent tooth pain. His wife kept telling him to go to the dentist, and he told her he would get to it when things at work got less busy. In reality, he was afraid of what he would find out about the state of his teeth, and the procedures he'd need to have done.

When he thought about the future-self problem, Paul realized that he had been telling himself that he was going to get over his fear, and that's when he would make the appointment. But when he looked at his actual behavior, he saw that he had been telling himself that for almost a decade. In that time, his teeth and gums had surely deteriorated from his refusal to go to the dentist. By waiting for his future fearless self, he was guaranteeing he'd have something to really be afraid of.

Once Paul admitted that there was no version of him that was ever going to want to go to the dentist, he decided to find a way to get his fearful self there. Paul got a recommendation from a coworker for a dentist who specialized in fearful patients, and even provided sedatives for the examination and treatment. Before, Paul would have felt too embarrassed to go to this dentist, but he knew it was the only way to get his real, present self to take care of his future self's health.

WHY THE FUTURE FEELS DIFFERENT

Why do we treat our future selves like different people? Part of the problem lies in our inability to access our future selves' thoughts and feelings. When we think of our future selves, our future needs and emotions don't feel as real and pressing as our present desires. The thoughts and feelings that shape our present selves' decisions aren't triggered until we feel the immediacy of an opportunity. Students making the choice about how much ketchup and soy sauce to drink didn't feel their stomachs lurch when the decision was for next semester. When donating the time of their future selves, the students weren't bombarded with thoughts of this weekend's big game or stress about next week's midterm. Without the internal cues of disgust and anxiety, we guess wrong about what we will be willing to do in the future.

Brain-imaging studies show that we even use different regions of the brain to think about our present selves and our future selves. When people imagine enjoying a future experience, the brain areas associated with thinking about oneself are surprisingly unengaged. It's as if we are picturing someone else enjoying the sunset or savoring the meal. The same is true when people are asked to consider whether certain traits describe their present selves or their future selves. When reflecting on the future self, the brain's activation is identical to when it is considering the traits of another person.* It's as if we are observing a person from the outside to decide what is true about them, rather than looking within to decide what is true of ourselves. The brain's habit of treating the future self like another person has major consequences for self-control. Studies show that the less active your brain's self-reflection system is when you contemplate

---

*In this particular study, the researchers used Natalie Portman and Matt Damon as the other person participants thought about, because pilot studies showed that these two celebrities were the two best-known and least-controversial people on the planet.

your future self, the more likely you are to say "screw you" to future you, and "yes" to immediate gratification.

A Fund-raiser Uses Future-Self Optimism for Good

Anna Breman, an economist at the University of Arizona, wondered whether there was a way for nonprofit organizations to take advantage of people's tendency to think of their future selves as more magnanimous than their present selves. Could fund-raisers exploit the future-self bias by asking people to pledge their future selves' money instead of giving money now? She worked with Diakonia, a Swedish charity that supports local sustainable projects in developing countries, to compare two different fund-raising strategies. In Give More Now, current donors were asked to increase their automatic monthly donations starting with the very next payment. In Give More Tomorrow, donors were also asked to increase their monthly donation, but it wouldn't kick in until two months later. Donors who received the Give More Tomorrow request increased their donations 32 percent more than the donors who were asked to Give More Today. When it comes to our own self-control, we need to be careful about what we expect from our future selves. But when it comes to getting other people to commit their money, time, or effort, you can take advantage of the future-self bias by asking them to commit far in advance.

When Your Future Self Is a Stranger

We all care more about our own well-being than that of a stranger—that's human nature. It is only logical, then, that we would put our present selves' wants above our future selves' welfare. Why invest in a stranger's future, especially at the expense of your own present comfort?

Hal Ersner-Hershfield, a psychologist at New York University, believes that this self-interest is behind one of the biggest challenges facing our aging society. People are living longer but retiring at the same age, and most have not financially prepared themselves for the extra years. It is estimated that two-thirds of Baby Boomers have not saved enough money to maintain their standard of living in retirement. In fact, a 2010 survey found that 34 percent of Americans had absolutely zero retirement savings, including 53 percent of those under the age of thirty-three, and 22 percent of those sixty-five or older. Ersner-Hershfield (a young guy himself, who at the time, did not have much saved) thought that maybe people were not saving for their future selves because it felt like putting money away for a stranger.

To find out, he created a measure of "future-self continuity"—the degree to which you see your future self as essentially the same person as your current self. Not everyone views the future self as a total stranger; some of us feel quite close and connected to our future selves. Figure 1 illustrates the wide range of relationships people have to their future selves. (Take a look at the figure, choose the pair of circles that seems most accurate to you, then come back.) Ersner-Hershfield has found that people with high future-self continuity—that is, their circles overlap more—save more money and rack up less credit card debt, building a significantly better financial future for their future selves to enjoy.

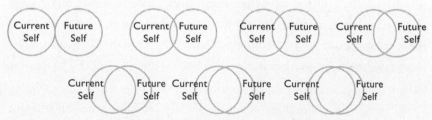

Figure 1. Everybody changes over time. Which of these pairs of circles best represents how similar your present self is to your future self twenty years from now?

If feeling estranged from your future self leads to short-sighted financial decisions, can getting to know your future self lead to greater savings? Ersner-Hershfield decided to test this possibility by introducing college students to their retirement-age selves. Working with professional computer animators using age-progression software, he created three-dimensional avatars of participants as they would look at retirement age.* Ersner-Hershfield's aim was to help his young participants feel like the age-progression really was them—not a relative (the most common response from students was, "That looks just like Uncle Joe [or Aunt Sally]!"), and not a creature from a horror movie. To get to know their future selves, the students interacted with their age-advanced avatars in an immersive virtual reality setup. The participants sat in front of a mirror, but they saw reflected their future selves. If the participant moved her head, her future self moved her head. If she turned sideways, her future self turned sideways. While participants watched their future selves in the mirror, an experimenter asked each participant questions, such as "What is your name?" "Where are you from?" and "What is your passion in life?" As the participant answered, it appeared as though the future self was speaking.

After spending time with their future selves, participants left the virtual reality lab and began a hypothetical budgeting task. They were given $1,000 and asked to divvy it up among present expenses, a fun splurge, a checking account, and a retirement account. Students who had interacted with their future selves put more than twice as much money into their retirement accounts as students who had spent time looking at their young selves in a real mirror. Getting to know their future selves made the students more willing to invest in them—and, by extension, themselves.

Although the technology is not yet widely available, one can imagine the day when every human resources office has new employees interact with their future selves before enrolling in the company's retirement plan. In the meantime, there are other ways to get to know your future self (see Willpower Experiment: "Meet Your Future Self"). Strengthening your future-self continuity can do more than fatten your savings—it can help you with any willpower challenge. High future-self continuity seems to propel people to be the best version of themselves *now*. For example,

---

*Charmingly, Ersner-Hershfield showed his future wife his own age-advanced avatar before he proposed. He also assured me that he is now saving plenty for retirement.

Ersner-Hershfield noticed that people high in future-self continuity were more likely to show up for the study on time, and people low in future-self continuity were more likely to blow the study off and have to reschedule. Struck by this accidental finding, he began to explore how future-self continuity affects ethical decision making. His most recent work shows that people with low future-self continuity behave less ethically in business role-play scenarios. They are more likely to pocket money found in the office, and more comfortable leaking information that could ruin another person's career. They also lie more in a game that rewards deception with money. It is as if feeling disconnected from our future selves gives us permission to ignore the consequences of our actions. In contrast, feeling connected to our future selves protects us from our worst impulses.

WILLPOWER EXPERIMENT: MEET YOUR FUTURE SELF

You can help yourself make wiser choices by sending yourself to the future (DeLorean not required*). Below are three ideas for making the future feel real, and for getting to know your future self. Pick one that appeals to you and try it out this week.

1. **Create a Future Memory.** Neuroscientists at the University Medical Center Hamburg-Eppendorf in Germany have shown that imagining the future helps people delay gratification. You don't even need to think about the future rewards of delaying gratification—just thinking about the future seems to work. For example, if you're trying to decide between starting a project now or putting it off, imagine yourself grocery shopping next week, or at a meeting you have scheduled. When you picture the future, the brain begins to think more concretely and immediately about the consequences of your present choices. The more real and vivid the future feels, the more likely you are to make a decision that your future self won't regret.

---

*It pains me to think I might have to explain this reference. Any reader who does not get it should plan to watch the 1985 classic film *Back to the Future*—your future self will thank you.

2. **Send a Message to Your Future Self.** The founders of FutureMe.org have created a way for people to e-mail their future selves. Since 2003, they've been holding on to e-mails people write to themselves, and delivering them on a future date chosen by the writer. Why not take advantage of the opportunity to think about what your future self will be doing, and how he or she will feel about the choices you're making now? Describe to your future self what you are going to do now to help yourself meet your long-term goals. What are your hopes for your future self? What do you think you will be like? You can also imagine your future self looking back on your present self. What would your future self thank you for, if you were able to commit to it today? Psychologist Hal Ersner-Hershfield says that even if you just briefly contemplate what you'd write in such a letter, you will feel more connected to your future self.

3. **Imagine Your Future Self.** Studies show that imagining your future self can increase your present self's willpower. One experiment asked couch potatoes to imagine either a hoped-for future self who exercised regularly and enjoyed excellent health and energy, or a feared future self who was inactive and suffering the health consequences. Both visualizations got them off the couch, and they were exercising more frequently two months later than a control group that did not imagine a future self. For your willpower challenge, can you imagine a hoped-for future self who is committed to the change, and reaping the benefits? Or a future self suffering the consequences of not changing? Let yourself daydream in vivid detail, imagining how you will feel, how you will look, and what pride, gratitude, or regret you will have for your past self's choices.

A TIME TO WAIT, AND A
TIME TO GIVE IN

We've been assuming that it is always better to delay gratification. But is it? Ran Kivetz, a marketing researcher at Columbia University, has found that some people have a very difficult time choosing current happiness over future rewards. They consistently put off pleasure in the name of work, virtue, or future happiness—but eventually, they regret their decisions. Kivetz calls this condition *hyperopia*—a fancy way of saying farsighted. Most people, as we've seen, are perpetually nearsighted. When the promise of reward is in front of their eyes, they cannot see past it to the value of delaying gratification. People who suffer from hyperopia are chronically farsighted—they cannot see the value of giving in today. This is as big a problem as being nearsighted; both lead to disappointment and unhappiness in the long run.

For people who have trouble saying yes to temptation, giving in requires as much self-control as saying no does for the rest of us. They must turn every strategy in this chapter on its head. People who are hyperopic—unlike the myopic majority—must precommit to indulgence. For example, you might choose a gift certificate over cash back when redeeming credit card reward points. That way, you will be forced to treat yourself to a luxury instead of squirreling away the cash for a future emergency. (However, you also need to make sure the gift certificate doesn't languish in the kitchen drawer, going unused because it never seems like the right time to splurge.) You can also use reframing to help make better decisions, just like people who want to avoid giving in to immediate gratification. Instead of focusing on the cost of an indulgence, the hyperopic person needs to reframe it as an investment. You might imagine how much pleasure you will receive from it over time, or think about the indulgence as a necessary way to restore yourself for work. (Marketers are well aware of this need, and are happy to position their luxury products in a way that reduces consumers' guilt.) And when you think about how your decisions today will affect your future self's happiness, you must imagine the regret you will feel if you do not indulge today.

I confess, I can get a little hyperopic myself. When I need to remind myself to indulge, I think back to a bottle of champagne that I carried around for five years. It was given to me by my boss when I received a fellowship to attend graduate school. When she handed it to me with a congratulatory note, it didn't feel right to break the bottle open. I was nervous about whether I would succeed in grad school, and in my mind, getting in was just the first hurdle. I told myself I'd drink it when I arrived at Stanford and felt settled in. So the bottle drove cross-country with me, from Boston to Northern California. I settled in to the psychology department, but the time still didn't feel right to drink the champagne. I hadn't done anything yet to celebrate. Maybe at the end of the first year, or when I published my first paper.

Well, that bottle of champagne moved with me four more times. Each time I packed it up, I thought, *I'll feel like I deserve to crack it open when I pass the next hurdle.* It wasn't until after I submitted my dissertation and received my diploma that I finally pulled the bottle out. By that time, it was undrinkable. As I poured it down the sink, I vowed to never let another bottle go to waste, or another milestone go uncelebrated.

UNDER THE MICROSCOPE: ARE YOU TOO FARSIGHTED FOR YOUR OWN GOOD?

Do you have a hard time taking a break from work because there is always more to do? Do you feel so guilty or anxious about spending money that you find it hard to purchase anything beyond the absolute basics? Do you ever look back at how you have spent your time and money, and wish you had been more focused on your present happiness instead of always putting it off? If so, take the willpower experiments in this chapter and turn them into strategies for self-indulgence. (And try not to put if off, will you?)

The Last Word

When we contemplate the future, our imaginations fail us in predictable ways. Far-off rewards seem less compelling, so we choose immediate gratification. We fail to predict how we will be tempted or distracted, so we fail to protect ourselves from abandoning our goals. To make wiser decisions, we need to better understand and support our future selves. And we need to remember that the future self who receives the consequences of our present self's actions is, indeed, still us, and will very much appreciate the effort.

CHAPTER SUMMARY

The Idea: Our inability to clearly see the future clearly leads us into temptation and procrastination.

Under the Microscope

- *How are you discounting future rewards?* For your willpower challenge, ask yourself what future rewards you put on sale each time you give in to temptation or procrastination.
- *Are you waiting for future you?* Is there an important change or task you're putting off, hoping that a future you with more willpower will show up?
- *Are you too farsighted for your own good?* Do you find it more difficult to indulge than to resist temptation?

Willpower Experiments

- *Wait ten minutes.* Institute a mandatory ten-minute wait for any temptation. Before the time is up, bring to mind the competing long-term reward of resisting temptation.
- *Lower your discount rate.* When you are tempted to act against your long-term interests, frame the choice as giving up the best possible long-term reward for resisting temptation.
- *Precommit your future self.* Create a new default, make it more difficult to reverse your preferences, or motivate your future self with reward or threat.
- *Meet your future self.* Create a future memory, write a letter to your future self, or just imagine yourself in the future.

EIGHT

Infected! Why Willpower Is Contagious

John, eighteen years old and just out of high school, stepped off a bus at the U.S. Air Force Academy in El Paso County, Colorado. He arrived with a single backpack containing the few items new cadets are allowed to bring: a small clock, a winter jacket, a supply of stamps and stationery, and a graphing calculator. He also brought with him something that wasn't in his backpack, and wasn't visible to the twenty-nine other new cadets assigned to a squadron with John. Over the course of the year, these cadets would live together, eat together, and study together. And what John brought with him would slowly spread to other members of his squadron, threatening their health and careers in the Air Force.

The scourge John brought with him? It wasn't smallpox, tuberculosis, or an STD. It was being out of shape. Although it's hard to believe that physical fitness could be contagious, a 2010 report from the National Bureau of Economic Research found that poor fitness spread through the U.S. Air Force Academy like an infectious disease. A total of 3,487 cadets were tracked for four years, from their high school fitness tests through their regular fitness exams at the academy. Over time, the least-fit cadet in a squadron gradually brought down the fitness levels of the other cadets. In fact, once a cadet arrived at the academy, the fitness level of the *least-fit* cadet in his squadron was a better predictor of his fitness performance than that cadet's own pre-academy fitness level.

This study is just one example of how behaviors we typically view as being under self-control are, in important ways, under social control as well. We like to believe that our choices are immune to the influence of others, and we pride ourselves on our independence and free will. But research from the fields of psychology, marketing, and medicine reveals that our individual choices are powerfully shaped by what other people think, want, and do— and what we think they want us to do. As you'll see, this social influence often gets us into trouble. However, it can also help us meet our willpower goals. Willpower failures may be contagious, but you can also catch self-control.

THE SPREAD OF AN EPIDEMIC

The Centers for Disease Control and Prevention are well known for tracking outbreaks like the H1N1 virus and the early AIDS epidemic. But they also keep track of long-term changes to our national health, including the obesity rates in every state in the country. In 1990, no state in the nation had an obesity rate equal to or higher than 15 percent. By 1999, eighteen states had a rate between 20 and 24 percent, but still no state had a rate equal to or higher than 25 percent. By 2009, only one state (Colorado) and the District of Columbia had a rate lower than 20 percent, and thirty-three states had a rate of 25 percent or higher.

Two scientists, Nicholas Christakis at Harvard Medical School and James Fowler at the University of California, San Diego, were struck by the language being used by health officials and the media to describe this trend: an obesity *epidemic*. They wondered whether weight gain could spread from person to person in much the same way as other contagious outbreaks, like the flu. To find out, they gained access to data from the Framingham Heart Study, which has tracked more than 12,000 residents of Framingham,

Massachusetts, for thirty-two years. It began in 1948 with 5,200 participants, and added new generations in 1971 and 2002. The members of this community have reported the intimate details of their lives for decades, including weight changes and their social connections to everyone else in the study.

When Christakis and Fowler looked at participants' weight over time, they saw what looked like a real epidemic. Obesity was infectious, spreading within families and from friend to friend. When a friend became obese, a person's own future risk of becoming obese increased by 171 percent. A woman whose sister became obese had a 67 percent increased risk, and a man whose brother became obese had a 45 percent increased risk.

Obesity wasn't the only thing going around the Framingham community. When one person started drinking more, the bar tabs and hangovers spread throughout the social network too. But they also found evidence for the contagiousness of self-control. When one person gave up cigarettes, it increased the odds that their friends and family would quit too. Christakis and Fowler have found the same pattern of contagion in other communities, and for willpower challenges as diverse as drug use, sleep deprivation, and depression. As unsettling as it may be, the implication is clear: Both bad habits and positive change can spread from person to person like germs, and nobody is completely immune.

UNDER THE MICROSCOPE: YOUR SOCIAL NETWORK

Not every willpower challenge is the result of a social "infection," but with most challenges, there is a social influence. For your own willpower challenge, consider:

- Do others in your social network share your willpower challenge?
- Looking back, did you pick up the habit from a friend or family member?
- Are there certain people you're more likely to indulge with?
- Have other people in your network recently attempted to improve on this willpower challenge too?

THE SOCIAL SELF

When it comes to self-control, we've seen that the human mind is not one unified self, but multiple selves who compete for control. There's the self who wants immediate gratification and the self who remembers your bigger goals. There's your present self, who may or may not seem to have much in common with your future self. As if that weren't a crowded enough crew, it turns out that you have a few other people living in your head too. I'm not talking about multiple personality disorder—I'm talking about your parents, your spouse, your children, your friends, your boss, and anyone else who is a part of your everyday world.

Humans are hardwired to connect with others, and our brains have adapted a nifty way to make sure we do. We have specialized brain cells—called mirror neurons—whose sole purpose is to keep track of what other people are thinking, feeling, and doing. These mirror neurons are sprinkled throughout the brain to help us understand the full range of other people's experiences.

For example, imagine that you and I are in the kitchen, and you see me reach my right hand for a knife. Your brain will automatically begin to encode this movement. The mirror neurons that correspond to movement and sensation in *your* right hand will be activated. In this way, your brain begins to craft an inner representation of what I'm doing. The mirror neurons re-create the movement like a detective might reenact a crime scene, trying to understand what happened and why. This allows you to guess why I'm reaching for the knife, and what might happen next. Am I going to attack you? Or is my intended victim the carrot cake on the counter?

Let's say I accidentally slice my right thumb as I grab the knife. Ouch! As you see this happen, mirror neurons in the pain regions of your brain will respond. You'll wince and know immediately what I'm feeling. The experience of pain is so real to the brain that the nerves in your spinal cord will even attempt to suppress incoming pain signals from your own right hand—just as if you had actually cut your hand! This is the empathy instinct that helps us understand and respond to other people's feelings.

After I bandage my thumb and serve myself a slice of cake, the mirror neurons in the reward system of your brain will be activated. Even if you don't like carrot cake yourself, if you know that it's my favorite (true), your brain will start anticipating a reward. When our mirror neurons encode the promise of reward in others, we long for a treat ourselves.

MIRRORING WILLPOWER FAILURES

In this simple scenario, we've seen three ways our social brains can catch willpower failures. The first is unintentional mimicry. The mirror neurons that detect another person's movement prime that very same movement in your own body. When you see me reach for the knife, you might unconsciously find yourself reaching out to lend me a hand. In many situations, we find ourselves automatically mirroring the physical gestures and actions of others. If you pay attention to body language, you'll notice that people in conversation start to adopt each other's positions. One person crosses his arms, and moments later, his conversation partner crosses her arms. She leans back, and soon enough, he leans back, too. This unconscious physical mirroring seems to help people understand each other better, and also creates a sense of connection and rapport. (One reason salespeople, managers, and politicians are trained to *intentionally* mimic other people's postures is that they know it will make it easier to influence the person they are mirroring.)

Our instinct to mimic other people's actions means that when you see someone else reach for a snack, a drink, or a credit card, you may find yourself unconsciously mirroring their behavior—and losing your will-power. For example, a recent study looked at what happens in smokers' brains when they see a movie character smoke. The brain regions that plan hand movements became activated, as if the smokers' brains were preparing to pull out a cigarette and light it. Just seeing someone smoke on screen launched a subconscious impulse to light up, giving the smokers' brains the added challenge of restraining that impulse.

The second way our social brains can lead us astray is the contagion of emotion. We saw that our mirror neurons respond to other people's pain, but they also respond to emotions. That's how a coworker's bad mood can become our bad mood—and make us feel like we're the ones who need a drink! It's also why television sitcoms use a laugh track—they're hoping the sound of someone else cracking up will tickle your funny bone. The automatic contagion of emotions also may help explain why social network researchers Christakis and Fowler have found that happiness and loneliness spread from friend to friend and through families. How can this lead to a willpower failure? When we catch a bad feeling, we're going to turn to our usual strategies for fixing it—and this may mean a shopping spree or chocolate bar is in your near future.

Finally, our brains can even catch temptation when we see others give in. Seeing someone else engage in your willpower challenge can put you in the mood to join them. When we imagine what other people want, their wants can trigger our wants, and their appetites can trigger our appetites. This is one reason we eat more with others than when we're alone, why gamblers raise their bets after seeing someone else win big, and why we spend more when shopping with friends.

UNDER THE MICROSCOPE: WHO ARE YOU MIRRORING?

This week, keep your eyes open for any evidence that you are mirroring other people's behavior—especially behavior related to your willpower challenge. Is a common indulgence the social glue that's holding a relationship together? Do you go overboard when others around you are doing the same?

A SMOKER UNDER SOCIAL INFLUENCE

Marc had recently started a new job behind the counter at a coffee shop. All the employees got one ten-minute break per four-hour shift. As Marc soon learned, most of them took their break out back where they could smoke.

People often ended a shift out back, talking and smoking a cigarette before they went home. Marc wasn't a regular smoker, though he occasionally had a cigarette or two at parties. But he found himself smoking if another employee was out back while he was on break, and he sometimes stuck around after work to smoke with his coworkers.

When our class got to the social influences on behavior, Marc recognized himself immediately. He never smoked when he was alone. It just seemed easier to smoke than to not smoke at work—it's what people did. Even the shop manager took smoke breaks. Marc hadn't given too much thought to where this social habit could be leading, but he definitely did not want to end up one of the completely hooked employees who lived for their smoke breaks. He decided to stop bumming cigarettes off his coworkers, who were not the least bit upset about no longer having to give him a smoke. Marc still made it a point to be social; he just didn't have to light up while he did it.

WHEN GOALS ARE INFECTIOUS

Human beings are natural mind readers. Whenever we observe other people in action, we use our social brains to guess at their goals. Why is that woman screaming at that man? Why is the waiter flirting with me? This guessing game helps us predict other people's behaviors and avoid social disasters. We need to be able to protect ourselves and others from social threats (Is the woman screaming, or the man being screamed at, dangerous? Who in this situation needs help?). We also need to choose the most appropriate response in an ambiguous situation (the flirtatious waiter probably wants a bigger tip, not an invitation to meet you in the restroom).

There is, however, a self-control side effect of this automatic mind reading: It activates those very same goals in us. Psychologists call this *goal contagion*. Research shows that it is surprisingly easy to catch a person's goals in a way that changes your own behavior. For example, in one study, students caught the goal to make money just from reading a story about another student who worked over spring break. These students then worked harder and faster to earn money in a laboratory task. Young men who read a story about a man trying to pick up a woman in a bar caught the goal of casual sex, becoming more likely to help an attractive young woman who interrupted the experiment. (The researchers confirmed that the young men believed that helping a woman increases the chances that she will sleep with them—a plausible hypothesis, although I'm pretty sure the effect size is smaller than most young men hope.) Other studies show that thinking about a friend who smokes marijuana increases college students' desire to get high, while thinking about a friend who does not smoke decreases their interest.

What does all this mean for your self-control? The good news is, goal contagion is limited to goals you already, at some level, share. You can't catch a brand-new goal from a brief exposure the way you can catch a flu virus. A nonsmoker is not going to catch a nicotine craving when a friend pulls out a cigarette. But another person's behavior can activate a goal in your mind that was not currently in charge of your choices. As we've seen, a willpower challenge always involves a conflict between two competing goals. You want pleasure now, but you want health later. You want to vent your anger at your boss, but you want to keep your job. You want to splurge, but you also want to get out of debt. Seeing another person pursue one of these competing goals can tip the balance of power in your own mind.

Goal contagion works in both directions—you can catch self-control as well as self-indulgence—but we seem to be especially susceptible to the contagion of temptation. If your lunch companion orders dessert, her goal for immediate gratification may team up with *your* goal for immediate gratification to outvote your goal to lose weight. Seeing someone else splurge on holidays gifts may reinforce your desire to delight your own kids on Christmas morning, and make you temporarily forget your goal to spend less.

WILLPOWER EXPERIMENT: STRENGTHEN YOUR IMMUNE SYSTEM

We don't always catch other people's goals. Sometimes seeing someone else give in to temptation can actually enhance our self-control. When you are firmly committed to a goal (e.g., losing weight), but aware that you have a conflicting goal (e.g., enjoying a deep-dish pizza), seeing someone do something that conflicts with your strongest goal will put your brain on high alert. It will activate your dominant goal even more strongly and start generating strategies to help you stick with it. Psychologists call this *counteractive control*, but you can think of it as an immune response to anything that threatens your self-control.

The best way to strengthen your immune response to other people's goals is to spend a few minutes at the beginning of your day thinking about your own goals, and how you could be tempted to ignore them. Like a vaccine that protects you from other people's germs, reflecting on your own goals will reinforce your intentions and help you avoid goal contagion.

CATCHING THE GOAL TO LOSE CONTROL

Sometimes we don't catch specific goals—eat a snack, spend money, seduce a stranger—but the more general goal to follow our impulses. Researchers at the University of Groningen in the Netherlands have shown this in a variety of real-world settings, using unsuspecting passersby as their subjects. They plant "evidence" of people behaving badly—for example, chaining bicycles to a fence right next to a prominent "No Bicycles" sign, and leaving grocery carts in a parking garage with a "Please Return Your Carts to the Store" policy. Their studies show that rule-breaking is contagious. People who stumble into the researchers' setup take their cues from what other people have done, and ignore the signs. They, too, chain up their bikes and leave their carts in the garage.

But the consequences go further than that. When people saw a bike chained to a no-bicycles fence, they were also more likely to take an illegal shortcut through the fence. When they saw carts in a parking garage, they were more likely to dump their trash on the floor of the garage. The contagious goal was bigger than the goal to break a specific rule. They caught the goal to do whatever they wanted, rather than what they were supposed to do.

When we observe evidence of other people ignoring rules and following their impulses, we are more likely to give in to *any* of our own impulses. This means that anytime we see someone behaving badly, our own self-control deteriorates (bad news for fans of reality television, where the three rules of high ratings are: Drink too much, pick a fight, and sleep with someone else's boyfriend). Hearing about someone cheating on their taxes might make you feel freer to cheat on your diet. Seeing other drivers go over the speed limit might inspire you to go over your budget. In this way, we can catch willpower weakness from others—even if our personal weakness is very different than the giving in that we observe. Importantly, we don't even need to see people in action. Like germs that linger on a doorknob long after a sick person passed through, an action can be passed on to us when we merely see evidence that others have done.

WILLPOWER EXPERIMENT: CATCH SELF-CONTROL

Research shows that thinking about someone with good self-control can increase your own willpower. Is there someone who can serve as a willpower role model for your challenge? Someone who has struggled with the same challenge and succeeded, or someone who exemplifies the kind of self-control you would like to have? (In my class, the most frequently nominated willpower role models are accomplished athletes, spiritual leaders, and politicians, though family members and friends may provide even more motivation, as you'll see in a little bit.) When you need a little extra willpower, bring your role model to mind. Ask yourself: What would this willpower wonder do?

WHY PEOPLE YOU LIKE ARE MORE
CONTAGIOUS THAN STRANGERS

In cold or flu season, you can catch a virus from any person you come into contact with—the coworker who coughs without covering her mouth, the cashier who swipes your credit card and hands it back teeming with germs. This is what epidemiologists call *simple contagion*. With simple contagion, it doesn't matter who introduces the infection. The germs of a total stranger have just as much influence as the germs of a loved one, and one exposure is enough to infect you.

The transmission of behaviors doesn't work this way. Social epidemics—like the spread of obesity or smoking—follow a pattern of *complex contagion*. It is not enough to come into contact with a person who is a "carrier" of the behavior. Your relationship to that person matters. In the Framingham community, behaviors weren't spreading over fences and backyards. The social epidemics spread through networks of mutual respect and liking, not the orderly network of a street grid. A coworker didn't have anywhere near the effect of a close friend, and even the friend of a friend's friend had more influence than a person you saw every day, but didn't like. This kind of selective infection is almost unheard-of in the world of diseases—it's as if your immune system could only defend itself against a virus you caught from someone you didn't know or didn't like. But that's exactly how behaviors spread. Social closeness matters more than geographic closeness.

Why are behaviors so contagious within close relationships? To stretch the immune system analogy a little further, we could say that our immune system only rejects the goals and behavior of other people *if it recognizes those other people as "not us."* After all, our physical immune system doesn't attack our own cells; what it recognizes as us, it leaves alone. But what it recognizes as *other*, it treats like a threat—isolating or destroying that virus or bacteria so you don't get sick. It turns out that when we think about people we love, respect, and feel similar to, our brains treat them more like us than like *not us.* You can see it in a brain scanner, watching adults think first about themselves, then about their mothers. The brain regions activated by self and mom are almost identical, showing that who we think we are includes the people we care about. Our sense of self depends on our relationships with others, and in many ways, we only know who we are by thinking about other people. Because we include other people in our sense of self, their choices influence our choices.

UNDER THE MICROSCOPE: WHO ARE YOU MOST LIKELY TO CATCH SOMETHING FROM?

Take a few moments to consider who your "close others" are. Who do you spend the most time with? Who do you respect? Who do you feel most similar to? Whose opinion matters most to you? Who do you trust or care about the most? Can you think of any behaviors—helpful or harmful— that you've picked up from them, or that they have caught from you?

ONE OF THE TRIBE

Imagine someone knocks on your door and asks you to answer a few questions about energy conservation. How often do you try to use less electricity? Do you conserve water by taking shorter showers? Have you insulated your house to reduce heat loss? Do you drive a car with high gas mileage? Then they ask you how strongly you agree that conserving energy will help the environment, save you money, and benefit future generations. Finally, they ask you two questions: Which reason most motivates your energy conservation? Oh, and how many of your neighbors do you think try to conserve energy?

Eight hundred California residents were asked these questions as part of a study on why people conserve. They were quite the altruistic bunch, claiming that their strongest motivation was to protect the environment, followed by helping future generations and saving money. "Because other people are doing it" came in dead last. But before we congratulate the Californians for being so civic-minded, consider this: The only survey question that predicted a person's actual energy conservation was how much they thought their neighbors tried to conserve. The other beliefs and motivations—saving money, saving the planet for their grandkids—had zero relationship to what people did. People thought they acted for noble reasons, but the only belief that mattered was a far less altruistic "Everyone else is doing it."

This is an example of what psychologists call *social proof*. When the rest of our tribe does something, we tend to think it's a smart thing to do. This is one of those useful survival instincts that come with having a social brain. After all, if you see your whole tribe heading east, you'd better follow. Trusting the judgment of others is the glue that makes social living work. You don't have to know everything yourself and can save your resources for whatever your specialty is, be it making the finest hippopotamus-hide loincloths, or the most accurate predictions about the stock market.

Social proof has enormous sway over our everyday behavior. It's why we often check out the "most read stories" box on news websites, and why we're more likely to go to the number-one movie in the country instead of the box-office bomb. It's why undecided voters can be persuaded by poll numbers, and why it counts as "news" when parents are fighting in the aisles over the hottest new toy. What other people want must be good. What other people think must be true. If we don't yet have an opinion, we might as well trust the tribe.

The researchers who went door-to-door asking about energy use decided to test the power of social proof for changing behavior. They created door hangers that urged residents of San Marcos, California, to take shorter showers, turn off unnecessary lights, and use fans instead of air-conditioning at night. Each door hanger came with a motivational message. Some asked the residents to protect the environment; others focused on how conserving energy would help future generations, or lower the residents' energy bills. The social proof door hangers included only one statement: "99% of people in your community reported turning off unnecessary lights to save energy."

A total of 371 households received one of these door hangers once a week for four weeks. Importantly, each household always received the same type of persuasive message—e.g., four social proof door hangers in a row, or four "help future generations" door hangers in a row. To find out which motivational appeal was most effective, the researchers took regular readings of the energy meters at each home. They also got a hold of the residents' electricity bills for the months before and after the door hangers were delivered. The only persuasive message that decreased a household's energy use was the "everyone else is doing it" appeal. The other appeals—for the reasons people say make them conserve energy—had no effect on behavior.

This study is one of many confirming that we *are* the lemmings our mothers always warned us not to be. "Would you jump off a bridge if all your friends were doing it?" We knew then, just as we know now, that the correct answer is supposed to be, "No, never! I am an independent-minded person, and other people have no influence over me!" But the more truthful answer is, yeah, maybe we would.

People rarely want to be reminded of this. In the classroom, I find that just about every student believes that he or she is the exception. We've been trained since birth to do it our way, to stand out from the crowd, to be a leader, not a follower. And yet our cultural obsession with independence cannot suppress our human desire to fit in. Our society may praise being above the influence of others, but we cannot separate ourselves from our social instincts. As the door hanger study shows, this needn't be a bad thing. Social proof can strengthen self-control when we believe that doing the right thing (or the harder thing) is the norm.

God Wants You to Lose Weight

Can you convince people to exercise and eat more fruits and vegetables by telling them it's what God wants? An intervention at Middle Tennessee State University is doing exactly that, with excellent results. The intervention asks people to consider how self-care and health are important values in their religion. For example, Christians may be asked to reflect on passages from the Bible such as "Do not join those who drink too much wine or gorge themselves on meat" (Proverbs 23:20 NIV) and "Let us purify ourselves from everything that contaminates body and spirit, perfecting holiness out of reverence for God" (2 Corinthians 7:1 NIV). They are asked to reflect on the behaviors in their own lives—such as eating junk food or not exercising—that are inconsistent with their professed faith and values. When they identify a disconnect between their faith and their actions, they are encouraged to create an action plan for changing that behavior. Believing that losing weight and exercising is what good Christians do is powerful social proof—far more motivating than getting a stern warning from a doctor after getting bad results on a cholesterol test.

Mark Ansel, the psychologist who developed this approach, argues that religious communities should take on more responsibility for supporting behavior change. Places of worship could offer fitness classes and nutrition talks alongside religious services, and social events should serve healthier food. He points out that for this approach to work, religious leaders will have to be good role models. Before they start preaching morning walks, they need to get in shape themselves—and just like they wouldn't be caught in a brothel, they'll need to think twice about stepping into the local McDonald's. After all, social proof requires proof.

An intervention at Stanford University took a very different approach to *reducing* a behavior among undergraduate students. Researchers designed two different flyers to discourage binge drinking. One took a rational approach, listing scary statistics about drinking like "One night of heavy drinking can impair your ability to think abstractly for thirty days." (Yes, this is a compelling argument to many grade-chasing undergraduates worried about their performance on the next calculus exam.) The other flyer linked drinking with the social lepers of university life: graduate students. This flyer showed a graduate student drinking, along with the warning, "Lots of graduate students at Stanford drink . . . and lots of them are sketchy. So think when you drink. . . . Nobody wants to be mistaken for this guy."

The two different flyers were posted separately in two different all-freshman dorms. Two weeks after the flyers went up, residents were asked to complete an anonymous survey about how many drinks they had consumed in the last week. Students in the dorm that was plastered with the sketchy grad student flyers reported drinking 50 percent less alcohol than students in the dorm that received the rational argument flyers. Were the students telling the truth? We can't know for sure, as the researchers didn't follow them to any parties. It's possible the undergrads didn't want to be mistaken, even in an anonymous research project, for a sketchy grad student. But if the reports were honest, this study suggests a new strategy for discouraging unhealthy behavior: Just convince people it's the habit of a group they would never want to be a member of.

> *These two interventions demonstrate the importance of social proof for supporting behavior change. We may be willing to give up our vices and cultivate new virtues if we believe that it will more firmly secure us a spot in our most cherished tribe.*

WHEN SELF-CONTROL ISN'T NORMAL

If we want people to have more willpower, we need to make them believe that self-control is the norm. But when was the last time you heard about a positive trend in behavior? The media prefer to scare us with shocking statistics about how we are all becoming lazier, less ethical, and less healthy. We hear the statistics all the time: 40 percent of Americans *never* exercise, and only 11 percent engage in vigorous exercise five times a week (the standard recommendation for health and weight loss). Only 14 percent of adults eat the recommended five servings of fruits and vegetables a day. Instead, the average adult consumes almost 100 pounds of sugar a year.

These statistics are meant to fill us with horror. But let's be honest: If we find ourselves in that majority, all our tribal brain hears is, "What a relief, I'm just like everyone else." The more we hear these kinds of statistics, the more firmly we start to believe that this is what people do, and it's OK if I do it too. When you are like 86 percent of other Americans, why would you need to change?

Learning that we are "normal" can even change our perception of ourselves. For example, as a nation, the fatter we get, the thinner we feel. A 2010 report in the *Archives of Internal Medicine* found that 37 percent of people who are clinically obese not only believe that they are *not* obese, but also believe that they have a low lifetime risk of becoming obese. Although this looks like a denial of reality, it simply reflects the new social reality. When everyone gains weight, our internal standards about what is "obese" shift upward, even if medical standards remain the same.

On the other side of the bell curve, if we're outside the "willpowerless" majority, we may even find ourselves boomeranging back to the middle. In one study, homeowners who were told on their energy bill that they consumed less energy than the average home started to leave on the lights and turn up the thermostat. The pull to the center can be more powerful than the desire to do the right thing.

When it comes to social proof, what we *think* other people do matters even more than what they actually do. For example, college students overestimate the prevalence of academic cheating among their peers. The best predictor of whether a student cheats is whether he believes other students cheat, not the severity of penalties or whether he thinks he will be caught. When students believe that their classmates cheat, a relatively honest class can become a class full of students who text their friends for answers during an exam (yes, I have caught a student trying this).

This phenomenon is not limited to the classroom. Most people overestimate the percentage of taxpayers who cheat on their tax returns. This leads to higher actual rates of cheating, as people conform to what they believe is the norm. It's not that we are irredeemable cheaters. When people are given accurate information about true norms, they correct their own behaviors. For example, when people are given accurate statistics about other taxpayers' honesty, they are more likely to file an honest return themselves.

UNDER THE MICROSCOPE: BUT MA, EVERYONE ELSE IS DOING IT!

Social proof can interfere with change if we believe that everyone else does whatever behavior we are trying to change. Do you ever tell yourself that your willpower challenge is no big deal, because it's the norm? Do you remind yourself of all the people you know who share the habit? If so, you may want to challenge this perception. The best way to do this is to find the folks who share the behavior you aspire to. Look for a new "tribe" you could join. It could be a support group, a class, a local club, an online community, or even subscribing to a magazine that supports your goals. Surrounding yourself with people who share your commitment to your goals will make it feel like the norm.

"SHOULD" POWER

Could imagining your former classmates' awe when you show up at your high school reunion fifty pounds lighter motivate you to get up every morning to exercise? Can your nine-year-old son's disappointment when you smoke keep you from sneaking a cigarette at work?

When contemplating a choice, we often imagine ourselves the object of other people's evaluations. Studies show that this can provide a powerful boost to self-control. People who imagine how proud they will feel when they accomplish a goal—from quitting smoking to donating blood—are more likely to follow through and succeed. Anticipated disapproval works too: People are more likely to use condoms when they imagine feeling ashamed if others knew that they had unprotected sex.

David Desteno, a psychologist at Northeastern University, argues that social emotions like pride and shame have a quicker and more direct influence over our choices than rational arguments about long-term costs and benefits. Desteno calls this *hot* self-control. Usually we think of self-control as the triumph of cool reason over hot impulses, but pride and shame rely on the emotional brain, not the logical prefrontal cortex. Social emotions may have evolved to help us make the choices that will keep us in good standing in our tribe, in the same way that fear helps us protect ourselves, and anger helps us defend ourselves. Imagining social acceptance or rejection can spur us to do the right thing.

Some businesses and communities have started to experiment with social shaming instead of standard penalties for illegal and socially destructive behavior. If you're caught shoplifting from a grocery store in Manhattan's Chinatown, you may be forced to pose for a photo with the item you tried to steal. It will be hung on a wall of shame near the store's cash register, bearing your name, address, and the description "Big Thief."

When Chicago police decided to publicize the names and photos of men arrested for soliciting prostitutes, they weren't so much trying to punish the men who were caught as they were hoping to strike fear in the hearts of men who were thinking about buying sex. As Chicago mayor Richard M. Daley said in a press conference defending the policy, "We're telling everyone who sets foot in Chicago, if you solicit a prostitute, you will be arrested. And when you are arrested, people will know. Your spouse, children, friends, neighbors, and employers will know." Survey research of Chicago men who have paid for sex suggests that this policy works. Having their photo or name printed in the local paper was rated as the strongest deterrent for buying sex (87 percent of the men interviewed said it would make them think twice). This trumped jail time, having their driver's license suspended, and having to pay a fine of $1,000 or more.*

---

*It's worth noting that half of the men interviewed were not alone the first time they visited a prostitute—they were with friends or relatives. Like obesity, smoking, and other social epidemics, the perception that buying sex is acceptable—and the behavior itself—spreads within social networks like a contagious disease.

THE LIMITS OF SHAME

Before we get too excited about the power of shame, it might be wise to remember a little something called the what-the-hell effect. There is a fine line between the self-control benefits of *anticipating* a negative social emotion like shame, and the willpower-draining effects of actually feeling ashamed. We've seen again and again that feeling bad leads to giving in—especially when feeling bad takes the form of guilt and shame. As a preventive measure, shame may work. But once the deed is done, shame is more likely to inspire self-sabotage than self-control. For example, gamblers who feel the most ashamed following a major loss are the most likely to "chase" the lost money by gambling more and borrowing money to try to recoup their losses.

Even when shame is anticipatory, it may fail us when we need it most. When health-conscious individuals are asked to imagine a chocolate cake in front of them, and then imagine the shame they would feel if they ate it, they are less likely to (hypothetically) eat it. However, when researchers actually placed a large piece of chocolate cake from the Cheesecake Factory on the table, complete with a bottle of water, fork, and napkin, shame had the opposite effect. Only 10 percent resisted the temptation. Anticipatory shame might be able to keep you from walking into the Cheesecake Factory, but when the temptation is in front of you, it has no power over the promise of reward. Once your dopamine neurons are firing, feeling bad intensifies your desire and makes you more likely to give in.

THE POWER OF PRIDE

Pride, on the other hand, pulls through even in the face of temptation. Forty percent of participants who imagined how proud they'd be for resisting the Cheesecake Factory cake didn't take a single bite. One reason pride helped is that it took people's minds off the cake. In contrast, shame paradoxically triggered anticipatory pleasure, and the participants reported more temptation-related thoughts like "It smells so good," and "It will taste great." Another reason boils down to biology: Laboratory studies reveal that guilt decreases heart rate variability, our physiological reserve of willpower. Pride, on the other hand, sustains and even increases this reserve.

For pride to work, we need to believe that others are watching, or that we will have the opportunity to report our success to others. Marketing researchers have found that people are much more likely to buy green products in public than in the privacy of online shopping. Buying green is a way to show others how altruistic and thoughtful we are, and we want the social credit for our high-minded purchases. Without the anticipated status boost, most people will skip the opportunity to save a tree. This research points to a helpful strategy for making resolutions stick: Go public with your willpower challenges. If you believe that others are rooting for your success and keeping an eye on your behavior, you'll be more motivated to do the right thing.

WILLPOWER EXPERIMENT: THE POWER OF PRIDE

Put the basic human need for approval to good use by imagining how proud you will feel when you succeed at your willpower challenge. Bring to mind someone in your tribe—a family member, friend, coworker, teacher—whose opinion matters to you, or who would be happy for your success. When you make a choice you're proud of, share it with your tribe by updating your Facebook status, Tweeting about it, or—for the Luddites among us—sharing the story in person.

THE SHAME OF OWING BACK TAXES

If there's time at the end of lectures, I invite my students to go public with their willpower goals. This can create a little bit of social pressure—many people feel compelled to act on a public announcement, especially if they know I'm going to ask them in front of the whole class how they are doing.

It also provides a form of anticipatory pride, as many students look forward to being able to describe their success in class.

One year, when there were about 150 students in the class, a woman announced her goal to file her back taxes. The following week, I didn't see her, and asked the class, "Where is the woman who was going to file her taxes?" She wasn't there, but *two other* people raised their hands to announce that they had taken the first step on their late taxes. The crazy thing was, neither of them had chosen late taxes as their willpower challenge. The woman's announcement in the previous lecture had inspired them—it was a classic case of goal contagion.

Now, where was the woman who had made the original pledge? I'm not sure, and because it was our last class, I never found out. I can only hope that she was meeting with a tax attorney, and not a casualty of shame. That, of course, is the other side of "should" power: The imagined eyes of others can be motivating, but if we fail, their imagined scorn can discourage us from showing our face in public again.

BEING KICKED OUT OF THE TRIBE

Willpower "failures" like addiction, obesity, and bankruptcy often come with a stigma in our society. We may wrongly assume that a person is weak, lazy, stupid, or selfish, and convince ourselves that they deserve to be shamed or excluded from the tribe. But we should be especially wary of shunning people who do not control their behavior in the way we would like. Besides being a pretty cruel way to treat people, it is a lousy strategy for motivating change. As Deb Lemire, president of the Association for Size Diversity and Health, says, "If shame worked, there'd be no fat people."

Research shows that being kicked out of the tribe drains willpower. For example, after people are socially rejected,* they are less likely to

---

*How do researchers reject study participants? They put a bunch of participants into a "get-acquainted task," then have them rate which people they would like to work with on the next task. The experimenters then tell some participants that no one has expressed an interest in working with them, so they would have to do the task alone. Nice, guys, real nice.

resist the temptation of freshly baked cookies, and they give up sooner on a challenging assignment. They also become more easily distracted during a concentration task. Studies show that the more racial minorities are exposed to prejudice, the less self-control they have—and just reminding minorities of discrimination depletes their willpower. Anytime we feel excluded or disrespected, we are at greater risk for giving in to our worst impulses.

Rather than shame people for their willpower failures, we would do far better by offering social support for willpower successes. One good example is a weight-loss intervention at the University of Pittsburgh that requires people to enroll with a friend or family member. The participants are given "support homework," such as sharing a healthy meal during the week and calling each other to check in and encourage each other. An impressive 66 percent of participants in this program had maintained their weight loss at a ten-month follow-up, compared with only 24 percent of participants in a control group who did not join with friends or family.

WILLPOWER EXPERIMENT: MAKE IT A GROUP PROJECT

You don't have to conquer your willpower challenge alone. Is there a friend, family member, or coworker who could join you in your willpower goals? You don't have to have the same goals; just checking in and encouraging each other can provide a boost of social support to your self-control. If you like your social support with a touch of competition, enlist others in a willpower face-off. Who will be the first to finish a procrastinated task, or the person to save the most money in one month?

E-MAIL CHECK-INS KEEP A GOAL ALIVE

One of my favorite e-mails from a former student came months after our class had ended. She wanted to let me know that an impromptu exercise I threw out in our last class meeting had made all the difference in helping her stick to her goals. In that final class, some students were concerned that once the course was over, they'd lose the motivation to keep up with the changes they had implemented. There is a big social component to the class, and knowing they can share their experiences—even just with the person sitting next to them—motivates many to have something to report.

So at the last class, as some students were getting anxious, I told everyone to exchange e-mail addresses with someone they didn't know. Then I said, "Tell this person what you are going to do in the next week that is consistent with your goals." Their assignment was to e-mail their partner and ask them: Did you do what you said you were going to do?

The student who e-mailed me months later said that the sole thing that kept her going that first week after the class ended was knowing she was going to have to tell this stranger whether or not she had kept her word. But then it turned into a true buddy system of support. They kept the weekly check-ins going for some time, despite the fact that they had no relationship outside of the class. By the time they stopped, the changes were a part of her life, and she no longer needed the extra accountability and support.

THE LAST WORD

To a remarkable degree, our brains incorporate the goals, beliefs, and actions of other people into our decisions. When we are with other people, or simply thinking about them, they become one more "self" in our minds competing for self-control. The flip side is also true: Our own actions influence the actions of countless other people, and each choice we make for ourselves can serve as inspiration or temptation for others.

CHAPTER SUMMARY

The Idea: Self-control is influenced by social proof, making both willpower and temptation contagious.

Under the Microscope

- *Your social network.* Do other people in your social circle share your willpower challenge?
- *Who are you mirroring?* Keep your eyes open for any evidence that you are mirroring other people's behavior.
- *Who are you most likely to catch something from?* Who are your "close others"? Are there any behaviors that you've picked up from them, or that they have caught from you?
- *But Ma, everyone else is doing it!* Do you use social proof to convince yourself that your willpower challenge is no big deal?

Willpower Experiments

- *Strengthen your immune system.* To avoid catching other people's willpower failures, spend a few minutes at the beginning of your day thinking about your goals.
- *Catch self-control.* When you need a little extra willpower, bring a role model to mind. Ask yourself: What would this willpower wonder do?
- *The power of pride.* Go public with your willpower challenges, and imagine how proud you will feel when you succeed at them.
- *Make it a group project.* Can you enlist others in a willpower challenge?

NINE

Don't Read This Chapter: The Limits of "I Won't" Power

The year was 1985, and the scene of the crime was a psychology laboratory at Trinity University, a small liberal arts school in San Antonio, Texas. Seventeen undergraduates were consumed with a thought they couldn't control. They knew it was wrong—they knew they shouldn't be thinking about it. But it was just so damn captivating. Every time they tried to think of something else, the thought bullied its way back into their consciousness. They just couldn't stop thinking about *white bears*.

White bears were hardly a regular concern of these college students, whose minds were more typically preoccupied by sex, exams, and the disappointment of New Coke. But white bears were irresistible to them at that moment—and all because they had been given the instruction "For the next five minutes, please try not to think about white bears."

These students were the first participants in a series of studies by Daniel Wegner, who is now a psychology professor at Harvard University. Early in his career, Wegner had come across a story about Russian novelist Leo Tolstoy. A young Tolstoy had been told by his older brother to sit in a corner until he could stop thinking about a white bear. His brother returned much later to discover Tolstoy still in the corner, paralyzed by his inability to stop thinking about a white bear. Wegner soon found that he couldn't get this story, and the question it raised, out of his mind: Why can't we control our thoughts?

Wegner set up a study nearly identical to Tolstoy's childhood test of mental control, asking participants to think about anything they wanted, except for a white bear. The following partial transcript from one woman thinking aloud reveals how difficult this was for most people:

> I'm trying to think of a million things to make me think about everything but a white bear and I keep thinking of it over and over and over. So . . . ummm, hey, look at this brown wall. It's like, every time I try and not think about a white bear, I'm still thinking about one.

This went on, with little variation, for fifteen minutes.

The inability to stop thinking about white bears might not strike you as the worst willpower failure in the world. But as we'll see, the problem with prohibition extends to any thought we try to ban. The latest research on anxiety, depression, dieting, and addiction all confirm: "I won't" power fails miserably when it's applied to the inner world of thoughts and feelings. As we enter that inner world, we will find we need a new definition of self-control—one that makes room for letting go of control.

ISN'T IT IRONIC

Wegner repeated his white bear thought experiment with other students, and when they too became obsessed with bears, he prohibited other thoughts. Each time, the mere act of trying not to think about something triggered a paradoxical effect: People thought about it more than when they weren't trying to control their thoughts, and even more than when they were intentionally trying to think about it. The effect was strongest when people were already stressed out, tired, or distracted. Wegner dubbed this effect *ironic rebound*. You push a thought away, and—BAM!—it boomerangs back.*

Ironic rebound explains many modern frustrations: the insomniac who finds herself more wide-awake the harder she tries to fall asleep; the dieter who banishes carbohydrates, only to find himself dreaming about Wonder bread and whoopie pies; the worrier who tries to block out her anxiety but gets drawn again and again into disaster fantasies. Wegner has even shown that suppressing thoughts about a crush while you are awake increases the likelihood of dreaming about them—more than *intentionally* fantasizing about the dreamboat does. This, no doubt, contributes to the Romeo and Juliet effect—the well-known psychological tendency to fall deeper in desire whenever a romance is forbidden.

Wegner has found evidence for ironic effects of attempting to suppress just about any instinct you can imagine. The job candidate who wants so badly to make a good impression is most likely to blurt out the very thing that makes the interviewer cringe. The speaker trying to be politically correct paradoxically activates every offensive stereotype in his mind. The person who most wants to keep a secret finds herself compelled to spill the beans. The waiter who tries the hardest to not tip his tray is most likely to end up with marinara sauce on his shirt. Wegner even (somewhat charitably) credits ironic effects for the scientific finding that the most homophobic men get the largest erections while watching gay porn.

WHY THOUGHT SUPPRESSION DOESN'T WORK

Why does trying to eliminate a thought or emotion trigger a rebound? Wegner's hunch is that it has something to do with how the brain handles

---

*When I told my father about this research, he instantly agreed with its conclusion and shared his own unscientific evidence: "When I was living in the Catholic seminary, they warned us to never, ever think about sex. So we were constantly telling each other not to think about sex. Of course, we ended up thinking about sex all the time, more than we ever would have outside the seminary." Maybe this explains why he never became a priest.

the command *not to* think about something. It splits the task into two parts, achieved by two different systems of the brain. One part of your mind will take on the job of directing your attention toward anything other than the forbidden thought. It's like the woman in Wegner's first study trying not to think of the white bear—"I'm trying to think of a million things to make me think about everything but a white bear . . . hey, look at this brown wall." Wegner calls this process the *operator*. The operator relies on the brain's system of self-control and—like all forms of effortful self-control—requires a good deal of mental resources and energy. Another part of your mind takes on the job of looking for any evidence that you are thinking, feeling, or doing whatever you don't want to think, feel, or do. It's like the young woman observing, "I keep thinking of it over and over and over . . . every time I try and not think about a white bear, I'm still thinking about one." Wegner calls this process the *monitor*. Unlike the operator, the monitor runs automatically and without much mental effort. The monitor is more closely related to the brain's automatic threat-detection system. This can sound good—automatic self-control!—until you realize how critical the cooperation is between operator and monitor. If, for any reason, the operator runs out of steam, the monitor is going to become a self-control nightmare.

Under ordinary circumstances, the operator and the monitor work in parallel. Let's say you're headed to the grocery store, and you've decided that you *will not* be tempted by the snack food aisle. While the operator is trying to focus, plan, and control your behavior ("I'm here at the grocery store to pick up cereal, nothing else. Where's the cereal aisle?"), the monitor is scanning your mind and your environment for warning signs. ("Danger! Danger! Cookies on aisle three! You love cookies! Is that your stomach growling? Alert! Alert! Beware of the cookies! *Cookies cookies cookies!*") If your mental resources are high, the operator can make good use of the monitor's hysteria. When the monitor points out possible temptations or troubling thoughts, the operator steps in to steer you toward your goals and out of trouble. But if your mental resources are taxed—whether by distractions, fatigue, stress, alcohol, illness, or other mental drains—the operator cannot do its job. The monitor, on the other hand, is like the Energizer Bunny. It keeps going and going and going.

A tired operator and an energized monitor create a problematic imbalance in the mind. As the monitor searches for forbidden content, it continuously brings to mind what it is searching for. Neuroscientists have shown that the brain is constantly processing the forbidden content just outside of conscious awareness. The result: You become primed to think, feel, or do whatever you are trying to avoid. So as soon as you pass the snack aisle in the grocery store, the monitor will remember the goal *not* to buy cookies, and fill your mind with *Cookies cookies cookies!* Without the operator's full strength to balance the monitor, it's like a Shakespearean tragedy in your very own brain. By trying to prevent your downfall, the monitor leads you straight to it.

IF I THINK IT, IT MUST BE TRUE

Trying not to think about something guarantees that it is never far from your mind. This leads to a second problem: When you try to push a thought away, and it keeps coming back to your mind, *you are more likely to assume that it must be true*. Why else would the thought keep resurfacing? We trust that our thoughts are important sources of information. When a thought becomes more frequent and harder to pull yourself away from, you will naturally assume that it is an urgent message that you should pay attention to.

This cognitive bias seems to be hardwired in the human brain. We estimate how likely or true something is by the ease with which we can bring it to mind. This can have unsettling consequences when we try to push a worry or desire out of our minds. For example, because it's easy to remember news stories about plane crashes (especially if you are a fearful flier handing over your boarding pass), we tend to overestimate the likelihood of being in a crash. The risk is actually about one in fourteen million, but most people believe the risk is higher than of dying from nephritis or septicemia—two of the top ten causes of death in the United States, but not diseases that easily pop into our minds.

Whatever fear or desire you try to push away will become more convincing and compelling. Wegner, the psychologist who discovered ironic rebound, once received a phone call from a distraught student who couldn't stop thinking about killing herself. A fleeting thought had gotten lodged in her brain, and she had become convinced that she must really, deep down, want to kill herself. Otherwise, why would the idea keep intruding into her thoughts? She called Wegner—perhaps the only psychologist she knew—for help. Now keep in mind, Wegner is a scientific psychologist, not a psychotherapist. He isn't trained to talk people off ledges or muddle around in the dark corners of other people's minds. So he talked to the student about what he knew: white bears. He told her about his experiments, and explained that the more you try to push away a thought, the more likely it is to fight its way back into consciousness. This doesn't mean the thought is true or important. The student was relieved to realize that how she reacted to the thought of suicide had strengthened it—but this did not mean she really wanted to kill herself.

For you, it might be the thought that a loved one has been in a car accident. Or the thought that a pint of Karamel Sutra ice cream is the only thing that will soothe your stress. If you panic and push the thought out of your mind, it is going to come back. And when it does, it will return with more authority. Because you are trying *not* to think about it, its reappearance seems even more meaningful. As a result, you're more likely to believe it is true. The worrier becomes more worried, and the ice-cream craver pulls out her spoon.

UNDER THE MICROSCOPE: INVESTIGATING IRONIC REBOUND

Is there something you try to keep out of your mind? If so, examine the theory of ironic rebound. Does suppression work? Or does trying to push something out of your mind make it come back stronger? (Yes, you are going to give the monitor the job of monitoring the monitor.)

Avoiding Ironic Rebound

How can you find your way out of this confounding dilemma? Wegner suggests an antidote to ironic rebound that is, itself, ironic: Give up. When you stop trying to control unwanted thoughts and emotions, they stop controlling you. Studies of brain activation confirm that as soon as you give participants permission to express a thought they were trying to suppress, that thought becomes less primed and less likely to intrude into conscious awareness. Paradoxically, permission to think a thought reduces the likelihood of thinking it.

This solution turns out to be useful for a surprisingly wide range of unwanted inner experiences. The willingness to think what you think and feel what you feel—without necessarily believing that it is true, and without feeling compelled to act on it—is an effective strategy for treating anxiety, depression, food cravings, and addiction. As we consider the evidence for each, we'll see that giving up control of our inner experiences gives us greater control over our outer actions.

I DON'T WANT TO FEEL THIS WAY

Can trying not to think sad thoughts make people depressed? It's not as far-fetched as it sounds. Studies show that the more you try to suppress negative thoughts, the more likely you are to become depressed. The more depressed people try to block out distressing thoughts, the more depressed they get. One of Wegner's first thought-suppression experiments showed this effect even in perfectly healthy subjects. He asked people to either think about the worst things that have happened to them, or to *not* think about those things. When people are stressed out or distracted, trying not to think sad thoughts makes them even sadder than when they are *trying* to feel sad. Another experiment found that when people try to push away self-critical thoughts ("I'm such a loser," "People think I'm stupid"), their self-esteem and mood plummet faster than when people openly contemplate such thoughts. This is true *even when people think they have succeeded at pushing the negative thoughts away*. Ironic rebound strikes again!

Trying to suppress anxiety also backfires. For example, people who try not to think about a painful medical procedure end up feeling more anxious and have more intrusive thoughts about the pain. People who try to suppress their fear before giving a public speech not only feel more anxious, but also have higher heart rates (and are therefore more likely to blow the big talk). We may try to push thoughts out of our minds, but the body gets the message anyway. And just as trying to suppress sad and self-critical thoughts makes depression worse, studies show that thought suppression increases the symptoms of serious anxiety disorders such as post-traumatic stress disorder and obsessive-compulsive disorder.

These findings can be hard to wrap our heads around. They go against every instinct we have to protect our minds from disturbing thoughts. What are we supposed to do with harmful thoughts if not get rid of them? But as we'll see, if we want to save ourselves from mental suffering, we need to make peace with those thoughts, not push them away.

THERE'S SOMETHING WRONG WITH ME

Philippe Goldin is one of the most outgoing neuroscientists you'll ever meet. This is not to say that brain geeks aren't a friendly bunch, but most don't offer bear hugs to whoever wanders into the lab. Goldin directs the Clinically Applied Affective Neuroscience Laboratory at Stanford University, which is a fancy way of saying that he uses what he knows about the brain to help people who suffer from depression and anxiety—social anxiety in particular. He's the last guy in the world you'd think would be interested in social anxiety disorder, a crippling form of shyness, but he's made a career trying to understand and treat the disorder.

The people who enroll in his studies are not just a little bit nervous in social situations. The mere thought of speaking to strangers can provoke a panic attack. You know that nightmare when you realize you are naked, and everyone is pointing and laughing at you? People with social anxiety disorder feel like they are living that nightmare 24/7. They have a constant fear of embarrassing themselves or being judged by others, and they are usually their own worst critics. They often suffer from depression. Most avoid any situation—from parties to crowds to speaking in public—that triggers their anxiety and self-doubt. As a result, their lives get smaller and smaller, and even things that most people take for granted—meetings at work, making a phone call—can become overwhelming.

Goldin studies what happens in anxiety sufferers' brains when they worry. He has found that people with social anxiety are worse at controlling their thoughts than the average person, and it shows in their brains. When confronted with a worry—say, imagining themselves being criticized—the stress center overreacts. When Goldin asks them to change what they're thinking, the system of attention control is underactivated. Borrowing from Wegner's theory of thought control, it's as if their "operator" is exhausted and cannot point their minds away from the worry. This would explain why people with anxiety disorders are so consumed by their fears—their attempts to push the thoughts away are especially ineffective.

Traditional therapy for social anxiety disorder focuses on challenging thoughts like "There's something wrong with me" to get rid of the anxiety. This only makes sense if you believe that trying *not* to think something works. Goldin takes a very different approach. He teaches social anxiety sufferers to observe and accept their thoughts and feelings—even the scary ones. The goal is not to get rid of the anxiety and self-doubt, but to develop a trust that they can handle these difficult thoughts and feelings. If they learn that there is no *inner* experience that they need to protect themselves from, they can find more freedom in the outer world. When a worry comes up, he instructs the anxiety sufferers to notice what they are thinking, feel the anxiety in their body, and then turn their attention to their breathing. If the anxiety persists, he encourages them to imagine their thoughts and emotions dissolving with the breath. He teaches them that if they don't fight the anxiety, it will naturally run its course.

Because Goldin is a neuroscientist, he's especially interested in how this approach might change the brain. Before and after the intervention, he puts the anxiety sufferers in an fMRI machine to watch their brains at work while they worry. These brain-scanning sessions could provoke anxiety and claustrophobia in even the calmest of people. His subjects are forced to lie immobilized on their backs, their heads trapped in the brain scanner. They have to clamp their mouths on dental wax to prevent them from moving their heads or talking. The machine around their heads makes a regular clanging sound that is best compared to a jackhammer. As if that's not bad enough, they are then asked to reflect on different statements about themselves that appear on a screen in front of their face: "I'm not OK the way I am." "People think I'm weird." "Something's wrong with me."

While the social anxiety sufferers are thinking about these statements, Goldin watches the activity in two regions of the brain: a network associated with reading comprehension, which would reveal how deeply a person was contemplating each statement, and the stress center, which would reveal how much that person was panicking.

When he compared each person's brain scan from before and after the training, he found an intriguing change. After the intervention, there was much more activity in the brain network associated with visual information processing. The social anxiety sufferers were paying *more* attention to the self-critical statements than they had before the training. Now, to most people, this would sound like a complete failure.

Except for one thing: There was also a major decrease in the stress center's activity. Even as the anxiety sufferers gave the negative thoughts their full attention, they were less upset by them. This change in the brain came with big benefits in everyday life. After the intervention, the anxiety sufferers felt less anxious overall, and they were spending less time criticizing themselves and worrying. When they stopped fighting their thoughts and emotions, they found more freedom from them.

WILLPOWER EXPERIMENT: FEEL WHAT YOU FEEL, BUT DON'T BELIEVE EVERYTHING YOU THINK

When an upsetting thought comes to mind, try the technique that Goldin teaches his subjects. Instead of instantly trying to distract yourself from it, let yourself notice the thought. Oftentimes, our most disturbing thoughts are familiar—the same worry, the same self-criticism, the same memory. "What if something goes wrong?" "I can't believe I did that. I'm so stupid." "If only that hadn't happened. What could I have done differently?" These thoughts pop up like a song that gets stuck in our heads, seemingly out of nowhere, but then is impossible to get rid of. Let yourself notice whether the upsetting thought is an old, familiar tune—that's your first clue that it is *not* critically important information you need to believe. Then shift your attention to what you are feeling in your body. Notice if there is any tension present, or changes to your heart rate or breathing. Notice if you feel it in your gut, your chest, your throat, or anywhere else in your body. Once you've observed the thought and feelings, shift your attention to your breathing. Notice how it feels to breathe in and breathe out. Sometimes the upsetting thought and feelings naturally dissipate when you do this. Other times, they will keep interrupting your attention to your breath. If this happens, imagine the thought and feelings like clouds passing through your mind and body. Keep breathing, and imagine the clouds dissolving or floating by. Imagine your breath as a wind that dissolves and moves the clouds effortlessly. You don't need to make the thought go away; just stay with the feeling of your breath.

Notice that this technique is not the same thing as believing or ruminating over a thought. The opposite of thought suppression is accepting the presence of the thought—not believing it. You're accepting that thoughts come and go, and that you can't always control what thoughts come to mind. You don't have to automatically accept the *content* of the thought. In other words, you might say to yourself, "Oh well, there's that thought again—worries happen. That's just the way the mind works, and it doesn't necessarily mean anything." You're not saying to yourself, "Oh well, I guess it's true. I am a terrible person and terrible things are going to happen to me, and I guess I need to accept it."

This same practice can be used for any distracting thought or upsetting emotion, including anger, jealousy, anxiety, or shame.

After trying this technique a few times, compare it with the results you get from trying to push away upsetting thoughts and emotions. Which is more effective at giving you peace of mind?

A Daughter Makes Peace with Her Anger

Valerie was exhausted from the events of the past year. Her mother had been diagnosed with early-stage Alzheimer's disease several years earlier, but things had gotten worse. Her mother's memory loss had accelerated, and she was no longer capable of being home by herself while Valerie worked. Valerie and her family had made the decision to have her mother moved into a long-term care facility. Although the medical team was always available, Valerie still felt responsible for visiting her mother every day and overseeing her medical care. Her other siblings didn't live as close to the facility, and her father had passed, so she was left in charge.

The whole situation made Valerie angry. Angry that she was losing her mother to the disease, and angry that she had to deal with this on her own. Even the visits were frustrating, as her mom's personality and memory were becoming unpredictable. On top of all that, she felt guilty for feeling angry. To deal with her exhaustion, anger, and guilt, she had been taking comfort in a daily stop at the grocery store on the way home from the long-term care facility. She loaded up on cupcakes, doughnuts, or whatever looked good in the bakery case, and ate them in her car in the parking lot. She had been telling herself it was the least she deserved for what she was going through, but really she was trying to drown her feelings before going home.

Valerie was afraid that if she didn't try to push away her feelings at the end of each visit, she would be completely overcome by them. If she let herself see the emotions, she might not be able to pull herself out of them. And yet they already were overwhelming her. So Valerie started to practice the breathing and cloud imagery after each visit with her mother, on a bench outside the facility. She let herself feel the heaviness and thickness of guilt, and the tightness of anger. Then she imagined her breath as a wind that could blow through these dark clouds. She imagined the feelings becoming less dense, less suffocating. As the guilt and anger dissolved, grief often came up—a feeling that did not go away with breathing. But Valerie found that when she allowed herself to feel the grief, she did not actually want to push it away. There was room for it.

In time, the grocery-store ritual lost its appeal and was replaced with a moment-by-moment willingness to feel whatever came up throughout the day. Valerie was even able to bring that same willingness to her visits with her mother, letting herself feel her frustration instead of telling herself she wasn't allowed to be angry at her mother. It didn't change the situation, but it took away some of the stress. When she wasn't trying to get rid of her feelings, she was better able to take care of both her mother and herself.

> *Trying to avoid unwanted feelings often leads to self-destructive behavior, whether it's a procrastinator trying to avoid anxiety, or a drinker trying to avoid feeling alone. For your willpower challenge, see if there is a feeling you are trying not to feel. What would happen if you gave yourself permission to feel it, using the breath and cloud imagery?*

DON'T EAT THE APPLE

James Erskine, a psychologist at St. George's University of London, is fascinated by Wegner's research on white bears. But he believes that thought suppression doesn't just make it more likely that we'll *think* something—it makes us compelled to *do* the very thing we're trying not to think of. He's long marveled at people's tendency to do the exact opposite of what they want to do (himself included, though this intrepid writer was unable to pry any details out of Erskine). His favorite author is Dostoyevsky, whose characters routinely vow not to do something, only to find themselves moments later doing that very thing. Of course, Dostoyevsky's characters are more likely to be conflicted over the urge to kill than the desire for dessert. Nevertheless, Erskine suspects that the process of ironic rebound is behind all of our self-sabotaging behavior, from breaking a diet to smoking, drinking, gambling, and having sex (presumably, with someone you're not supposed to be swapping DNA with).

Erskine first demonstrated how dangerous thought suppression is to self-control with one of the world's most craved substances: chocolate. (To appreciate the near universality of chocolate cravings, consider this: For a study designed to examine the differences between people who crave chocolate and people who don't, it took researchers a year just to find eleven men who didn't like chocolate.) Erskine invited women into his laboratory for a taste test of two similar chocolate candies.* Before the chocolate was brought in, he asked the women to think out loud for five minutes. He told some women to express any thoughts of chocolate, and others to suppress any thoughts of chocolate. (A third of the women were given no special thought-control instructions, for comparison.)

At first, thought suppression appeared to work. Women who tried not to think about chocolate reported fewer thoughts about chocolate—in one study, they had an average of only nine thoughts, compared with fifty-two by the women who were told to express any thoughts about chocolate. But anyone rooting for suppression should not get their hopes up. The real measure of success is the taste test.

The experimenter then presented each woman with two bowls con-

---

*Candy connoisseurs may be interested in knowing that Erskine uses Maltesers, spheres of malt honeycomb surrounded by milk chocolate; Cadburys Shots, spheres of milk chocolate in a crispy sugar shell; and Galaxy Minstrels, a similar chocolate treat marketed by its manufacturers as "sophisticated silliness."

taining twenty individually wrapped chocolates. They were left alone in the room with a survey about the chocolates, and invited to eat as many chocolates as necessary to answer the questions. In each study, the results were the same: Women ate almost twice as many chocolates if they tried not to think about chocolate before the taste test. Dieters showed the biggest rebound of all, revealing that the people most likely to use thought suppression as a defense strategy against temptation are the most vulnerable to its unwanted effects. A 2010 survey found that dieters are much more likely than nondieters to try to suppress thoughts about food. And— as Wegner's white bears would predict—dieters who suppress thoughts about food have the *least* control around food. They experience more intense food cravings and are more likely to binge-eat than those who do not try to control their thoughts.

The Problem with Dieting

Although dieting is a long-standing American pastime, as a method of losing weight, it stinks. A 2007 review of all research on food-restriction or calorie-restriction diets declared that there is little to no evidence for weight loss or health benefits of dieting, and growing evidence that dieting does harm. The vast majority of dieters not only regain the weight they lose while dieting, but gain more. In fact, dieting is a better way to *gain* weight than to lose it. People who go on diets gain more weight over time than people who start at the same weight but never diet. Several long-term studies have found that yo-yo dieting raises blood pressure and unhealthy cholesterol levels, suppresses the immune system, and increases the risk of heart attack, stroke, diabetes, and all-cause mortality. (And, if you recall, dieting also increases your chances of cheating on your spouse—though you won't see any of these side effects listed on your Jenny Craig contract.)

Many researchers—like Erskine—have come to the conclusion that what makes dieting so ineffective is the very thing people expect to be most effective: outlawing fattening foods. From the very first forbidden fruit, prohibition has led to problems, and science is now confirming that restricting a food automatically increases your cravings for it. For example, women asked to not eat chocolate for one week experience a surge in chocolate cravings and eat twice as much chocolate ice cream, cookies, and cake during a taste test as women who had not been depriving themselves. This doesn't happen because the brain and body suddenly realize they cannot function without the exact amino acids and micronutrients in chocolate-chip cookie dough ice cream. (If cravings really worked this way, millions of Americans would have the overwhelming desire for fresh fruits and vegetables.) No, the rebound is more psychological than physiological. The more you try to avoid the food, the more your mind will be preoccupied by it.

Erskine points out that many dieters are fooled into thinking thought suppression works because they often feel successful—at least initially—at getting rid of their food thoughts. It's not just dieters who can convince themselves that suppression works; we're all susceptible to this illusion. Because it is possible to temporarily push away a thought, we assume that the strategy is itself fundamentally sound. Our eventual failure to control our thoughts and behavior is interpreted as evidence that we didn't try hard enough to suppress—not that suppression doesn't work. This leads us to try harder, setting ourselves up for an even stronger rebound.

UNDER THE MICROSCOPE: WHAT'S ON YOUR MOST-WANTED LIST?

The science suggests that when we outlaw a food, we increase desire. Is this true in your experience? Have you ever tried to lose weight by cutting out a food group or favorite snack? If so, how long did that last—and how did it end? Is there anything on your do-not-eat list right now? If so, how has outlawing it influenced your cravings for it? If you don't diet, is there anything you're prohibiting? Has it killed your desire, or fed it?

The Power of Acceptance

What are we to do with our thoughts and cravings if not push them away? Maybe we should embrace them. That's the conclusion of a study that gave one hundred students transparent boxes of Hershey's Kisses to keep with them at all times for forty-eight hours. Their challenge: Don't eat a single Kiss, or any other chocolate. (To be sure there were no cheaters, the experimenters subtly marked each Kiss so they would know if anyone tried to replace eaten Kisses.) The experimenters didn't send the students off defenseless; they gave them advice on how to handle their temptation. Some students were told to distract themselves whenever they wanted to eat a Kiss. They were also told to argue with thoughts of eating. For example, if they had the thought, *Those chocolates look so good. I'll eat just one!* they should try to replace it with the thought, *You are not allowed to eat the chocolates, and you don't need one.* In other words, these students were told to do exactly what most of us do when we want to control our appetites.

Other students got a lesson in the white-bear phenomenon. Experimenters explained ironic rebound and encouraged the students not to push away thoughts about eating chocolate. Instead, they should notice when they were craving chocolate, accept whatever thoughts or feelings they had about the chocolate, *but also remember that they didn't have to act on those thoughts and feelings.* While not controlling their thoughts, they still had to control their behavior.

Over the forty-eight-hour test of their willpower, the students who gave up thought control had the fewest cravings for chocolate. Interestingly, the students who were helped the most by the acceptance strategy were those who ordinarily had the least self-control around food. When students who typically struggled the most with food cravings tried to distract or argue with themselves, it was a disaster. But when they let go of thought suppression, they were less tempted by the Kisses and less stressed out about having to carry around chocolate they couldn't eat. Most incredibly, not a single student using the acceptance strategy ate a Kiss, despite staring at the promise of reward for two days straight.

WILLPOWER EXPERIMENT: ACCEPT THOSE CRAVINGS—JUST DON'T ACT ON THEM

In the Hershey's Kisses study, students who learned about the white-bear rebound effect were given the following four-step advice for handling their cravings. This week, try applying this advice to your own most challenging cravings, be they chocolate, cappuccinos, or checking e-mail.

1. Notice that you are thinking about your temptation or feeling a craving.
2. Accept the thought or feeling without trying to immediately distract yourself or argue with it. Remind yourself of the white-bear rebound effect.
3. Step back by realizing that thoughts and feelings aren't always under your control, but you can choose whether to act on them.
4. Remember your goal. Remind yourself of whatever your commitment is, as the students reminded themselves of their agreement not to eat the Hershey's Kisses.

A CHOCOHOLIC TAKES INSPIRATION FROM HERSHEY'S KISSES

Caroline was grateful to have a strategy against constant exposure to chocolate. In her office, it was common custom to have a candy bowl on your desk. Caroline didn't keep one on her desk, but she couldn't visit anyone else without facing temptation. It was a constant source of stress—would she or wouldn't she? If she took one piece, would she find some pretense to sneak back for another? It had gotten to the point where she would e-mail or call a coworker who was less than fifty feet away, just to avoid a fully stocked bowl of temptation. The week after we discussed the Hershey's Kiss study, I got an excited e-mail from Caroline. She told me that just thinking about the study had given her newfound self-control. She could look right at the chocolates on a coworker's desk, even lean down and inhale the scent, and not give in. Her coworkers would pop another piece of candy and sigh about how little willpower they had. In contrast, Caroline couldn't believe how much willpower she had. She didn't know if it was accepting her cravings, or just thinking about those students carrying around their boxes of Hershey's Kisses, that was boosting her willpower—but either way, she was thrilled.

> *Students often tell me that bringing a specific study to mind—even imagining the participants in the study—gives them greater self-control. If a study stands out to you, bring it to mind in tempting situations.*

THE NO-DIETING DIET

Is it even possible to lose weight or improve your health if you don't outlaw fattening foods? A new approach suggests that it is—and I'm not talking about some miracle pill that claims to help you burn fat and lift weights in your sleep. Researchers at Laval University in Quebec have been studying a unique intervention that focuses on what participants *should* eat. The program doesn't hand out a list of forbidden foods, and it doesn't focus on cutting calories. Instead, it emphasizes how foods can create health and provide pleasure. It also asks participants to think about what they *can* do to improve their health—like exercise—instead of thinking in terms of what they shouldn't do or eat.

In essence, the program turns an "I won't" power challenge into an "I will" power challenge. Instead of waging war against their appetites, they make it their mission to pursue health.

Studies of this approach show that turning "I won't" into "I will" works. Two-thirds of the participants who have been followed lost weight and maintained that loss at a sixteen-month follow-up. (Compare that with the results of your most recent diet; I believe it takes the average dieter sixteen *days* to be back where he or she started.) They also report fewer food cravings after completing the program, and are less likely to lose control around food in situations—like stress and celebration—that typically trigger overeating. Importantly, the women who developed the most flexible attitudes toward food lost the most weight. Ending prohibition gave them more, not less, control over what they ate.

WILLPOWER EXPERIMENT: TURN YOUR "I WON'T" INTO "I WILL"

Even nondieters can take a lesson from the success of turning an "I won't" challenge into an "I will" challenge. For your biggest "I won't" power challenge, try one of the following strategies for flipping your focus:

- *What could you do instead of the "I won't" behavior that might satisfy the same needs?* Most bad habits are an attempt to meet a need, whether it's reducing stress, having fun, or seeking approval. You can get the focus off of prohibiting your bad habit by replacing it with a new (hopefully, healthier) habit. One of my students was trying to quit coffee and turned to tea as a substitute. It had all the same benefits—being a good excuse for a break, giving him more energy, easy to get anywhere—without as much caffeine.
- *If you weren't doing the bad habit, what might you be doing instead?* Most of our addictions and distractions take time and energy away from something else we could be doing. Sometimes focusing on that missed opportunity is more motivating than trying to quit the bad habit. One of my students felt like she was wasting her time getting sucked into reality television shows. She had more success at turning off the TV when she set a goal for what she should use the time for instead—learning to be a better cook. (She started by substituting cooking shows for the shows she had been watching—a good first step—then transitioned from couch to kitchen.)
- *Can you redefine the "I won't" challenge so that it becomes an "I will" challenge?* Sometimes the very same behavior can be thought of in two different ways. For example, one of my students redefined "not being late" as "being the first person there" or "arriving five minutes early." This may not sound like much of a difference, but he found himself far more motivated—and less likely to be late—when he turned being on time

into a race he could win. If you focus on what you want to do, instead of what you don't want to do, you sidestep the dangers of ironic rebound.

If you take on this experiment, commit to spending this week focusing on positive action rather than prohibition. At the end of the week, consider how well you did with both the original "I won't" challenge and the new "I will" challenge.

NO SMOKING, PLEASE

Sarah Bowen, a research scientist in the Addictive Behaviors Research Center at the University of Washington, had thought very carefully about how to best set up her torture chamber. She chose a basic conference room with a long table that could seat twelve people. She covered the windows and took everything off the walls so there would be nothing to distract her subjects.

One by one, they arrived. At her request, each carried an unopened pack of his or her favorite brand of cigarettes. All of them wanted to quit smoking, but hadn't quit yet. Bowen had asked the smokers to abstain for at least twelve hours to make sure they showed up in a nicotine-deprived state. She knew they were eager to light one and inhale, but they had to wait until everyone arrived.

When the smokers were all there, Bowen seated them around the table. Each chair faced the outer walls so the smokers could not see one another. She told them to put away any books, phones, food, or drinks, and gave them each a pencil and paper to answer questions. They were not to speak to one another, no matter what happened. Then the torture began.

"Take out your pack and look at it," Bowen instructed. They did. "Now pack it," she said, referring to the smoker's ritual of pounding the pack to settle the tobacco in each cigarette. "Now remove the cellophane," she commanded. "Now open the pack." She continued walking the smokers through each step, from breathing in the first smell of the opened pack to pulling out a cigarette, holding it, looking at it, and smelling it. Putting the cigarette in their mouths. Taking out a lighter. Bringing the lighter to the cigarette without igniting it. At each step, she forced participants to stop and wait for several minutes. "People were not having a good time," Bowen told me. "I could literally see their craving. They were doing anything to distract themselves: playing with the pencils, looking around, fidgeting." Bowen wasn't enjoying the smokers' agony, but she needed to be sure they were suffering the kind of intense craving that can derail attempts to quit. Bowen's real aim was to investigate whether mindfulness can help smokers resist cravings.

Before the torture test, half of the smokers had received a brief training in a technique called "surfing the urge." They were instructed to pay close attention to the urge to smoke, without trying to change it or get rid of it—an approach that we've seen can be quite helpful for dealing with worries and food cravings. Instead of distracting themselves from the urge or hoping that it would just go away, they should really get a good look at it. What thoughts were going through their mind? What did the urge feel like in the body? Was there nausea, or a gnawing in their stomach? Did they feel tension in their lungs or throat? Bowen explained to the smokers that urges always pass eventually, whether or not you give in to them. When they felt a strong craving, they should imagine the urge as a wave in the ocean. It would build in intensity, but ultimately crash and dissolve. The smokers were to picture themselves riding the wave, not fighting it but also not giving in to it. Bowen then asked these smokers to apply the surfing-the-urge technique during the craving induction.

An hour and a half later, after being fully put through the wringer, all of the smokers were released from Bowen's torture chamber. She didn't ask them to cut back on cigarettes, and she didn't even encourage them to use the surfing-the-urge technique in everyday life. But Bowen did give them one last task: Keep track of how many cigarettes they smoked each day for the following week, along with their daily mood and the intensity of urges to smoke.

For the first twenty-four hours, there was no difference in the number of cigarettes smoked by the two groups. But starting with the second day, and continuing throughout the week, the surfing-the-urge group smoked fewer cigarettes. By day seven, the control group showed no change, but those surfing the urge had cut back 37 percent. Giving their cravings their full attention helped them take positive steps toward quitting smoking. Bowen also looked at the relationship between the smokers' moods and their urges to smoke. Surprisingly, smokers who had learned to surf the urge no longer showed the typical correlation between feeling bad and giving in. Stress no longer automatically led to lighting up. This is one of the best side effects of surfing the urge: You learn how to accept and handle all your difficult inner experiences, and no longer need to turn to unhealthy rewards for comfort.

Although this smoking study was a scientific experiment, not a full-blown intervention, Bowen also leads longer programs for people in residential substance-abuse programs. ("We do imagery instead of actual exposure to the triggers," she told me. "For many reasons, we can't bring in crack pipes.") Bowen's most recent study randomly assigned 168 men and women to either treatment as usual for substance-abuse recovery or to a mindfulness program that taught them surfing the urge and other strategies for handling stress and urges. Over a four-month follow-up, the mindfulness group had fewer cravings and was less likely to relapse than the treatment-as-usual group. Once again, the training disrupted the automatic link between feeling bad and wanting to use. For the people who learned to surf the urge, stress no longer increased the risk of relapse.

WILLPOWER EXPERIMENT: SURF THE URGE

Whatever your drug of choice, surfing the urge can help you ride out cravings without giving in. When the urge takes hold, pause for a moment to sense your body. What does the urge feel like? Is it hot or cold? Do you feel tension anywhere in your body? What's happening with your heart rate, your breathing, or your gut? Stay with the sensations for at least one minute. Notice whether the feelings fluctuate in intensity or quality. Not acting on an urge can sometimes increase its intensity—like an attention-seeking child throwing a temper tantrum. See if you can stay with these sensations without trying to push them away, and without acting on them. As you practice surfing the urge, the breath can be a wonderful source of support. You can surf the sensations of breathing—noticing how it feels to inhale and exhale—alongside the sensations of the urge.

When you first practice this strategy, you may surf the urge *and still give in*. In Bowen's smoking study, everybody smoked as soon as they left the torture chamber. Don't use your first few attempts as a final verdict on the value of this approach. Surfing the urge is a skill that builds with time, like any new form of self-control. Want to practice the skill before a craving hits? You can get a good sense of the technique just by sitting still and waiting for the urge to scratch your nose, cross your legs, or shift your weight. Apply the same principles of surfing the urge to this impulse—feel it, but don't automatically give in.

SURFING THE URGE TO COMPLAIN

Therese knew that her habit of constantly criticizing her husband was putting a strain on their relationship. They had been married for five years, but the last year had been especially tense. They argued frequently about how things should be done around the house and how to discipline their four-year-old son. Therese couldn't help but feel that her husband was going out of his way to irritate her by doing things the wrong way. In turn, he was tired of always being corrected and never being thanked. Even though Therese wanted him to change his behavior, she realized that it was her behavior that was threatening their marriage.

She decided to try surfing the urge to criticize. When she felt the impulse rising, she paused and felt the tension in her body. It was strongest in her jaw, face, and chest. She watched the sensations of irritation and frustration. They felt like heat and pressure building. It was as if she had to say the criticism to get it out of her system, like a volcano that needed to erupt. She had been acting on the belief that she had to get the complaint out of her, that she had to express it or it would fester inside her. Therese tested the idea that, like cravings, the impulse would actually pass on its own even if she didn't act on it. When Therese surfed the urge, she let herself say the complaint internally. Sometimes she saw it as ridiculous, and sometimes it felt really true. Either way, she let it be in her mind without arguing and without expressing it. Then she imagined her irritation as a wave and rode out the feelings. She found that the impulse would subside if she breathed and stayed with the feeling in her body.

> *Surfing the urge is not just for addiction; it can help you handle any destructive impulse.*

INNER ACCEPTANCE, OUTER CONTROL

As you begin to experiment with the power of acceptance, it's important to remember that the opposite of suppression is not self-indulgence. All of the successful interventions we've seen in this chapter—accepting anxiety and cravings, ending restrictive dieting, and surfing the urge—teach people to give up a rigid attempt to control their *inner* experiences. They don't encourage people to believe their most upsetting thoughts or lose control of their behavior. Nobody's telling socially anxious people to stay home worrying, or encouraging dieters to eat junk food for breakfast, lunch, and dinner, or telling recovering addicts, "Get high if you want to!"

In many ways, these interventions tie together everything that we've seen so far about how willpower works. They rely on the mind's ability to observe ourselves with curiosity, not judgment. They offer a way to handle the biggest enemies of willpower: temptation, self-criticism, and stress. They ask us to remember what we really want so we can find the strength to do what is difficult. The fact that this same basic approach helps such a wide range of willpower challenges, from depression to drug addiction, confirms that these three skills—self-awareness, self-care, and remembering what matters most—are the foundation for self-control.

THE LAST WORD

Trying to control our thoughts and feelings has the opposite effect of what most people expect. And yet rather than catch on to this, most of us respond to our failures with more commitment to this misguided strategy. We try even harder to push away thoughts and feelings we don't want to have in a vain attempt to keep our minds safe from danger. If we truly want peace of mind and better self-control, we need to accept that it is impossible to control what comes into our mind. All we can do is choose what we believe and what we act on.

CHAPTER SUMMARY

The Idea: Trying to suppress thoughts, emotions, and cravings backfires and makes you more likely to think, feel, or do the thing you most want to avoid.

Under the Microscope

- *Investigate ironic rebound.* Is there something you try to avoid thinking about? Does suppression work, or does trying to push something out of your mind make it come back stronger?
- *What's on your Most-Wanted list?* In your experience, is it true that outlawing something increases desire for it?

Willpower Experiments

- *Feel what you feel, but don't believe everything you think.* When an upsetting thought comes to mind, notice it and how it feels in your body. Then turn your attention to your breathing, and imagine the thought dissolving or passing by.
- *Accept those cravings—just don't act on them.* When a craving hits, notice it and don't try to immediately distract yourself or argue with it. Remind yourself of the white-bear rebound effect, and remember your goal to resist.
- *Surf the urge.* When an urge takes hold, stay with the physical sensations and ride them like a wave, neither pushing them away nor acting on them.

TEN

Final Thoughts

We started our journey together in the savannah of the Serengeti, being chased by a saber-toothed tiger. Now we find ourselves here, on the last few pages, ending our tour. Along the way, we've seen chimps display extraordinary self-control, and quite a few humans lose control. We've visited laboratories where dieters must resist chocolate cake, and anxiety sufferers must face their fears. We've watched as neuroscientists discovered the promise of reward, and neuromarketers discovered its payoff. We've come across interventions that use pride, forgiveness, exercise, meditation, peer pressure, money, sleep, and even God to motivate people to change their ways. We've met psychologists who shock rats, torture smokers, and tempt four-year-olds with marshmallows—all in the name of the science of willpower.

I hope this tour has provided more than a voyeur's glimpse into the fascinating world of research. Each of these studies teaches us something about ourselves and our own willpower challenges. They help us recognize our natural capacity for self-control, even if we sometimes struggle to use it. They help us understand our failures and point at possible solutions. They even tell us something about what it means to be human. For example, we've seen again and again that we are not one self, but multiple selves. Our human nature includes both the self that wants immediate gratification, and the self with a higher purpose. We are born to be tempted, and born to resist. It is just as human to feel stressed, scared, and out of control as it is to find the strength to be calm and in charge of our choices. Self-control is a matter of understanding these different parts of ourselves, not fundamentally changing who we are. In the quest for self-control, the usual weapons we wield against ourselves—guilt, stress, and shame—don't work. People who have the greatest self-control aren't waging self-war. They have learned to accept and integrate these competing selves.

If there *is* a secret for greater self-control, the science points to one thing: the power of paying attention. It's training the mind to recognize when you're making a choice, rather than running on autopilot. It's noticing how you give yourself permission to procrastinate, or how you use good behavior to justify self-indulgence. It's realizing that the promise of reward doesn't always deliver, and that your future self is not a superhero or a stranger. It's seeing what in your world—from sales gimmicks to social proof—is shaping your behavior. It's staying put and sensing a craving when you'd rather distract yourself or give in. It's remembering what you really want, and knowing what really makes you feel better. Self-awareness is the one "self" you can always count on to help you do what is difficult, and what matters most. And that is the best definition of willpower I can think of.

THE LAST WORD

In the spirit of scientific inquiry, I always end my Science of Willpower course by asking the students what stands out to them from everything they've observed and every experiment they've tried. More recently, a scientist friend of mine suggested that the only reasonable conclusion to a book about scientific ideas is: *Draw your own conclusions.* So as tempting as it is to have the last word, I'll exercise my "I won't" power, and ask you instead:

- Has your thinking about willpower and self-control changed?
- Which willpower experiment was the most helpful?
- What was your big a-ha moment?
- What are you going to take with you?

As you move forward, keep the mind-set of a scientist. Try new things, collect your own data, and listen to the evidence. Stay open to surprising ideas, and learn from both your failures and your successes. Keep what works, and share what you know with others. With all our human quirks and modern temptations, this is the best we can do—but when we do it with an attitude of curiosity and self-compassion, it is more than enough.

ACKNOWLEDGMENTS

Everyone I'm related to got thoroughly thanked in the last book, and nothing has changed—I'm still grateful for a lifetime of support. So thanks now to some new people, who made this book possible:

To my agent, Ted Weinstein, who every author should be so lucky to have as an advocate. He gets credit for shaping the proposal, helping the book find just the right publisher and editor, and making sure I wasn't procrastinating on my deadlines.

To the entire publishing team at Avery, and especially my editor, Rachel Holtzman, for championing the book, providing brilliant editorial guidance, and (no small matter) appreciating the humor of a study that asks preschoolers to resist marshmallows. I hate to think what might have become of this book in the hands of someone who didn't love science.

To readers of my first drafts: Brian Kidd, who was unfailingly enthusiastic about every word and laughed at all the jokes, and Constance Hale, whose insightful feedback helped me clean up the mess.

To illustrator Tina Pavlatos, of Visual Anatomy Limited, for the wonderful brain pictures in this book, and for demonstrating exceptional patience when I kept asking for a slightly different angle on the medial prefrontal cortex.

To all of the scientists who talked with me via phone, e-mail, or in person, either directly for the book or over the years helping me shape my understanding of the science, including Jo Barton, Sarah Bowen, Daniel Effron, James Erskine, Hal Ersner-Hershfield, Matthew Gailliot, Philippe Goldin, James Gross, Kate Janse Van Rensburg, Brian Knutson, Jason Lillis, Eileen Luders, Antoine Lutz, Traci Mann, Benoît Monin, Kristin Neff, Robert Sapolsky, Suzanne Segerstrom, Brian Shelley, and Greg Walton. Deep gratitude for your contributions to the field, and if I erred in my description of the nuances of your work, I apologize.

To the folks at Stanford who have supported my teaching over the years: a special thanks to Stanford Continuing Studies for nurturing "The Science of Will-power," especially Associate Dean and Director Dan Colman, who first approved the course idea; and to the Stanford Center for Teaching and Learning, the School of Medicine's Health Improvement Program, the Stanford Center for Compassion and Altruism Research and Education, and the Psychology One Program for giving me the tools, opportunities, and encouragement to focus on becoming a better teacher.

The last and largest "thank you" goes to all the students who took the course "The Science of Willpower," without whom there would be no book. Especially to those of you who asked tough questions, bravely shared your embarrassing stories in front of a lecture hall full of strangers, and even brought in homemade fudge on the last night of class so we could all practice—or abandon—willpower in celebration.

NOTES

Introduction: Welcome to Willpower 101

Page 1—Willpower survey: 2010 American Psychological Association. "Americans Report Willpower and Stress as Key Obstacles to Meeting Health-Related Resolutions." National U.S. survey conducted by Harris Interactive, 3/2–3/4/2010.

Page 4—People who think they have a lot of self-control don't: Nordgren, L. F., F. van Harreveld, and J. van der Pligt. "The Restraint Bias: How the Illusion of Self-Restraint Promotes Impulsive Behavior." *Psychological Science* 20 (2009): 1523–28. See also Saito, H., Y. Kimura, S. Tashima, N. Takao, A. Nakagawa, T. Baba, and S. Sato. "Psychological Factors That Promote Behavior Modification by Obese Patients." *BioPsychoSocial Medicine* 3 (2009): 9.

Chapter 1. I Will, I Won't, I Want:
What Willpower Is, and Why It Matters

Page 11—How social complexity led to brain evolution: Dunbar, R. I. M. "The Social Brain: Mind, Language, and Society in Evolutionary Perspective." *Annual Review of Anthropology* 32 (2003): 163–81. See also Dunbar, R. I. M., and S. Shultz. "Evolution in the Social Brain." *Science* 317 (2007): 1344–47.

Page 12—The benefits of self-control: Tangney, J. P., R. F. Baumeister, and A. L. Boone.

"High Self-Control Predicts Good Adjustment, Less Pathology, Better Grades, and Interpersonal Success." *Journal of Personality* 72 (2004): 271–324. See also Kern, M. L., and H. S. Friedman. "Do Conscientious Individuals Live Longer? A Quantitative Review." *Health Psychology* 27 (2008): 505–12.

Page 12—Self-control and academic success: Duckworth, A. L., and M. E. Seligman. "Self-Discipline Outdoes IQ in Predicting Academic Performance of Adolescents." *Psychological Science* 16 (2005): 939–44.

Page 12—Self-control and leadership: Kirkpatrick, S. A., and E. A. Locke. "Leadership: Do Traits Matter?" *Academy of Management Executive* 5 (1991): 48–60.

Page 12—Self-control and marriage: Tucker, J. S., N. R. Kressin, A. Spiro, and J. Ruscio. "Intrapersonal Characteristics and the Timing of Divorce: A Prospective Investigation." *Journal of Social and Personal Relationships* 15 (1998): 211–25.

Page 13—The prefrontal cortex makes us want to do the harder things: Sapolsky, R. M. "The Frontal Cortex and the Criminal Justice System." *Philosophical Transactions of the Royal Society of London. Series B, Biological Sciences* 359 (2004): 1787–96.

Page 14—Specialization of different regions of the prefrontal cortex: Suchy, Y. "Executive Functioning: Overview, Assessment, and Research Issues for Non-Neuropsychologists." *Annals of Behavioral Medicine* 37 (2009): 106–16.

Page 14—Details about the case of Phineas Gage: Macmillan, M. "Restoring Phineas Gage: A 150th Retrospective." *Journal of the History of the Neurosciences: Basic and Clinical Perspectives* 9 (2000): 46–66.

Page 15—Original case report by Gage's doctor: Harlow, J. M. "Passage of an Iron Rod through the Head." *Boston Medical and Surgical Journal* 39 (1848): 389–93.

Page 16—How the human brain evolved: Cohen, J. D. "The Vulcanization of the Human Brain: A Neural Perspective on Interactions Between Cognition and Emotion." *Journal of Economic Perspectives* 19 (2005): 3–24.

Pages 17–18—The problem of two minds: Cohen, J. D. "Neural Perspective on Cognitive Control and the Multiplicity of Selves" (Invited Address at the Annual Meeting of the American Psychological Association, San Diego, California, August 13, 2010).

Page 19—Case of no fear: Anson, J. A., and D. T. Kuhlman. "Post-Ictal Klüver-Bucy Syndrome after Temporal Lobectomy." *Journal of Neurology, Neurosurgery & Psychiatry* 56 (1993): 311–13.

Page 18—How pain prevents spending: Knutson, B., S. Rick, G. E. Wimmer, D. Prelec, and G. Loewenstein. "Neural Predictors of Purchases." *Neuron* 53 (2007): 147–56.

Page 20—Food choices: Wansink, B., and J. Sobal. "Mindless Eating." *Environment and Behavior* 39 (2007): 106–23.

Page 21—Distraction and impulsive choices: Shiv, B., and A. Fedorikhin. "Heart and Mind in Conflict: The Interplay of Affect and Cognition in Consumer Decision Making." *Journal of Consumer Research* 26 (1999): 278–92. See also Shiv, B., and

S. M. Nowlis. "The Effect of Distractions While Tasting a Food Sample: The Interplay of Informational and Affective Components in Subsequent Choice." *Journal of Consumer Research* 31 (2004): 599–608.

Page 24—Juggling changes the brain: Taubert, M., B. Draganski, A. Anwander, K. Muller, A. Horstmann, A. Villringer, and P. Ragert. "Dynamic Properties of Human Brain Structure: Learning-Related Changes in Cortical Areas and Associated Fiber Connections." *Journal of Neuroscience* 30 (2010): 11670–77.

Page 24—Memory games change the brain: Takeuchi, H., A. Sekiguchi, Y. Taki, S. Yokoyama, Y. Yomogida, N. Komuro, T. Yamanouchi, S. Suzuki, and R. Kawashima. "Training of Working Memory Impacts Structural Connectivity." *Journal of Neuroscience* 30 (2010): 3297–303.

Page 24—Benefits of meditation: Brefczynski-Lewis, J. A., A. Lutz, H. S. Schaefer, D. B. Levinson, and R. J. Davidson. "Neural Correlates of Attentional Expertise in Long-Term Meditation Practitioners." *Proceedings of the National Academy of Sciences* 104 (2007): 11483–88. See also Baron Short, E., S. Kose, Q. Mu, J. Borckardt, A. Newberg, M. S. George, and F. A. Kozel. "Regional Brain Activation During Meditation Shows Time and Practice Effects: An Exploratory fMRI Study." *Evidence-based Complementary and Alternative Medicine* 7 (2007): 121–27. See also Moore, A., and P. Malinowski. "Meditation, Mindfulness and Cognitive Flexibility." *Consciousness and Cognition* 18 (2009): 176–86.

Pages 24–25—Meditation and the brain: Luders, E., A. W. Toga, N. Lepore, and C. Gaser. "The Underlying Anatomical Correlates of Long-Term Meditation: Larger Hippocampal and Frontal Volumes of Gray Matter." *Neuroimage* 45 (2009): 672–78. See also Holzel, B. K., U. Ott, T. Gard, H. Hempel, M. Weygandt, K. Morgen, and D. Vaitl. "Investigation of Mindfulness Meditation Practitioners with Voxel-Based Morphometry." *Social Cognitive and Affective Neuroscience* 3 (2008): 55–61. See also Lazar, S. W., C. E. Kerr, R. H. Wasserman, J. R. Gray, D. N. Greve, M. T. Treadway, M. McGarvey, et al. "Meditation Experience Is Associated with Increased Cortical Thickness." *NeuroReport* 16 (2005): 1893–97. See also Pagnoni, G., and M. Cekic. "Age Effects on Gray Matter Volume and Attentional Performance in Zen Meditation." *Neurobiology of Aging* 28 (2007): 1623–27.

Page 27—Meditation and self-control: Tang, Y. Y., Q. Lu, X. Geng, E. A. Stein, Y. Yang, and M. I. Posner. "Short-Term Meditation Induces White Matter Changes in the Anterior Cingulate." *Proceedings of the National Academy of Sciences* 107 (2010): 15649–52.

Page 27—Meditation and self-awareness: Holzel, B. K., J. Carmody, M. Vangel, C. Congleton, S. M. Yerramsetti, T. Gard, and S. W. Lazar. "Mindfulness Practice Leads to Increases in Regional Brain Gray Matter Density." *Psychiatry Research* 191 (2011): 36–43.

Chapter 2. The Willpower Instinct:
Your Body Was Born to Resist Cheesecake

Page 32—Fight-or-flight stress response: Sapolsky, R. M. *Why Zebras Don't Get Ulcers: An Updated Guide to Stress, Stress Related Diseases, and Coping.* 2nd ed. New York: W. H. Freeman, 1998.

Page 33—Stress impairs prefrontal cortex: Arnsten, A. F. "Stress Signaling Pathways That Impair Prefrontal Cortex Structure and Function." *Nature Reviews Neuroscience* 10 (2009): 410–22.

Page 35—Pause-and-plan response: Segerstrom, S. C., J. K. Hardy, D. R. Evans, and N. F. Winters. "Pause and Plan: Self-Regulation and the Heart." In: Gendolla, G. and R. Wright, eds. *Motivational Perspectives on Cardiovascular Response.* Washington, DC: American Psychological Association, in press.

Page 37—Self-control requires energy: Madsen, P. L., S. G. Hasselbalch, L. P. Hagemann, K. S. Olsen, J. Bulow, S. Holm, G. Wildschiodtz, O. B. Paulson, and N. A. Lassen. "Persistent Resetting of the Cerebral Oxygen/Glucose Uptake Ratio by Brain Activation: Evidence Obtained with the Kety-Schmidt Technique." *Journal of Cerebral Blood Flow and Metabolism* 15 (1995): 485–91.

Page 38—Resisting sweets requires increase in heart-rate variability: Segerstrom, S. C., and L. S. Nes. "Heart Rate Variability Reflects Self-Regulatory Strength, Effort, and Fatigue." *Psychological Science* 18 (2007): 275–81.

Page 39—Heart rate variability distinguishes alcoholics at risk of relapse: Ingjaldsson, J. T., J. C. Laberg, and J. F. Thayer. "Reduced Heart Rate Variability in Chronic Alcohol Abuse: Relationship with Negative Mood, Chronic Thought Suppression, and Compulsive Drinking." *Biological Psychiatry* 54 (2003): 1427–36.

Page 39—High heart rate variability helps self-control: Thayer, J. F., A. L. Hansen, E. Saus-Rose, and B. H. Johnsen. "Heart Rate Variability, Prefrontal Neural Function, and Cognitive Performance: The Neurovisceral Integration Perspective on Self-Regulation, Adaptation, and Health." *Annals of Behavioral Medicine* 37 (2009): 141–53.

Page 39—High heart rate variability helps persistence: Segerstrom, S. C., and L. S. Nes. "Heart Rate Variability Reflects Self-Regulatory Strength, Effort, and Fatigue." *Psychological Science* 18 (2007): 275–81. See also Geisler, F. C. M., and T. Kubiak. "Heart Rate Variability Predicts Self-Control in Goal Pursuit." *European Journal of Personality* 23 (2009): 623–33.

Page 39—Depression, mood, and heart rate variability: Taylor, C. B. "Depression, Heart Rate–Related Variables and Cardiovascular Disease." *International Journal of Psychophysiology* 78 (2010): 80–88. See also Grippo, A. J., C. S. Carter, N. McNeal, D. L. Chandler, M. A. Larocca, S. L. Bates, and S. W. Porges. "24-Hour Autonomic Dysfunction and Depressive Behaviors in an Animal Model of Social Isolation: Implications for the Study of Depression and Cardiovascular Disease." *Psychosomatic Medicine* (2010).

Page 39—Chronic pain, illness, and heart rate variability: Solberg Nes, L., C. R. Carlson, L. J. Crofford, R. de Leeuw, and S. C. Segerstrom. "Self-Regulatory Deficits in Fibromyalgia and Temporomandibular Disorders." *Pain* 151 (2010): 37–44.

Page 39—Meditation increases heart rate variability: Peressutti, C., J. M. Martin-Gonzalez, J. M. García-Manso, and D. Mesa. "Heart Rate Dynamics in Different Levels of Zen Meditation." *International Journal of Cardiology* 145 (2010): 142–46. See also Tang, Y.-Y., Y. Ma, Y. Fan, H. Feng, J. Wang, S. Feng, Q. Lu, et al. "Central and Autonomic Nervous System Interaction Is Altered by Short-Term Meditation." *Proceedings of the National Academy of Sciences* 106 (2009): 8865–70.

Page 40—Breathing and heart rate variability: Song, H.-S., and P. M. Lehrer. "The Effects of Specific Respiratory Rates on Heart Rate and Heart Rate Variability." *Applied Psychophysiology and Biofeedback* 28 (2003): 13–23.

Page 40—Breathing helps PTSD and substance abuse: Zucker, T., K. Samuelson, F. Muench, M. Greenberg, and R. Gevirtz. "The Effects of Respiratory Sinus Arrhythmia Biofeedback on Heart Rate Variability and Post-traumatic Stress Disorder Symptoms: A Pilot Study." *Applied Psychophysiology and Biofeedback* 34 (2009): 135–43.

Pages 42–43—Exercise as self-control training: Oaten, M., and K. Cheng. "Longitudinal Gains in Self-Regulation from Regular Physical Exercise." *British Journal of Health Psychology* 11 (2006) 717–33.

Page 42—Exercise and cravings: Janse Van Rensburg, K., A. Taylor, and T. Hodgson. "The Effects of Acute Exercise on Attentional Bias Towards Smoking-Related Stimuli During Temporary Abstinence from Smoking." *Addiction* 104 (2009): 1910–17. See also Taylor, A. H., and A. J. Oliver. "Acute Effects of Brisk Walking on Urges to Eat Chocolate, Affect, and Responses to a Stressor and Chocolate Cue. An Experimental Study." *Appetite* 52 (2009): 155–60.

Page 42—Exercise is an antidepressant: Nabkasorn, C., N. Miyai, A. Sootmongkol, S. Junprasert, H. Yamamoto, M. Arita, and K. Miyashita. "Effects of Physical Exercise on Depression, Neuroendocrine Stress Hormones and Physiological Fitness in Adolescent Females with Depressive Symptoms." *The European Journal of Public Health* 16 (2006): 179–84.

Page 43—Exercise and heart rate variability: Hansen, A. L., B. H. Johnsen, J. J. Sollers, K. Stenvik, and J. F. Thayer. "Heart Rate Variability and Its Relation to Prefrontal Cognitive Function: The Effects of Training and Detraining." *European Journal of Applied Physiology* 93 (2004): 263–72.

Page 43—Exercise and the brain: Colcombe, S. J., K. I. Erickson, N. Raz, A. G. Webb, N. J. Cohen, E. McAuley, and A. F. Kramer. "Aerobic Fitness Reduces Brain Tissue Loss in Aging Humans." *The Journals of Gerontology Series A: Biological Sciences and Medical Sciences* 58 (2003): M176–M180. See also Colcombe, S. J., K. I. Erickson, P. E. Scalf, J. S. Kim, R. Prakash, E. McAuley, S. Elavsky, et al. "Aerobic Exercise

Training Increases Brain Volume in Aging Humans." *The Journals of Gerontology Series A: Biological Sciences and Medical Sciences* 61 (2006): 1166–70. See also Hillman, C. H., K. I. Erickson, and A. F. Kramer. "Be Smart, Exercise Your Heart: Exercise Effects on Brain and Cognition." *Nature Reviews Neuroscience* 9 (2008): 58–65.

Page 43—Five minutes of exercise helps: Barton, J., and J. Pretty. "What Is the Best Dose of Nature and Green Exercise for Improving Mental Health? A Multi-Study Analysis." *Environmental Science & Technology* 44 (2010): 3947–55.

Page 46—Sleep and energy: Spiegel, K., E. Tasali, R. Leproult, and E. Van Cauter. "Effects of Poor and Short Sleep on Glucose Metabolism and Obesity Risk." *Nature Reviews Endocrinology* 5 (2009): 253–61. See also Knutson, K. L., and E. Van Cauter. "Associations Between Sleep Loss and Increased Risk of Obesity and Diabetes." *Annals of the New York Academy of Sciences* 1129 (2008): 287–304.

Page 46—Sleep deprivation and brain function: Durmer, J. S., and D. F. Dinges. "Neurocognitive Consequences of Sleep Deprivation." *Seminars in Neurology* 25 (2005): 117–29.

Page 46—Mild prefrontal dysfunction: Killgore, W. D. S., E. T. Kahn-Greene, E. L. Lipizzi, R. A. Newman, G. H. Kamimori, and T. J. Balkin. "Sleep Deprivation Reduces Perceived Emotional Intelligence and Constructive Thinking Skills." *Sleep Medicine* 9 (2008): 517–26.

Pages 46–47—Sleep deprivation and alcohol intoxication: Elmenhorst, D., E.-M. Elmenhorst, N. Luks, H. Maass, E.-W. Mueller, M. Vejvoda, J. Wenzel, and A. Samel. "Performance Impairment During Four Days Partial Sleep Deprivation Compared with the Acute Effects of Alcohol and Hypoxia." *Sleep Medicine* 10 (2009): 189–97.

Page 46—Sleep deprivation and stress: Yoo, S.-S., N. Gujar, P. Hu, F. A. Jolesz, and M. P. Walker. "The Human Emotional Brain without Sleep—A Prefrontal Amygdala Disconnect." *Current Biology* 17 (2007): R877–78.

Page 47—Recovery from poor sleep: Altena, E., Y. D. Van Der Werf, E. J. Sanz-Arigita, et al. "Prefrontal Hypoactivation and Recovery in Insomnia." *Sleep 31* (2008): 1271–76.

Page 47—Meditation, sleep, and substance abuse: Britton, W. B., R. R. Bootzin, J. C. Cousins, B. P. Hasler, T. Peck, and S. L. Shapiro. "The Contribution of Mindfulness Practice to a Multicomponent Behavioral Sleep Intervention Following Substance Abuse Treatment in Adolescents: A Treatment-Development Study." *Substance Abuse* 31 (2010): 86–97.

Page 49—Self-control and immune function: Segerstrom, S. C., J. K. Hardy, D. R. Evans, N. F. Winters. "Pause and Plan: Self-Regulation and the Heart." In: Gendolla, G., and R. Wright, eds. *Motivational Perspectives on Cardiovascular Response*. Washington, DC: American Psychological Association, in press. See also Segerstrom,

S. C. "Resources, Stress, and Immunity: An Ecological Perspective on Human Psychoneuroimmunology." *Annals of Behavioral Medicine* 40 (2010): 114–125.

Page 50—Relaxation benefits: Kiecolt-Glaser, J. K., L. Christian, H. Preston, C. R. Houts, W. B. Malarkey, C. F. Emery, and R. Glaser. "Stress, Inflammation, and Yoga Practice." *Psychosomatic Medicine* 72 (2010): 113–21.

Page 50—Athletes recover faster: Martarelli, D., M. Cocchioni, S. Scuri, and P. Pompei. "Diaphragmatic Breathing Reduces Exercise-Induced Oxidative Stress." *Evidence-Based Complementary and Alternative Medicine* 2011 (2011): 1-10.

Page 50—Physiological relaxation response: Benson, H. *The Relaxation Response*. New York: Morrow, 1975.

Page 52—Stress survey: American Psychological Association. *"Stress in America."* 1–64: Washington DC, 2010.

Page 52—9/11 and stress: Lampert, R., S. J. Baron, C. A. McPherson, and F. A. Lee. "Heart Rate Variability During the Week of September 11, 2001." *Journal of the American Medical Association* 288 (2002): 575.

Page 52—9/11 and substance use: Vlahov, D., S. Galea, H. Resnick, J. Ahern, J. A. Boscarino, M. Bucuvalas, J. Gold, and D. Kilpatrick. "Increased Use of Cigarettes, Alcohol, and Marijuana among Manhattan, New York, Residents After the September 11th Terrorist Attacks." *American Journal of Epidemiology* 155 (2002): 988–96.

Page 52—Economic crisis and stress: "WASA Snacking Satisfaction Survey." Survey conducted 2/10–2/23/2009 by Kelton Research, New York. www.wasacrispbread.com/downloads/SurveyFactSheet.pdf. See also American Legacy Foundation. "Current Economic Situation Prompts Increased Smoking, Delay in Quit Attempts Middle and Low-Income Americans Hit Hardest." 11/7/2008. www.legacyforhealth.org/2753.aspx.

Page 52—Americans sleeping less: National Sleep Foundation: Sleep in America Poll. Washington, (2008).

Page 52—Sleep deprivation and obesity: Leproult, R., and E. Van Cauter. "Role of Sleep and Sleep Loss in Hormonal Release and Metabolism," ed. S. Loche, M. Cappa, L. Ghizzoni, M. Maghnie, and M. O. Savage. *Pediatric Neuroendocrinology: Endocrine Development* 17 (2010): 11–21.

Page 53—Sleep deprivation mimics ADHD: Brennan, A. R., and A. F. T. Arnsten. "Neuronal Mechanisms Underlying Attention Deficit Hyperactivity Disorder." *Annals of the New York Academy of Sciences* 1129 (2008): 236–45.

Chapter 3. Too Tired to Resist:
Why Self-Control Is Like a Muscle

Page 55—Studying and self-control: Oaten, M., and K. Cheng. "Academic Examination Stress Impairs Self-Control." *Journal of Social and Clinical Psychology* 24 (2005): 254–79.

Page 56—Smoking and ice cream: Duffy, J., and S. M. Hall. "Smoking Abstinence, Eating Style, and Food Intake." *Journal of Consulting and Clinical Psychology* 56 (1988): 417–21.

Page 56—Drinking and endurance: Muraven, M., and D. Shmueli. "The Self-Control Costs of Fighting the Temptation to Drink." *Psychology of Addictive Behaviors* 20 (2006): 154–60.

Page 56—Dieters cheat: Gailliot, M. T., and R. F. Baumeister. "Self-Regulation and Sexual Restraint: Dispositionally and Temporarily Poor Self-Regulatory Abilities Contribute to Failures at Restraining Sexual Behavior." *Personality and Social Psychology Bulletin* 33 (2007): 173–86.

Page 57—Self-control runs out: Baumeister, R. F., T. F. Heatherton, and D. M. Tice. *Losing Control: How and Why People Fail at Self-Regulation.* San Diego: Academic Press, 1994.

Page 57—Shopping decisions drain willpower: Vohs, K. D., R. F. Baumeister, B. J. Schmeichel, J. M. Twenge, N. M. Nelson, and D. M. Tice. "Making Choices Impairs Subsequent Self-Control: A Limited-Resource Account of Decision Making, Self-Regulation, and Active Initiative." *Journal of Personality and Social Psychology* 94 (2008): 883–98.

Page 57—The brain gets tired: Inzlicht, M. I., and J. N. Gutsell. "Running on Empty: Neural Signals for Self-Control Failure." *Psychological Science* 18 (2007): 933–37.

Page 60—Lemonade restores willpower: Gailliot, M. T., R. F. Baumeister, C. N. DeWall, J. K. Maner, E. A. Plant, D. M. Tice, L. E. Brewer, and B. J. Schmeichel. "Self-Control Relies on Glucose as a Limited Energy Source: Willpower Is More Than a Metaphor." *Journal of Personality and Social Psychology* 92 (2007): 325–36.

Page 60—Low blood sugar and bad behavior: DeWall, C. N., T. Deckman, M. T. Gailliot, and B. J. Bushman. "Sweetened Blood Cools Hot Tempers: Physiological Self-Control and Aggression." *Aggressive Behavior* 37 (2011): 73–80. See also Gailliot, M. T., B. Michelle Peruche, E. A. Plant, and R. F. Baumeister. "Stereotypes and Prejudice in the Blood: Sucrose Drinks Reduce Prejudice and Stereotyping." *Journal of Experimental Social Psychology* 45 (2009): 288–90. See also DeWall, C. N., R. F. Baumeister, M. T. Gailliot, and J. K. Maner. "Depletion Makes the Heart Grow Less Helpful: Helping as a Function of Self-Regulatory Energy and Genetic Relatedness." *Personality and Social Psychology Bulletin* 34 (2008): 1653–62.

Page 61—Self-control's energy costs: Kurzban, R. "Does the Brain Consume Additional Glucose During Self-Control Tasks?" *Evolutionary Psychology* 8 (2010): 244–59.

Page 62—Neurons detect glucose availability: Routh, V. N. "Glucose Sensing by the Brain: Implications for Diabetes." *UMDNJ Research* 8 (2007): 1–3.

Pages 62–63—Energy budget model of self-control: Wang, X. T., and R. D. Dvorak. "Sweet Future: Fluctuating Blood Glucose Levels Affect Future Discounting." *Psychological Science* 21 (2010): 183–88.

Page 65—People make riskier investments when they're hungry: Symmonds, M., J. J. Emmanuel, M. E. Drew, R. L. Batterham, and R. J. Dolan. "Metabolic State Alters Economic Decision Making under Risk in Humans." *PLoS ONE* 5 (2010): e11090.

Page 65—Hungry people more interested in cheating: Gailliot, M. T. "Hunger Impairs and Food Improves Self-Control in the Laboratory and Across the World: The Hyperbole of Reducing World Hunger as a Self-Control Panacea." (2011, under review).

Page 65—A good guide for a willpower-boosting diet: Pollan, M. *Food Rules: An Eater's Manual.* New York: Penguin, 2009.

Page 66—Setting deadlines strengthens self-control: Oaten, M., and K. Cheng. "Improved Self-Control: The Benefits of a Regular Program of Academic Study." *Basic and Applied Social Psychology* 28 (2006): 1–16.

Pages 66–67—Examples of willpower training programs: Baumeister, R. F., M. Gailliot, C. N. DeWall, and M. Oaten. "Self-Regulation and Personality: How Interventions Increase Regulatory Success, and How Depletion Moderates the Effects of Traits on Behavior." *Journal of Personality* 74 (2006): 1773–801. See also Muraven, M., R. F. Baumeister, and D. M. Tice. "Longitudinal Improvement of Self-Regulation through Practice: Building Self-Control Strength through Repeated Exercise." *The Journal of Social Psychology* 139 (1999): 446–57. See also Muraven, M. "Building Self-Control Strength: Practicing Self-Control Leads to Improved Self-Control Performance." *Journal of Experimental Social Psychology* 46 (2010): 465–68. See also Oaten, M., and K. Cheng. "Improvements in Self-Control from Financial Monitoring." *Journal of Economic Psychology* 28 (2007): 487–501.

Page 67—Training self-control to reduce violence: Finkel, E. J., C. N. DeWall, E. B. Slotter, M. Oaten, and V. A. Foshee. "Self-Regulatory Failure and Intimate Partner Violence Perpetration." *Journal of Personality and Social Psychology* 97 (2009): 483–99.

Page 69—Resisting candy to strengthen self-control: Geyskens, K., S. Dewitte, M. Pandelaere, and L. Warlop. "Tempt Me Just a Little Bit More: The Effect of Prior Food Temptation Actionability on Goal Activation and Consumption." *Journal of Consumer Research* 35 (2008): 600–10.

Page 70—Why we fatigue: Noakes, T. D., A. St. Clair Gibson, and E. V. Lambert. "From Catastrophe to Complexity: A Novel Model of Integrative Central Neural Regulation of Effort and Fatigue During Exercise in Humans: Summary and Conclusions." *British Journal of Sports Medicine* 39 (2005): 120–24.

Page 71—Fatigue is an emotion: Noakes, T. D., J. E. Peltonen, and H. K. Rusko. "Evidence That a Central Governor Regulates Exercise Performance During Acute Hypoxia and Hyperoxia." *The Journal of Experimental Biology* 204 (2001): 3225–34.

Page 72—Willpower athletes don't show exhaustion: Job, V., C. S. Dweck, and G. M. Walton. "Ego Depletion—Is It All in Your Head? Implicit Theories About Willpower Affect Self-Regulation." *Psychological Science* 21 (2010): 1686–93.

Page 73—Motivation helps overcome exhaustion: Muraven, M., and E. Slessareva. "Mechanisms of Self-Control Failure: Motivation and Limited Resources." *Personality and Social Psychology Bulletin* 29 (2003): 894–906.

Page 76—"The Forest Game": Crelley, D., S. Lea, and P. Fisher. "Ego Depletion and the Tragedy of the Commons: Self Regulation Fatigue in Public Goods Games." Presented at the 2008 World Meeting of the International Association for Research in Economic Psychology and the Society for Advancement of Behavioral Economics, Rome.

Page 77—For a dramatic telling of the Easter Island tragedy, see Diamond, J. *Collapse: How Societies Choose to Fail or Succeed.* New York: Viking, 2004. *For an economic model,* see Bologna, M., and J. C. Flores. "A Simple Mathematical Model of Society Collapse Applied to Easter Island." *EPL (Europhysics Letters)* 81 (2008): 480–86.

Page 78—"Choice architecture": Thaler, R. H., and C. R. Sunstein. *Nudge: Improving Decisions About Health, Wealth, and Happiness.* New York: Knopf, 2008.

Page 79—Placement increases purchases: Just, D. R., and B. Wansink. "Smarter Lunchrooms: Using Behavioral Economics to Improve Meal Selection." *Choices* 24 (2009).

Chapter 4. License to Sin:
Why Being Good Gives Us Permission to Be Bad

Pages 82–83—Sexist survey and moral licensing: Monin, B., and D. T. Miller. "Moral Credentials and the Expression of Prejudice." *Journal of Personality and Social Psychology* 81 (2001)33–43.

Page 84—How feeling virtuous licenses being bad: Fishbach, A., and R. Dhar. "Goals as Excuses or Guides: The Liberating Effect of Perceived Goal Progress on Choice." *Journal of Consumer Research* 32 (2005): 370–77. See also Fishbach, A., and Y. Zhang. "Together or Apart: When Goals and Temptations Complement Versus Compete." *Journal of Personality and Social Psychology* 94 (2008): 547–59.

Page 84—Past good behavior lets us off the hook: Sachdeva, S., R. Iliev, and D. L. Medin. "Sinning Saints and Saintly Sinners." *Psychological Science* 20 (2009): 523–28.

Page 85—Indulging on purpose: Mukhopadhyay, A., and G. V. Johar. "Indulgence as Self-Reward for Prior Shopping Restraint: A Justification-Based Mechanism." *Journal of Consumer Psychology* 19 (2009): 334–45.

Page 85—I deserve a treat: Mick, D. G., and M. Demoss. "Self-Gifts: Phenomenological Insights from Four Contexts." *Journal of Consumer Research* 17 (1990): 322–32.

Page 85—Imagining altruistic behavior licenses us to indulge: Khan, U., and R. Dhar. "Licensing Effect in Consumer Choice." *Journal of Marketing Research* 43 (2006): 259–66.

Pages 86–87—Moral judgments: Haidt, J. "The Emotional Dog and Its Rational Tail: A Social Intuitionist Approach to Moral Judgment." *Psychological Review* 108 (2001): 814–34.

Page 89—Weight loss licenses chocolate: Fishbach, A., and R. Dhar. "Goals as Excuses or Guides: The Liberating Effect of Perceived Goal Progress on Choice." *Journal of Consumer Research* 32 (2005): 370–77.

Pages 88–90—Progress versus commitment: Fishbach, A., and R. Dhar. "Goals as Excuses or Guides: The Liberating Effect of Perceived Goal Progress on Choice." *Journal of Consumer Research* 32 (2005): 370–77. See also Fishbach, A., R. Dhar, and Y. Zhang. "Subgoals as Substitutes or Complements: The Role of Goal Accessibility." *Journal of Personality and Social Psychology* 91 (2006): 232–42.

Page 91—Remember the why: Mukhopadhyay, A., J. Sengupta, and S. Ramanathan. "Recalling Past Temptations: An Information-Processing Perspective on the Dynamics of Self-Control." *Journal of Consumer Research* 35 (2008): 586–99.

Page 93—Credit for future behavior: Fishbach, A., and R. Dhar. "Goals as Excuses or Guides: The Liberating Effect of Perceived Goal Progress on Choice." *Journal of Consumer Research* 32 (2005): 370–77.

Page 93—Salad increases unhealthy choices: Wilcox, K., B. Vallen, L. Block, and G. J. Fitzsimons. "Vicarious Goal Fulfillment: When the Mere Presence of a Healthy Option Leads to an Ironically Indulgent Decision." *Journal of Consumer Research* 36 (2009): 380–93.

Page 93—Future choice licenses self-indulgence: Khan, U., and R. Dhar. "Where There Is a Way, Is There a Will? The Effect of Future Choices on Self-Control." *Journal of Experimental Psychology* 136 (2007): 277–88.

Page 94—We'll have more free time in the future: Zauberman, G., and J. J. G. Lynch. "Resource Slack and Propensity to Discount Delayed Investments of Time Versus Money." *Journal of Experimental Psychology* 134 (2005): 23–37.

Page 95—An ideal future: Tanner, R. J., and K. A. Carlson. "Unrealistically Optimistic Consumers: A Selective Hypothesis Testing Account for Optimism in Predictions of Future Behavior." *Journal of Consumer Research* 35 (2009): 810–22.

Page 96—Reduce variability of behavior, e.g., smoke same number of cigarettes every day: Rachlin, H. *The Science of Self-Control*. Cambridge: Harvard University Press, 2000, 126–27.

Page 97—Healthy choice licenses indulgence: Chandon, P., and B. Wansink. "The Biasing Health Halos of Fast-Food Restaurant Health Claims: Lower Calorie Estimates and Higher Side-Dish Consumption Intentions." *Journal of Consumer Research* 34 (2007): 301–14.

Page 99—Negative calories for cheeseburgers: Chernov, A. "The Dieter's Paradox." *Journal of Consumer Psychology* (in press).

Page 99—Chocolate for charity: Mukhopadhyay, A., and G. V. Johar. "Indulgence as Self-Reward for Prior Shopping Restraint: A Justification-Based Mechanism." *Journal of Consumer Psychology* 19 (2009): 334–45.

Page 100—Organic Oreos get a halo: Schuldt, J. P., and N. Schwarz. "The 'Organic'

Path to Obesity? Organic Claims Influence Calorie Judgments and Exercise Recommendations." *Judgment and Decision Making* 5 (2010): 144–50.

Page 102—Going green licenses stealing: Mazar, N., and C. B. Zhong. "Do Green Products Make Us Better People?" *Psychological Science* 21 (2010): 494–98.

Page 103—Green licensing in real world: Kotchen, M. J. "Offsetting Green Guilt." *Stanford Social Innovation Review* 7 (2009): 26–31.

Pages 103–104—When does green licensing happen? Gans, J. S., and V. Groves. "Carbon Offset Provision with Guilt-Ridden Consumers." *Social Science Research Network* (2010). www.papers.ssrn.com/sol3/papers.cfm?abstract_id=969494.

Chapter 5. The Brain's Big Lie: Why We Mistake Wanting for Happiness

Pages 107–108—The rat that liked shocks: Olds, J. "Pleasure Center in the Brain." *Scientific American* 195 (1956): 105–16. See also Olds, J. " 'Reward' from Brain Stimulation in the Rat." *Science* 122 (1955): 878.

Pages 108–109—Rats shock themselves: Olds, J. "Self-Stimulation of the Brain: Its Use to Study Local Effects of Hunger, Sex, and Drugs." *Science* 127 (1958): 315–24.

Page 109—Human experiments with self-shocking: Heath, R. G. "Electrical Self-Stimulation of the Brain in Man." *American Journal of Psychiatry* 120 (1963): 571–77. See also Bishop, M. P., S. T. Elder, and R. G. Heath. "Intracranial Self-Stimulation in Man." *Science* 140 (1963): 394–96.

Page 109—Case report: Heath, R. G. "Pleasure and Brain Activity in Man. Deep and Surface Electroencephalograms During Orgasm." *Journal of Nervous and Mental Disease* 154 (1972): 3–18.

Page 112—Dopamine creates wanting: Berridge, K. C. "The Debate over Dopamine's Role in Reward: The Case for Incentive Salience." *Psychopharmacology* 191 (2007): 391–431.

Page 112—Pleasure without dopamine: Berridge, K. C. " 'Liking' and 'Wanting' Food Rewards: Brain Substrates and Roles in Eating Disorders." *Physiology & Behavior* 97 (2009): 537–50.

Page 112—Anticipating reward: Knutson, B., G. W. Fong, C. M. Adams, J. L. Varner, and D. Hommer. "Dissociation of Reward Anticipation and Outcome with Event-Related fMRI." *NeuroReport* 12 (2001): 3683–87.

Page 114—Video games release dopamine: Koepp, M. J., R. N. Gunn, A. D. Lawrence, V. J. Cunningham, A. Dagher, T. Jones, D. J. Brooks, C. J. Bench, and P. M. Grasby. "Evidence for Striatal Dopamine Release During a Video Game." *Nature* 393 (1998): 266–68.

Page 115—Gamer death: BBC News. 2005. "S. Korean Dies After Games Session." www.news.bbc.co.uk/2/hi/technology/4137782.stm.

Page 115—Parkinson's disease case reports: Nirenberg, M. J., and C. Waters. "Compulsive Eating and Weight Gain Related to Dopamine Agonist Use." *Movement Disorders* 21 (2006): 524–29. See also Bostwick, J. M., K. A. Hecksel, S. R. Stevens, J. H. Bower, and J. E. Ahlskog. "Frequency of New-Onset Pathologic Compulsive Gambling or Hypersexuality After Drug Treatment of Idiopathic Parkinson Disease." *Mayo Clinic Proceedings* 84 (2009): 310–16.

Page 116—Sexy images and financial risks: Knutson, B., G. E. Wimmer, C. M. Kuhnen, and P. Winkielman. "Nucleus Accumbens Activation Mediates the Influence of Reward Cues on Financial Risk-Taking." *NeuroReport* 19 (2008): 509–13.

Page 117—Lottery dreams and eating: Briers, B., M. Pandelaere, S. Dewitte, and L. Warlop. "Hungry for Money: The Desire for Caloric Resources Increases the Desire for Financial Resources and Vice Versa." *Psychological Science* 17 (2006): 939–43.

Page 117—Dopamine and immediate gratification: Berridge, K. C. "Wanting and Liking: Observations from the Neuroscience and Psychology Laboratory." *Inquiry: An Interdisciplinary Journal of Philosophy* 52 (2009): 378–98.

Page 117—Food samples study: Wadhwa, M., B. Shiv, and S. M. Nowlis. "A Bite to Whet the Reward Appetite: The Influence of Sampling on Reward-Seeking Behaviors." *Journal of Marketing Research* 45 (2008): 403–13.

Page 118—TV ads make us snack: Harris, J. L., J. A. Bargh, and K. D. Brownell. "Priming Effects of Television Food Advertising on Eating Behavior." *Health Psychology* 28 (2009): 404–13.

Page 123—Fish bowl: Petry, N. M., B. Martin, J. L. Cooney, and H. R. Kranzler. "Give Them Prizes, and They Will Come: Contingency Management for Treatment of Alcohol Dependence." *Journal of Consulting and Clinical Psychology* 68 (2000): 250–57. See also Petry, N. M. "Contingency Management Treatments." *The British Journal of Psychiatry* 198 (2006): 97–98.

Page 125—Dopamine and stress: Kash, T. L., W. P. Nobis, R. T. Matthwes, and D. G. Winder. "Dopamine Enhances Fast Excitatory Synaptic Transmission in the Extended Amygdala by a CRF-R1-Dependent Process." *The Journal of Neuroscience* 28 (2008): 13856–65.

Page 125—Chocolate is stressful: Rodríguez, S., M. C. Fernández, A. Cepeda-Benito, and J. Vila. "Subjective and Physiological Reactivity to Chocolate Images in High and Low Chocolate Cravers." *Biological Psychology* 70 (2005): 9–18.

Page 128—Stale popcorn: Wansink, B., and J. Kim. "Bad Popcorn in Big Buckets: Portion Size Can Influence Intake as Much as Taste." *Journal of Nutrition Education and Behavior* 37: 242–45.

Page 129—Test the promise of reward: Smith, B. W., B. M. Shelley, L. Leahigh, and B. Vanleit. "A Preliminary Study of the Effects of a Modified Mindfulness Intervention on Binge Eating." *Complementary Health Practice Review* 11 (2006): 133–43. See also Dalen, J., B. W. Smith, B. M. Shelley, A. L. Sloan, L. Leahigh, and D. Begay.

"Pilot Study: Mindful Eating And Living (MEAL): Weight, Eating Behavior, and Psychological Outcomes Associated with a Mindfulness-Based Intervention for People with Obesity." *Complementary Therapies in Medicine* 18 (2010): 260–64.

Page 130—An addict loses desire: Miller, J. M., S. R. Vorel, A. J. Tranguch, E. T. Kenny, P. Mazzoni, W. G. van Gorp, and H. D. Kleber. "Anhedonia After a Selective Bilateral Lesion of the Globus Pallidus." *American Journal of Psychiatry* 163 (2006): 786–88. As in other stories and cases in this book, the name used in the text is a pseudonym.

Page 131—Underactive reward system: Heller, A. S., T. Johnstone, A. J. Shackman, S. N. Light, M. J. Peterson, G. G. Kolden, N. H. Kalin, and R. J. Davidson. "Reduced Capacity to Sustain Positive Emotion in Major Depression Reflects Diminished Maintenance of Fronto-Striatal Brain Activation." *Proceedings of the National Academy of Sciences* 106 (2009): 22445–50.

Chapter 6. What the Hell:
How Feeling Bad Leads to Giving In

Page 134—Stress survey: American Psychological Association (APA) study, "Stress in America." American Psychological Association. Washington, DC: 2007.

Page 135—Chocolate leads to guilt: Macdiarmid, J. I., and M. M. Hetherington. "Mood Modulation by Food: An Exploration of Affect and Cravings in 'Chocolate Addicts.'" *British Journal of Clinical Psychology* 34 (1995): 129–38.

Page 135—Stress and smoking: Erblich, J., C. Lerman, D. W. Self, G. A. Diaz, and D. H. Bovbjerg. "Stress-Induced Cigarette Craving: Effects of the Drd2 Taqi Rflp and Slc6a3 Vntr Polymorphisms." *The Pharmacogenomics Journal* 4 (2004): 102–09.

Page 135—Stress and eating: Oliver, G., J. Wardle, and E. L. Gibson. "Stress and Food Choice: A Laboratory Study." *Psychosomatic Medicine* 62 (2000): 853–65.

Page 135—Stressed-out rats: Yap, J. J., and K. A. Miczek. "Stress and Rodent Models of Drug Addiction: Role of VTA-Accumbens-PFC-Amygdala Circuit." *Drug Discovery Today: Disease Models* 5 (2008): 259–70.

Page 135—Real-world stress triggers relapse: Oaten, M., and K. Cheng. "Academic Examination Stress Impairs Self-Control." *Journal of Social and Clinical Psychology* 24 (2005): 254–79.

Page 136—Stress and cravings: Sinha, R., C. Lacadie, P. Skudlarski, R. Fulbright, B. Rounsaville, T. Kosten, and B. Wexler. "Neural Activity Associated with Stress-Induced Cocaine Craving: A Functional Magnetic Resonance Imaging Study." *Psychopharmacology* 183 (2005): 171–80.

Page 136—Feeling bad makes cake look good: Chun, H., V. M. Patrick, and D. J. MacInnis. "Making Prudent Vs. Impulsive Choices: The Role of Anticipated Shame and Guilt on Consumer Self-Control." *Advances in Consumer Research* 34 (2007): 715–19.

Page 136—Shopping to relieve anxiety: Pine, K. J. "Report on a Survey into Female

Economic Behaviour and the Emotion Regulatory Role of Spending." *Sheconomics* website, 2009, pp. 1–24. www.sheconomics.com/downloads/womens_emotions.pdf.

Page 137—Goal to feel better trumps self-control: Tice, D. M., and E. Bratslavsky. "Giving In to Feel Good: The Place of Emotion Regulation in the Context of General Self-Control." *Psychological Inquiry: An International Journal for the Advancement of Psychological Theory* 11 (2000): 149–59.

Page 139—Terror management theory: Burke, B. L., A. Martens, and E. H. Faucher. "Two Decades of Terror Management Theory: A Meta-Analysis of Mortality Salience Research." *Personality and Social Psychology Review* 14 (2010): 155–95.

Page 140—Death and comfort eating: Mandel, N., and D. Smeesters. "The Sweet Escape: Effects of Mortality Salience on Consumption Quantities for High- and Low-Self-Esteem Consumers." *Journal of Consumer Research* 35 (2008): 309–23.

Page 140—Death and status symbols: Mandel, N., and S. J. Heine. "Terror Management and Marketing: He Who Dies with the Most Toys Wins." *Advances in Consumer Research* 26 (1999): 527–32.

Page 140—September 11, 2001, and shopping: Arndt, J., S. Solomon, T. Kasser, and K. M. Sheldon. "The Urge to Splurge: A Terror Management Account of Materialism and Consumer Behavior." *Journal of Consumer Psychology* 14 (2004): 198–212.

Page 140—Sad film prompts impulse purchase: Cryder, C. E., J. S. Lerner, J. J. Gross, and R. E. Dahl. "Misery Is Not Miserly: Sad and Self-Focused Individuals Spend More." *Psychological Science* 19 (2008): 525–30.

Page 141—Warning labels may backfire: Hansen, J., S. Winzeler, and S. Topolinski. "When the Death Makes You Smoke: A Terror Management Perspective on the Effectiveness of Cigarette on-Pack Warnings." *Journal of Experimental Social Psychology* 46 (2010): 226–28.

Page 143—The what-the-hell effect: Polivy, J., and C. P. Herman. "Dieting and Binging: A Causal Analysis." *American Psychologist* 40 (1985): 193–201. See also guilt survey: Steenhuis, I. "Guilty or Not? Feelings of Guilt About Food Among College Women." *Appetite* 52 (2009): 531–34

Page 144—Drinking and guilt: Muraven, M., R. L. Collins, E. T. Morsheimer, S. Shiffman, and J. A. Paty. "The Morning After: Limit Violations and the Self-Regulation of Alcohol Consumption." *Psychology of Addictive Behaviors* 19 (2005): 253–62.

Page 144—Eating more than others triggers what-the-hell effect: Polivy, J., C. P. Herman, and R. Deo. "Getting a Bigger Slice of the Pie. Effects on Eating and Emotion in Restrained and Unrestrained Eaters." *Appetite* 55 (2010): 426–30.

Page 144—Rigged scale triggers what-the-hell effect: McFarlane, T., J. Polivy, and C. P. Herman. "Effects of False Weight Feedback on Mood, Self-Evaluation, and Food Intake in Restrained and Unrestrained Eaters." *Journal of Abnormal Psychology* 107 (1998): 312–18.

Page 145—Breaking the what-the-hell cycle: Adams, C. E., and M. R. Leary. "Promoting

Self-Compassionate Attitudes toward Eating among Restrictive and Guilty Eaters." *Journal of Social and Clinical Psychology* 26 (2007): 1120–44.

Page 147—Self-criticism and self-control: Trumpeter, N., P. J. Watson, and B. J. O'Leary. "Factors within Multidimensional Perfectionism Scales: Complexity of Relationships with Self-Esteem, Narcissism, Self-Control, and Self-Criticism." *Personality and Individual Differences* 41 (2006): 849–60. See also Wills, T. A., F. X. Gibbons, J. D. Sargent, M. Gerrard, H.-R. Lee, and S. Dal Cin. "Good Self-Control Moderates the Effect of Mass Media on Adolescent Tobacco and Alcohol Use: Tests with Studies of Children and Adolescents." *Health Psychology* 29 (2010): 539–49. Cetýn, B., H. B. Gunduz, and A. Akin. "An Investigation of the Relationships between Self-Compassion, Motivation, and Burnout with Structural Equation Modeling." *Abant Ýzzet Baysal Universitesi Eðitim Fakultesi Dergisi Cilt* 8 (2008): 39–45.

Page 148—Self-criticism and depression: Gilbert, P., K. McEwan, M. Matos, and A. Rivis. "Fears of Compassion: Development of Three Self-Report Measures." *Psychology and Psychotherapy* (2010). Epub ahead of print.

Page 148—Guilt and procrastination: Wohl, M. J. A., T. A. Pychyl, and S. H. Bennett. "I Forgive Myself, Now I Can Study: How Self-Forgiveness for Procrastinating Can Reduce Future Procrastination." *Personality and Individual Differences* 48 (2010): 803–08.

Page 148—Self-forgiveness and accountability: Leary, M. R., E. B. Tate, C. E. Adams, A. B. Allen, and J. Hancock. "Self-Compassion and Reactions to Unpleasant Self-Relevant Events: The Implications of Treating Oneself Kindly." *Journal of Personality and Social Psychology* 92 (2007): 887–904. See also Allen, A. B., and M. R. Leary. "Self-Compassion, Stress, and Coping." *Social and Personality Psychology Compass* 4 (2010): 107–18. See also Neff, K. D., K. L. Kirkpatrick, and S. S. Rude. "Self-Compassion and Adaptive Psychological Functioning." *Journal of Research in Personality* 41 (2007): 139–54. See also Chamberlain, J. M., and D. A. F. Haaga. "Unconditional Self-Acceptance and Responses to Negative Feedback." *Journal of Rational-Emotive & Cognitive-Behavior Therapy* 19 (2001): 177–89.

Page 152—Resolving to change feels good: Polivy, J., and C. P. Herman. "If at First You Don't Succeed: False Hopes of Self-Change." *American Psychologist* 57 (2002): 677–89.

Page 154—Plan for failure: Gollwitzer, P. M., and G. Oettingen. "Planning Promotes Goal Striving." In Vohs, K. D., and R. F. Baumeister, eds. *Handbook of Self-Regulation: Research, Theory, and Applications*. New York: Guilford, 2011.

Chapter 7. Putting the Future on Sale:
The Economics of Instant Gratification

Page 156—Humans versus chimps: Rosati, A. G., J. R. Stevens, B. Hare, and M. D. Hauser. "The Evolutionary Origins of Human Patience: Temporal Preferences in Chimpanzees, Bonobos, and Human Adults." *Current Biology* 17 (2007): 1663–68.

Page 157—Only humans think about future: Gilbert, D. *Stumbling on Happiness.* New York: Knopf, 2006.

Page 158—Reversal of preferences: Ainslie, G. "Specious Reward: A Behavioral Theory of Impulsiveness and Impulse Control." *Psychological Bulletin* 82 (1975): 463–96.

Page 159—"Bounded rationality": Mullainathan, S., and R. H. Thaler. "Behavioral Economics." Working Paper No. 00-27 (2000). www.ssrn.com/abstract=245828.

Pages 159–160—Brain responds to immediate rewards: Cohen, J. D. "The Vulcanization of the Human Brain: A Neural Perspective on Interactions between Cognition and Emotion." *Journal of Economic Perspectives* 19 (2005): 3–24.

Page 160—Future versus immediate rewards: McClure, S. M., D. I. Laibson, G. Loewenstein, and J. D. Cohen. "Separate Neural Systems Value Immediate and Delayed Monetary Rewards." *Science* 306 (2004): 503–07.

Page 161—Put the candy away: Painter, J. E., B. Wansink, and J. B. Hieggelke. "How Visibility and Convenience Influence Candy Consumption." *Appetite* 38 (2002): 237–38.

Page 161—"Ten-minute delay": McClure, S. M., K. M. Ericson, D. I. Laibson, G. Loewenstein, and J. D. Cohen. "Time Discounting for Primary Rewards." *Journal of Neuroscience* 27 (2007): 5796–804.

Page 163—"The Marshmallow Test": Mischel, W., Y. Shoda, and M. I. Rodriguez. "Delay of Gratification in Children." *Science* 244 (1989): 933–38.

Page 164—Follow-up to the marshmallow test: Mischel, W., Y. Shoda, and P. K. Peake. "The Nature of Adolescent Competencies Predicted by Preschool Delay of Gratification." *Journal of Personality and Social Psychology* 54 (1988): 687–96. See also Eigsti, I. M., V. Zayas, W. Mischel, Y. Shoda, O. Ayduk, M. B. Dadlani, M. C. Davidson, J. Lawrence Aber, and B. J. Casey. "Predicting Cognitive Control from Preschool to Late Adolescence and Young Adulthood." *Psychological Science* 17 (2006): 478–84.

Page 164—Discount rate predicts self-control problems: Ikeda, S., M.-I. Kang, and F. Ohtake. "Hyperbolic Discounting, the Sign Effect, and the Body Mass Index." *Journal of Health Economics* 29 (2010): 268–84. See also Kirby, K. N., N. M. Petry, and W. K. Bickel. "Heroin Addicts Have Higher Discount Rates for Delayed Rewards Than Non-Drug-Using Controls." *Journal of Experimental Psychology: General* 128 (1999): 78–87. See also Alessi, S. M., and N. M. Petry. "Pathological Gambling Severity Is Associated with Impulsivity in a Delay Discounting Procedure." *Behavioural Processes* 64 (2003): 345–54. See also Zauberman, G., and B. K. Kim. "Time Perception and Retirement Saving: Lessons from Behavioral Decision Research." Pension Research Council Working Paper 2010-35. (2010): www.ssrn.com/abstract=1707666. See also Zimbardo, P. G., and J. N. Boyd. "Putting Time in Perspective: A Valid, Reliable Individual-Differences Metric." *Journal of Personality and Social Psychology* 77 (1999): 1271–88.

Page 165—Think about the future reward first: Weber, E. U., E. J. Johnson, K. F. Milch,

H. Chang, J. C. Brodscholl, and D. G. Goldstein. "Asymmetric Discounting in Intertemporal Choice." *Psychological Science* 18 (2007): 516–23.

Page 166—Precommitment: Schelling, T. C. "Egonomics, or the Art of Self-Management." *The American Economic Review* 68 (1978): 290–94.

Page 167—Constrain your future self: Ainslie, G. "Specious Reward: A Behavioral Theory of Impulsiveness and Impulse Control." *Psychological Bulletin* 82 (1975): 463–96.

Page 168—A writer's strategy: Grossman, L. "Jonathan Franzen: Great American Novelist." *Time*. August 12, 2010.

Page 170—ATM intervention: Rosen, M. I., B. J. Rounsaville, K. Ablondi, A. C. Black, and R. A. Rosenheck. "Advisor-Teller Money Manager (ATM) Therapy for Substance Use Disorders." *Psychiatric Services* 61 (2010): 707–13. See also Black, A. C., and M. I. Rosen. "A Money Management-Based Substance Use Treatment Increases Valuation of Future Rewards." *Addictive Behaviors* 36 (2011): 125–28.

Pages 171–174—Thinking about present vs. future selves: Mitchell, J. P., J. Schirmer, D. L. Ames, and D. T. Gilbert. "Medial Prefrontal Cortex Predicts Intertemporal Choice." *Journal of Cognitive Neuroscience* 23 (2011): 857–66. See also D'Argembeau, A., D. Stawarczyk, S. Majerus, F. Collette, M. Van der Linden, and E. Salmon. "Modulation of Medial Prefrontal and Inferior Parietal Cortices When Thinking About Past, Present, and Future Selves." *Social Neuroscience* 5 (2010): 187–200. See also Ersner-Hershfield, H., G. E. Wimmer, and B. Knutson. "Saving for the Future Self: Neural Measures of Future Self-Continuity Predict Temporal Discounting." *Social Cognitive and Affective Neuroscience* 4 (2009): 85–92.

Page 172—Future selves are strangers: Pronin, E., C. Y. Olivola, and K. A. Kennedy. "Doing unto Future Selves as You Would Do unto Others: Psychological Distance and Decision Making." *Personality and Social Psychology Bulletin* 34 (2008): 224–36.

Page 175—Brain activation and self-control choice: Mitchell, J. P., J. Schirmer, D. L. Ames, and D. T. Gilbert. "Medial Prefrontal Cortex Predicts Intertemporal Choice." *Journal of Cognitive Neuroscience* 23 (2011): 857–66.

Pages 176–178—Retirement savings survey: Harris Interactive Poll. "Number of Americans Reporting No Personal or Retirement Savings Rises." Survey of 2,151 adults in the U. S. conducted between November 8 and 15, 2010. Reported online February 2, 2011.

Page 177—Future-self continuity measure illustration: Courtesy Jon Baron and Hal Ersner-Hershfield. Ersner-Hershfield, H., M. T. Garton, K. Ballard, G. R. Samanez-Larkin, and B. Knutson. "Don't Stop Thinking About Tomorrow: Individual Differences in Future Self-Continuity Account for Saving." *Judgment and Decision Making* 4 (2009): 280–86.

Page 177—Meeting future self helps students save for retirement: Ersner-Hershfield, H., D. G. Goldstein, W. F. Sharpe, J. Fox, L. Yeykelvis, L. L. Carstensen, and J. Bailenson. "Increasing Saving Behavior Through Age-Progressed Renderings of the Future Self." *Journal of Marketing Research,* in press.

Page 179—Imagining the future helps people delay gratification: Peters, J., and C. Buchel. "Episodic Future Thinking Reduces Reward Delay Discounting Through an Enhancement of Prefrontal-Mediotemporal Interactions." *Neuron* 66 (2010): 138–48.

Page 180—Visualizing future self increases exercise: Murru, E. C., and K. A. Martin Ginis. "Imagining the Possibilities: The Effects of a Possible Selves Intervention on Self-Regulatory Efficacy and Exercise Behavior." *Journal of Sport & Exercise Psychology* 32 (2010): 537–54.

Page 181—Hyperopia. Kivetz, R., and A. Keinan. "Repenting Hyperopia: An Analysis of Self-Control Regrets." *Journal of Consumer Research* 33 (2006): 273–82.

Page 182—Strategies to avoid hyperopic regret: Kivetz, R., and I. Simonson. "Self-Control for the Righteous: Toward a Theory of Precommitment to Indulgence." *Journal of Consumer Research* 29 (2002): 199–217. See also Haws, K. L., and C. Poynor. "Seize the Day! Encouraging Indulgence for the Hyperopic Consumer." *Journal of Consumer Research* 35 (2008): 680–91. See also Keinan, A., and R. Kivetz. "Remedying Hyperopia: The Effects of Self-Control Regret on Consumer Behavior." *Journal of Marketing Research* 45 (2008): 676–89.

Chapter 8. Infected! Why Willpower Is Contagious

Pages 184–185—Air Force fitness study: Carrell, S. E., M. Hoekstra, and J. E. West. "Is Poor Fitness Contagious? Evidence from Randomly Assigned Friends." Working Paper 16518, National Bureau of Economic Research (2010).

Page 185—Obesity rates in the U.S.: The Centers for Disease Control and Prevention statistics, www.cdc.gov/obesity/data/trends.html#State.

Pages 185–186—Contagion of obesity: Christakis, N. A., and J. H. Fowler. "The Spread of Obesity in a Large Social Network over 32 Years." *New England Journal of Medicine* 357 (2007): 370–79.

Page 186—Social contagion studies: Fowler, J. H., and N. A. Christakis. "Estimating Peer Effects on Health in Social Networks: A Response to Cohen-Cole and Fletcher; and Trogdon, Nonnemaker, and Pais." *Journal of Health Economics* 27 (2008): 1400–05. See also Rosenquist, J. N., J. Murabito, J. H. Fowler, and N. A. Christakis. "The Spread of Alcohol Consumption Behavior in a Large Social Network." *Annals of Internal Medicine* 152 (2010): 426–33. See also Christakis, N. A., and J. H. Fowler. "The Collective Dynamics of Smoking in a Large Social Network." *New England Journal of Medicine* 358 (2008): 2249–58. See also Mednick, S. C., N. A. Christakis, and J. H. Fowler. "The Spread of Sleep Loss Influences Drug Use in Adolescent Social Networks." *PLoS ONE* 5 (2010): e9775. See also Rosenquist, J. N., J. H. Fowler, and N. A. Christakis. "Social Network Determinants of Depression." *Molecular Psychiatry* (2010): Online advance publication.

Page 187—Mirror neurons: Cattaneo, L., and G. Rizzolatti. "The Mirror Neuron System." *Archives of Neurology* 66 (2009): 557–60.

Pages 187–188—Pain anticipation and empathy: Avenanti, A., A. Sirigu, and S. M. Aglioti. "Racial Bias Reduces Empathic Sensorimotor Resonance with Other-Race Pain." *Current Biology* 20 (2010): 1018–22.

Page 188—Seeing smokers on screen: Wagner, D. D., S. Dal Cin, J. D. Sargent, W. M. Kelley, and T. F. Heatherton. "Spontaneous Action Representation in Smokers When Watching Movie Characters Smoke." *Journal of Neuroscience* 31 (2011): 894–98.

Page 189—Emotions spread to others in social networks: Fowler, J. H., and N. A. Christakis. "Dynamic Spread of Happiness in a Large Social Network: Longitudinal Analysis over 20 Years in the Framingham Heart Study." *BMJ* 337 (2008): a2338. See also Cacioppo, J. T., J. H. Fowler, and N. A. Christakis. "Alone in the Crowd: The Structure and Spread of Loneliness in a Large Social Network." *Journal of Personality and Social Psychology* 97 (2009): 977–91.

Page 190—Goal contagion: Aarts, H., P. M. Gollwitzer, and R. R. Hassin. "Goal Contagion: Perceiving Is for Pursuing." *Journal of Personality and Social Psychology* 87 (2004): 23–37. See also Pontus Leander, N., J. Y. Shah, and T. L. Chartrand. "Moments of Weakness: The Implicit Context Dependencies of Temptations." *Personality and Social Psychology Bulletin* 35 (2009): 853–66.

Page 192—A self-control immune response: Fishbach, A., and Y. Trope. "Implicit and Explicit Mechanisms of Counteractive Self-Control." In Shah, James Y., and W. Gardner, eds., *Handbook of Motivation Science*, eds. James Y. Shah and W. Gardner. New York: Guilford, 2007.

Page 192—Rule-breaking is contagious: Keizer, K., S. Lindenberg, and L. Steg. "The Spreading of Disorder." *Science* 322 (2008): 1681–85.

Page 193—Think about someone with good self-control: vanDellen, M. R., and R. H. Hoyle. "Regulatory Accessibility and Social Influences on State Self-Control." *Personality and Social Psychology Bulletin* 36 (2010): 251–63.

Page 194—Complex contagion: Centola, D. "The Spread of Behavior in an Online Social Network Experiment." *Science* 329 (2010): 1194–97.

Page 194—Mom is part of "self": Vanderwal, T., E. Hunyadi, D. W. Grupe, C. M. Connors, and R. T. Schultz. "Self, Mother and Abstract Other: An fMRI Study of Reflective Social Processing." *NeuroImage* 41 (2008): 1437–46.

Pages 195–196—Energy conservation survey: Nolan, J. M., P. W. Schultz, R. B. Cialdini, N. J. Goldstein, and V. Griskevicius. "Normative Social Influence Is Underdetected." *Personality and Social Psychology Bulletin* 34 (2008): 913–23.

Page 197—God wants you to lose weight: Anshel, M. H. "The Disconnected Values (Intervention) Model for Promoting Healthy Habits in Religious Institutions." *Journal of Religion and Health* 49 (2010): 32–49.

Page 198—"Scary" health statistics: Schoenborn, C. A., and P. F. Adams. "Health Behaviors of Adults: United States, 2005–2007." *Vital and Health Statistics: Series 10, Data from the National Health Survey* 245 (2010): 1–132. See also Centers for Disease Control and Prevention State Indicator Report on Fruits and Vegetables, 2009. www.cdc.gov/Features/FruitsAndVeggies/. United States Department of Agriculture Economic Research Service, Briefing Rooms, Sugar and Sweeteners (2010). www.ers.usda.gov/Briefing/Sugar/Data.htm.

Page 198—Don't be a sketchy grad student: Berger, J., and L. Rand. "Shifting Signals to Help Health: Using Identity Signaling to Reduce Risky Health Behaviors." *Journal of Consumer Research* 35 (2008): 509–18.

Page 200—The obese don't feel obese: Powell, T. M., J. A. de Lemos, K. Banks, C. R. Ayers, A. Rohatgi, A. Khera, D. K. McGuire, et al. "Body Size Misperception: A Novel Determinant in the Obesity Epidemic." *Archives of Internal Medicine* 170 (2010): 1695–97.

Page 200—Boomerang to the middle: Schultz, P. W., J. M. Nolan, R. B. Cialdini, N. J. Goldstein, and V. Griskevicius. "The Constructive, Destructive, and Reconstructive Power of Social Norms." *Psychological Science* 18 (2007): 429–34. See also Costa, D. L., and M. E. Kahn. "Energy Conservation 'Nudges' and Environmentalist Ideology: Evidence from a Randomized Residential Electricity Field Experiment." Working paper 15939, National Bureau of Economic Research (2010).

Page 200—Academic cheating norms: Hard, S. F., J. M. Conway, and A. C. Moran. "Faculty and College Student Beliefs About the Frequency of Student Academic Misconduct." *The Journal of Higher Education* 77 (2006): 1058–80.

Page 200—Beliefs predict cheating: McCabe, D. L., L. K. Treviño, and K. D. Butterfield. "Honor Codes and Other Contextual Influences on Academic Integrity: A Replication and Extension to Modified Honor Code Settings." *Research in Higher Education* 43 (2002): 357–78.

Page 200—Cheating on taxes: Wenzel, M. "Misperceptions of Social Norms About Tax Compliance: From Theory to Intervention." *Journal of Economic Psychology* 26 (2005): 862–83.

Page 200—Correcting misperceived norms: Perkins, H. W. "Social Norms and the Prevention of Alcohol Misuse in Collegiate Contexts." *Journal of Studies on Alcohol Supplement* 14 (2002): 164–72.

Page 201—Anticipated shame promotes safe sex: Hynie, M., T. K. MacDonald, and S. Marques. "Self-Conscious Emotions and Self-Regulation in the Promotion of Condom Use." *Personality and Social Psychology Bulletin* 32 (2006): 1072–84.

Page 202—"Big Thief!" poster: Kilgannon, C., and J. E. Singer. "Stores' Treatment of Shoplifters Tests Rights." *New York Times*, June 21, 2010. www.nytimes.com/2010/06/22/nyregion/22shoplift.html.

Page 202—Public shaming for men who use prostitutes: "Should cities shame johns by putting their faces on billboards, television, and the Internet after their arrest?" www.prostitution.procon.org/view.answers.php?questionID=000845.

Page 202—Public shaming discourages paying for sex: Durchslag, R., and S. Goswami. "Deconstructing the Demand for Prostitution: Preliminary Insights from Interviews with Chicago Men Who Purchase Sex." In *Chicago Alliance Against Sexual Exploitation*. Chicago, 2008.

Page 203—Shame and gambling: Yi, S., and V. Kanetkar. "Coping with Guilt and Shame After Gambling Loss." *Journal of Gambling Studies* (2011, in press). DOI: 10.1007/s10899-010-9216-y.

Page 203—Shame, guilt, and chocolate cake: Chun, H., V. M. Patrick, and D. J. MacInnis. "Making Prudent Vs. Impulsive Choices: The Role of Anticipated Shame and Guilt on Consumer Self-Control." *Advances in Consumer Research* 34 (2007): 715–19. See also Patrick, V. M., H. H. Chun, and D. J. MacInnis. "Affective Forecasting and Self-Control: Why Anticipating Pride Wins over Anticipating Shame in a Self-Regulation Context." *Journal of Consumer Psychology* 19 (2009): 537–45.

Page 203—Imagining pride helps goal achievement: Bagozzi, R. P., U. M. Dholakia, and S. Basuroy. "How Effortful Decisions Get Enacted: The Motivating Role of Decision Processes, Desires, and Anticipated Emotions." *Journal of Behavioral Decision Making* 16 (2003): 273–95.

Page 204—Guilt, pride, and heart rate variability: Fourie, M. M., H. G. L. Rauch, B. E. Morgan, G. F. R. Ellis, E. R. Jordaan, and K. G. F. Thomas. "Guilt and Pride Are Heartfelt, but Not Equally So." *Psychophysiology* (2011, in press). DOI: 10.1111/j.1469-8986.2010.01157.x.

Page 204—We want others to see us doing good, e.g., buying green products: Griskevicius, V., J. M. Tybur, and B. Van den Bergh. "Going Green to Be Seen: Status, Reputation, and Conspicuous Conservation." *Journal of Personality and Social Psychology* 98 (2010): 392–404.

Page 205—"If shame worked, there'd be no fat people": Personal phone interview with Deb Lemire, president of the Association for Size Diversity and Health. 2/26/2010.

Page 205—Social rejection drains willpower: Baumeister, R. F., C. N. DeWall, N. J. Ciarocco, and J. M. Twenge. "Social Exclusion Impairs Self-Regulation." *Journal of Personality and Social Psychology* 88 (2005): 589–604.

Page 206—Prejudice drains willpower: Inzlicht, M., L. McKay, and J. Aronson. "Stigma as Ego Depletion: How Being the Target of Prejudice Affects Self-Control." *Psychological Science* 17 (2006): 262–69.

Page 206—Social support improves self-control: Wing, R. R., and R. W. Jeffery. "Benefits of Recruiting Participants with Friends and Increasing Social Support for Weight Loss and Maintenance." *Journal of Consulting and Clinical Psychology* 67 (1999): 132–38.

Chapter 9. Don't Read This Chapter:
The Limits of "I Won't" Power

Pages 209–210—Tolstoy story: Recounted in preface to Wegner, D. M. *White Bears and Other Unwanted Thoughts: Suppression, Obsession, and the Psychology of Mental Control.* New York: Guilford, 1994.

Page 210—White bear study transcript: From p. 3 of Wegner, D. M. *White Bears and Other Unwanted Thoughts: Suppression, Obsession, and the Psychology of Mental Control.* New York: Guilford, 1994.

Page 211—Ironic rebound examples: Wegner, D. M. "How to Think, Say, or Do Precisely the Worst Thing for Any Occasion." *Science* 325 (2009): 48–50.

Page 211—Dreaming of crushes: Wegner, D. M., R. M. Wenzlaff, and M. Kozak. "Dream Rebound: The Return of Suppressed Thoughts in Dreams." *Psychological Science* 15 (2004): 232–36.

Page 211—Homophobic men and gay porn: Adams, H. E., L. W. Wright, Jr., and B. A. Lohr. "Is Homophobia Associated with Homosexual Arousal?" *Journal of Abnormal Psychology* 105 (1996): 440–45.

Pages 212–213—Brain processes forbidden content: Giuliano, R. J., and N. Y. Wicha. "Why the White Bear Is Still There: Electrophysiological Evidence for Ironic Semantic Activation During Thought Suppression." *Brain Research* 1316 (2010): 62–74.

Page 213—If I think it, it must be true: Tversky, A., and D. Kahneman. "Availability: A Heuristic for Judging Frequency and Probability." *Cognitive Psychology* 5 (1973): 207–32.

Page 213   Plane crash statistics: Barnett, A. "Cross National Differences in Aviation Safety Records." *Transportation Science* 44 (2010): 322–32.

Page 214—Suicidal student story: Jaffe, E. "The Science Behind Secrets." *APS Observer*, July 2006.

Page 215—Accepting thoughts helps them go away: Giuliano, R. J., and N. Y. Wicha. "Why the White Bear Is Still There: Electrophysiological Evidence for Ironic Semantic Activation During Thought Suppression." *Brain Research* 1316 (2010): 62–74.

Page 215—Thought suppression and depression: Wegner, D. M., and S. Zanakos. "Chronic Thought Suppression." *Journal of Personality* 62 (1994): 616–40. See also Muris, P., H. Merckelbach, and R. Horselenberg. "Individual Differences in Thought Suppression. The White Bear Suppression Inventory: Factor Structure, Reliability, Validity and Correlates." *Behaviour Research and Therapy* 34: 501–13.

Page 215—Suppressing sad thoughts makes people sad: Wegner, D. M., R. Erber, and S. Zanakos. "Ironic Processes in the Mental Control of Mood and Mood-Related Thought." *Journal of Personality and Social Psychology* 65 (1993): 1093–104.

Page 215—Thought suppression and self-esteem: Borton, J. L. S., L. J. Markowitz, and

J. Dieterich. "Effects of Suppressing Negative Self-Referent Thoughts on Mood and Self–Esteem." *Journal of Social and Clinical Psychology* 24 (2005): 172–90.

Page 216—Suppressing anxiety increases anxiety: Koster, E. H. W., E. Rassin, G. Crombez, and G. W. B. Näring. "The Paradoxical Effects of Suppressing Anxious Thoughts During Imminent Threat." *Behaviour Research and Therapy* 41 (2003): 1113–20. See also Hofmann, S. G., S. Heering, A. T. Sawyer, and A. Asnaani. "How to Handle Anxiety: The Effects of Reappraisal, Acceptance, and Suppression Strategies on Anxious Arousal." *Behaviour Research and Therapy* 47 (2009): 389–94.

Pages 216–217—Thought suppression and psychological disorders: Beck, J. G., B. Gudmundsdottir, S. A. Palyo, L. M. Miller, and D. M. Grant. "Rebound Effects Following Deliberate Thought Suppression: Does PTSD Make a Difference?" *Behavior Therapy* 37 (2006): 170–80. See also Becker, E. S., M. Rinck, W. T. Roth, and J. Margraf. "Don't Worry and Beware of White Bears: Thought Suppression in Anxiety Patients." *Journal of Anxiety Disorders* 12 (1998): 39–55. See also Tolin, D. F., J. S. Abramowitz, A. Przeworski, and E. B. Foa. "Thought Suppression in Obsessive-Compulsive Disorder." *Behaviour Research and Therapy* 40 (2002): 1255–74.

Page 217—Social anxiety in the brain: Goldin, P. R., T. Manber, S. Hakimi, T. Canli, and J. J. Gross. "Neural Bases of Social Anxiety Disorder: Emotional Reactivity and Cognitive Regulation During Social and Physical Threat." *Archives of General Psychiatry* 66 (2009): 170–80.

Pages 217–218—Acceptance reduces stress of social anxiety: Goldin, P. R., W. Ramel, and J. J. Gross. "Mindfulness Meditation Training and Self-Referential Processing in Social Anxiety Disorder: Behavioral and Neural Effects." *Journal of Cognitive Psychotherapy* 23 (2009): 242–57. See also Goldin, P. R., and J. J. Gross. "Effects of Mindfulness-Based Stress Reduction (MBSR) on Emotion Regulation in Social Anxiety Disorder." *Emotion* 10 (2010): 83–91.

Page 222—Suppressing thoughts of chocolate: Erskine, J. A. K. "Resistance Can Be Futile: Investigating Behavioural Rebound." *Appetite* 50 (2008): 415–21. See also Erskine, J. A. K., and G. J. Georgiou. "Effects of Thought Suppression on Eating Behaviour in Restrained and Non-Restrained Eaters." *Appetite* 54 (2010): 499–503.

Page 222—Chocolate cravers study: Rezzi, S., Z. Ramadan, F. P. Martin, L. B. Fay, P. van Bladeren, J. C. Lindon, J. K. Nicholson, and S. Kochhar. "Human Metabolic Phenotypes Link Directly to Specific Dietary Preferences in Healthy Individuals." *Journal of Proteome Research* 6 (2007): 4469–77.

Page 223—Dieting and thought suppression: Barnes, R. D., and S. Tantleff-Dunn. "Food for Thought: Examining the Relationship between Food Thought Suppression and Weight-Related Outcomes." *Eating Behaviors* 11 (2010): 175–79.

Page 223—Dieting doesn't work: Mann, T., A. J. Tomiyama, E. Westling, A. M. Lew, B. Samuels, and J. Chatman. "Medicare's Search for Effective Obesity Treatments: Diets Are Not the Answer." *American Psychologist* 62 (2007): 220–33.

Pages 223–224—Restriction increases cravings: Hill, A. J. "The Psychology of Food Craving." *Proceedings of the Nutrition Society* 66 (2007): 277–85. See also Polivy, J., J. Coleman, and C. P. Herman. "The Effect of Deprivation on Food Cravings and Eating Behavior in Restrained and Unrestrained Eaters." *International Journal of Eating Disorders* 38 (2005): 301–09.

Page 225—Hershey's Kisses study: Forman, E. M., K. L. Hoffman, K. B. McGrath, J. D. Herbert, L. L. Brandsma, and M. R. Lowe. "A Comparison of Acceptance- and Control-Based Strategies for Coping with Food Cravings: An Analog Study." *Behaviour Research and Therapy* 45 (2007): 2372–86.

Page 227—Ending food prohibition: Provencher, V., C. Begin, A. Tremblay, L. Mongeau, L. Corneau, S. Dodin, S. Boivin, and S. Lemieux. "Health-at-Every-Size and Eating Behaviors: 1-Year Follow-up Results of a Size Acceptance Intervention." *Journal of the American Dietetic Association* 109 (2009): 1854–61. See also Gagnon-Girouard, M. P., C. Begin, V. Provencher, A. Tremblay, L. Mongeau, S. Boivin, and S. Lemieux. "Psychological Impact of a 'Health-at-Every-Size' Intervention on Weight-Preoccupied Overweight/Obese Women." *Journal of Obesity* 2010 (2010).

Page 229—The smokers' torture test: Bowen, S., and A. Marlatt. "Surfing the Urge: Brief Mindfulness-Based Intervention for College Student Smokers." *Psychology of Addictive Behaviors* 23 (2009): 666–71.

Page 231—Mindfulness prevents relapse: Bowen, S., N. Chawala, S. E. Collins, K. Witkiewitz, S. Hsu, J. Grow, S. Clifasefi, et al. "Mindfulness-Based Relapse Prevention for Substance Use Disorders: A Pilot Efficacy Trial." *Substance Abuse* 30 (2009): 295–305. See also Witkiewitz, K., and S. Bowen. "Depression, Craving, and Substance Use Following a Randomized Trial of Mindfulness-Based Relapse Prevention." *Journal of Consulting and Clinical Psychology* 78 (2010): 362–74.

Chapter 10: Final Thoughts

Page 237—"Only reasonable conclusion to a book about scientific ideas is: Draw your own conclusions": Credit for this suggestion goes to Brian Kidd, Senior Bioinformatics Research Specialist, Institute for Infection Immunity and Transplantation, Stanford University.

INDEX